Stranger in
a Strange State

Stranger in a Strange State

The Politics of Carpetbagging from Robert Kennedy to Scott Brown

Christopher J. Galdieri

Published by State University of New York Press, Albany

For information, contact State University of New York Press, Albany, NY
www.sunypress.edu

Library of Congress Cataloging-in-Publication Data

Names: Galdieri, Christopher J., author.
Title: Stranger in a strange state : the politics of carpetbagging from
  Robert Kennedy to Scott Brown / Christopher J. Galdieri.
Description: Albany : State University of New York Press, [2019] | Includes
  bibliographical references and index.
Identifiers: LCCN 2018027701 | ISBN 9781438474038 (hardcover : alk. paper) |
  ISBN 9781438474045 (ebook)
Subjects: LCSH: Political campaigns—United States. | Political candidates—United
  States. | Elections—United States.
Classification: LCC JK2281 .G35 2019 | DDC 324.70973—dc23
LC record available at https://lccn.loc.gov/2018027701

10 9 8 7 6 5 4 3 2 1

For Kate and Veronica and Alexander

Contents

Illustrations

Acknowledgments

When Scott Brown decided to run for the Senate in New Hampshire, I thought there was probably an academic paper to be written about carpetbagging. As I started thinking about the project, I quickly realized there was enough going on to justify a book, not just about Brown, but also about his fellow carpetbaggers and the unusual enterprise of carpetbagging. This is an imperfect attempt to thank everyone who helped me turn that initial idea into the physical or electronic book you hold in your hands.

My colleagues at Saint Anselm College have provided me with encouragement and support at every step of the way, from reading my proposal to critiquing chapter drafts to telling me to stop worrying and turn in the manuscript. Particular thanks are due to my fellow faculty in the Politics Department, including Erik Cleven, Christine Gustafson, Anne Holthoefer, Peter Josephson, Dale Kuehne, and Jennifer Lucas, as well as Tauna Starbuck Sisco of the Sociology Department and countless others who listened to me talk about this project at lunch and during pub nights. I also received helpful early feedback on this project from colleagues at a New Faculty Forum research colloquium.

Chris Chapp kindly shared his own book proposal with me, so I could see what a book proposal looked like before I wrote one. Petrice Flowers and Carrie Booth Walling also gave helpful proposal advice. Bethany Albertson and Shirin Deylami were very patient with me as I talked about this project with them in the lobby of the Hilton at the 2014 meeting of the American Political Science Association, as was Andrew Rehfeld when I cornered him in the lobby of the Marriot to pick his brain about representation and constituency. Maurice Cunningham and Kevin Parsneau provided useful comments after a presentation at the American Elections Conference at Saint Anselm College in 2015. Libby Sharrow gave me excellent advice on conducting archival research, and I should have done a better job following it. Abigail

Malangone and the archival staff at the John F. Kennedy Presidential Library and Museum helped me navigate the records of Robert Kennedy's 1964 campaign. Melinda Malik and the interlibrary loan desk at Geisel Library tracked down every single article and book I needed for this project, no matter how obscure. Katie Brandt Gott and Maria Rosales critiqued a chapter I was having a particularly difficult time drafting, and Dante Scala provided helpful feedback on other chapters. Adam Sexton shared some of his personal recollections of the 2014 New Hampshire Senate campaign. Barbara Carvalho shared Marist College's polling on the carpetbagger question in New York in 2000. Steve Wrinn helped demystify academic publishing for me. Encounters with Dahlia Lithwick, Celeste Ng, and John Scalzi provided encouragement at times when I needed it. My Facebook friends' supportive and snarky comments on my daily word count announcements likewise helped keep me writing. Melissa Proulx unlocked the mystery of .eps files for me. And special mention must be made of Madison Mangels, who went through the manuscript with a keen eye and four different colors of Post-it notes to flag any statements that needed clarification or correction. If any such errors remain, the fault is mine, not hers.

Thanks are also due to the political reporters whose accounts of these campaigns were very crucial to my research. Journalism is often called the first draft of history, and I hope I've done justice to their coverage.

Throughout the conception, writing, and editing of this project, I often took myself to the True Brew Café at Gibson's Bookstore in Concord, New Hampshire, to do my work. Thanks to the staff there for giving an itinerant scholar a table, wifi, and an electrical outlet, even when I was working on a nonfiction book during National Novel Writing Month. Support your local independent bookstores.

Additional thanks are due to the dean's office at Saint Anselm College, the New Hampshire Institute of Politics, and the Department of Politics at Saint Anselm College for their generous financial support.

Further thanks to the State University of New York Press; my editor there, Michael Rinella, who knew exactly when to ask for updates and was very generous with my interpretations of deadlines; and to SUNY's production and editorial staff. Thanks also to the anonymous reviewers for their helpful recommendations about improving the manuscript.

Thanks as well to Dr. John Disceaux and Bill Potts; to Bernadette Fox; to Gordon Cole and Dougie Jones and Margaret Lanterman; and to Yorkie and Kelly; as well as to Tracyanne Campbell, Gavin Dunbar, Carey Lander, Kenny McKeeve, and Lee Thomson; and to Colin Hay, Robert Earl Keen, Jens Lekman, Lyle Lovett, Nick Offerman, and Gwenno Mererid Saunders.

Finally, thanks to my parents, James and Donna Galdieri, for instilling in me a lifelong love of politics. And thanks to my wife, the formidable Katherine Alexandra Eads Galdieri, and our daughter, the amazing Veronica Rose Eads Galdieri, for living with me during what turned out to be a years-long gestation process. A final thank you goes to our son, Alexander Christopher Eads Galdieri, who had the good sense to arrive after the manuscript was completed.

Chapter 1

Don't Be a Stranger

November 4, 2014, was a very good night to be a Republican. When the votes were tallied, Republicans had picked up 9 seats in the United States Senate and won control of that body for the first time in a decade. Incumbent Democrats lost in Arkansas, Alaska, Colorado, North Carolina, and, after a December runoff, Louisiana, while Republicans swept the seats opened up by the retirements of longtime incumbent Democrats in Iowa, Montana, West Virginia, and South Dakota. In the House of Representatives, Republicans expanded their majority to 247 seats, the party's largest since just after World War II. Controversial Republican governors in Florida, Kansas, Maine, and Wisconsin won second terms in the face of fierce opposition, and, in state after state, Republicans won or tightened their control of state legislatures. Republicans even won governor's races in Democratic-leaning states like Illinois, Massachusetts, and Maryland. It was the sort of triumphant night that a political party is lucky to enjoy once every decade so, when the political stars align just right, and every close race breaks in the same direction. While many Democrats had hoped that they could use sophisticated voter mobilization and targeting techniques to win enough close races to hold onto a bare Senate majority, those hopes were dashed. Election night 2014 was a night when Republicans simply could not lose—except in New Hampshire.

New Hampshire turned out to be one of the Democrats' few bright spots that night. While Republicans did win control of the state legislature, that control proved precarious; in December, Democrats joined a group of breakaway Republicans to elect a more traditional, mainstream Republican as Speaker of the House, rather than allow conservative firebrand Bill O'Brien to return to that position. While incumbent Carol Shea-Porter lost in the state's

First Congressional District, Ann McLane Kuster easily held onto her seat in the Second. New Hampshire's governor, Maggie Hassan, won a second term and instantly found herself being courted by national Democrats as a prospect for the state's 2016 Senate race. But the real focus on election night in New Hampshire, as it had been for over a year, was on the state's epic Senate race between Jeanne Shaheen and Scott Brown. Early on, many had expected the race to be a sleepy one in which Shaheen, a fixture of state politics for decades, would be easily re-elected. But Brown's candidacy, combined with the Republican wave that rose throughout 2014, had upended the race. By the end of the campaign, Brown had transformed the contest into one of the marquee races of the year. Each candidate spent millions of dollars, a half-dozen or more would-be presidents visited the state to campaign on behalf of each candidate, and the televised debates between the candidates were moderated not just by local reporters but also by national network news figures such as Chuck Todd and George Stephanopoulos.

It was late on election night when Brown took to the podium in a ballroom at Manchester's Radisson Hotel to concede the race. While television networks had called the election for Shaheen hours earlier, an apparent, and brief, tightening of the vote count delayed Brown's concession. Much of Brown's speech sounded familiar to anyone who has ever observed the ritual of the concession speech: the congratulations to the winner; the thanking of family, staff, and supporters; and the promise to fight again another day. One passage, however, stands out: "I was born here, and as a new candidate for office here I'm so very thankful for the people who are willing to come out and help give me a shot and give us an opportunity to try to make a better state."[1]

It is, of course, not unusual for candidates to mention their state in an election night speech. But in Brown's case, the question of where he was born and where he lived was inextricably bound up in questions about why he was running. While Brown was indeed a New Hampshire resident at the time of the 2014 election, that residency was of recent vintage; it was not until December of 2013—less than a year before the election—that Brown sold his home in Massachusetts and officially switched his full-time residency to what had formerly been his family's vacation home in Rye, New Hampshire.[2] Prior to that well-publicized move, Brown had been a resident of Massachusetts, the state immediately south of New Hampshire. The two states have many ties; thousands of people commute into Massachusetts from New Hampshire every day, and thousands more visit New Hampshire from Massachusetts to camp, go to the beach, hike, and engage in other tourist activities. Even Maggie Hassan, re-elected as governor that same night, had been a lifelong resident of Massachusetts until she moved to New Hampshire in the 1990s. But Brown was no mere transplant to the state. He had not simply lived in Massachusetts before he moved to New Hampshire; he had represented Massachusetts in the United States Senate from 2010 to 2013.

How did a former Massachusetts senator find himself running for office in New Hampshire? Brown's road to election night 2014 began on another election night, January 19, 2010. Scott Brown's victory in the 2010 special election to the United States Senate seat vacated by the death of Edward Kennedy, who had held the seat for nearly a half-century, sent shockwaves through American politics. Brown became the first Republican to win a Senate seat in Massachusetts since Edward Brooke's election to a second term in 1972. That alone made Brown's election surprising. But what made his election even more important was that it increased the size of the Republicans' caucus from forty votes to forty-one, giving the GOP the votes needed to filibuster any Democratic nomination or proposal; this, in turn, gave the Senate minority, which had spent the first year of Barack Obama's presidency able to do little more than withhold their votes from, but not stop, the Democrats' policy proposals, a newfound power to kill or extract policy concessions on any bill before the Senate. Sober analysts declared Brown's victory the end of President Obama's health care reform overhaul; more triumphant or hysterical commentators announced that Brown's win had essentially ended Obama's presidency just one year after it had begun. Despite his junior status, Brown quickly became something of a national figure, in demand on national and cable news and on the campaign trail with other Republican candidates; his election drew so much attention that Jon Hamm played Brown in a *Saturday Night Live* sketch that aired just after the special election.

Once he was sworn in, Brown became the most junior member of an institution where seniority equals power. But Brown gained influence as one of the handful of Republicans whose votes were in play on such Democratic initiatives as Wall Street reform and the repeal of the military's "Don't Ask, Don't Tell" policy regarding gays in the military. As a member of the Republicans' Capitol Hill softball team, Brown wore a jersey emblazoned with the number "41," and more than one commentator suggested that Brown could someday appear on a national Republican ticket as a candidate for president or vice president.

But any national dreams would have to wait until after Brown won re-election to a full term. And those dreams appeared to end in 2012 when Brown lost his bid for a full term to Elizabeth Warren. Brown's celebrity and influence within the Senate (influence which declined after the election of a

Republican House in 2010 effectively ended the prospects of major legislation for the remainder of Barack Obama's presidency) were simply not enough to withstand the overwhelmingly Democratic tilt of the Massachusetts elector- ate in a presidential election year. In the aftermath of his loss, speculation turned to Brown's next act: Would he run in the special election in 2013 for Massachusetts's other Senate seat, vacated by John Kerry's appointment as Secretary of State? Would he forgo the 2013 special election but run for a full term in 2014? Would he run for governor, an office to which the citizens of Massachusetts have repeatedly elected more-or-less moderate Republicans like Brown? Would he stand down from the pursuit of elected office and seek to influence public affairs in other ways as a private citizen?

The answer, it turned out, was none of the above. Instead, Brown began a months-long flirtation with the idea of seeking another term in the Senate in the neighboring state of New Hampshire—a campaign which, had it suc- ceeded, would have made him the first person to represent two different states in the Senate since the direct election of senators began in the early twentieth century. By the spring of 2014, that flirtation had turned into a full-blown candidacy. Brown's opponent, incumbent Democrat Jeanne Shaheen, was quick to mock Brown's candidacy. At a Jefferson-Jackson dinner in Novem- ber 2013, Shaheen joked that immigration reform was necessary because of people crossing the border to take jobs that belong to New Hampshirites.[3] After Brown officially started running, she and her supporters remarked on the campaign trail that the Constitution says there should be two senators for each state, not two states for each senator.[4] At a St. Patrick's Day lunch in Salem, Governor Maggie Hassan joined in when she told an audience, "It's great to be here in Salem, straddling the border of New Hampshire and Massachusetts—but enough about Scott Brown."[5]

Brown and his supporters countered these criticisms by pointing to other politicians who had moved to a new state to find greener political pastures than they might have found elsewhere—Hillary Clinton, for example, who had sought and won a Senate seat in New York in 2000, despite having no ties to the state when she moved to New York to begin her candidacy in 1999. Jim Merrill, a prominent figure in New Hampshire Republican politics, argued that "Scott Brown has more connections to New Hampshire than Hillary Clinton had to New York when she first ran for Senate."[6] If Clinton could do it, Republicans argued, why couldn't Brown? What's the difference between Hillary Clinton and Scott Brown?

That is the question that this book addresses. Why was Hillary Clinton, who had been first lady of Arkansas for years and had never lived in New York before she became a candidate for the United States Senate in that state, able to succeed in her campaign, while Brown, who had owned a vacation home in New Hampshire long before he became a candidate there, failed? Both met any reasonable definition of the term "carpetbagger," so it is not simply that carpetbaggers are inevitably rejected by the voters of their new states. Nor are Clinton and Brown the only examples of candidates with strong ties to one state who moved to a second in order to run for the Senate. Comparing the campaigns of recent history's most prominent instances of carpetbaggers and examining the reasons each succeeded or failed will explain whether success or failure is simply a matter of candidate quality and skill—which would mean that Clinton, for example, won because she was a good candidate and Brown a poor one—or whether other contextual factors explain these outcomes—which would mean that Clinton's win and Brown's loss had as much to do with economic and political conditions in the country and in their new states, the candidates they ran against, and other factors above and beyond their individual skills as candidates. This examination will also shed light on the reasons carpetbaggers undertake their uphill battles in unfamiliar states in the first place. What would lead an experienced, talented politician to pursue such an unorthodox route to elective office?

What is it about carpetbaggers and carpetbagging that provokes such instant suspicion at best and hostility at worst? Few other professions are tied to geography in the way politics is: A physician who completes a residency in Boston and then practices medicine in Portsmouth raises no eyebrows; nor does an attorney who goes to law school in Minneapolis and then joins a firm in Fargo. But a politician who changes states is immediately and roundly criticized. Are these simply convenient attacks for their opponents to make, attacks that would be replaced with attacks on the carpetbagger's record or character or appearance in the absence of the fact of their carpetbagging? Or do these attacks tell us something about how Americans think about representation?

This book undertakes the first extensive examination of carpetbagging as a political phenomenon. It examines nine cases in which a candidate moved to a new state for the express purpose of running for office or ran in one state after first holding office in another. Some of these candidates had represented another state in the past and sought to return to the Washington stage. Others were already national figures in need of a new platform to continue their political careers. Some were heavily recruited or eagerly received by their new state's branch of their chosen political party. Others blunderbussed into a new state and expected others to duck and cover and get out of their way. And, of course, some succeeded in their campaigns, while others—most others, in point of fact—failed.

But this is not simply a book about these candidates and their campaigns or about the oddity of candidates who run for office in one state despite strong ties to another. Instead, this is a book about what these candidates and campaigns tell us about larger issues and concerns in American politics. Most campaigns, of course, do not include a carpetbagger, and so these issues remain unexamined in those campaigns. But when there is a carpetbagger in the race—when one of the candidates has come to a state expressly in order to run there—these issues come to the surface in ways that they otherwise would not. Carpetbagger races thus provide an unusual opportunity to study and consider some of the central issues of American democracy.

One such issue is representation. What do citizens actually want and expect from their representatives? Is a representative to be someone who goes to Washington and reflects the will of the voters? Someone who exercises independent judgment? Someone who falls somewhere in between? And on the other side of the equation, how do candidates seeking to become representatives of the people talk not just about representation but also about representing? How does a candidate convince citizens that he or she will be a good, faithful, and effective representative? Every candidate for office must do this to some extent. But this concern uniquely comes to the fore when a carpetbagger runs for office, since the carpetbagger must convince voters of his or her capacity to represent a state without the benefit of years of experience living there.

This leads to another issue—localism, or the politics of presence—that is tightly tied to representation. In American politics, representation is almost always linked to a particular location. Elected representatives are chosen by the people, but those people are generally the residents of a specific state, or electoral district, who choose representatives to speak for their particular interests in Congress, state legislatures, or other local governments. In many of these legislative bodies, the interests of a representative's constituents will compete or come into conflict with the interests of other representatives' constituents. In a political system where representation is not just something a representative does, but something a representative does for people united by—possibly united only by—the fact of where they live, then the geographic ties of a representative or would-be representative are more than a matter of state pride or that slippery and elusive type of "authenticity" so often discussed by political pundits. In a normal campaign, those ties remind voters that candidates should be acting in the interests of their state's citizens. When a carpetbagger runs for office, however, the issue looms larger and becomes more complex. A carpetbagger cannot address the question of state ties by reminding voters of his or her history in a state or with testimonials from local officials and residents about his or her role in getting things done for the state. Instead, a carpetbagger must convince voters that he or she does, in fact, have voters' best interests at heart through the campaign he or she runs.

But that effort is complicated by another crucial aspect of American elections that carpetbaggers bring to the surface: ambition. All politicians, of course, are ambitious. But someone who packs up a carpetbag and moves to a new state for the sole purpose of running for office is displaying ambition on a scale that is impossible for voters to ignore or for candidates to obscure with happy rhetoric about public service. This is not to say that all carpetbaggers are drunk with ambition; rather, it is to say that the nature of their candidacies puts their ambition at the front and center of their campaigns in a way that few other candidates do. A carpetbagger must be able to address questions of ambition and, by extension, the purity of his or her motives in a convincing way in order to have even a chance of winning the support of voters. One way a carpetbagger might be able to address this issue is by securing the support of established figures in the carpetbagger's party. The support of party actors is often an important factor in the campaigns of any candidate for any office. But the need to temper an appearance of unchecked ambition makes this support even more necessary for a carpetbagger than it is for other types of candidates.

Crossing state boundaries was not always an all-but-insurmountable barrier in American politics. Early in American history, it was more common for individuals to serve in Congress as representatives of more than one state over the course of a career. Daniel Webster, for example, first represented New Hampshire in the House of Representatives before being elected to represent neighboring Massachusetts in the Senate. The high-water mark for multistate representation was set by James Shields, who over the course of his long political career was elected to represent not two but three different states—Illinois, Minnesota, and finally Missouri—in the United States Senate. And throughout Scott Brown's 2014 campaign, more than one journalist mentioned Shields as a precedent. A closer look at Shields's elections, however, helps explain why more recent examples are so much harder to come by.

First, each of Shields's elections took place during the era in which state legislatures, rather than voters, elected members of the Senate. As a result, in his second and third elections in Minnesota and Missouri, Shields did not have to worry about convincing millions of voters that he would be a good representative. Instead, the decision was made by a small number of legislators, all of whom were themselves elected officials with their own particular electoral and policy interests. It is important to put his elections in historical context as well. Shields was first elected by the Illinois legislature and served from 1849 to 1855; he sought but did not win a second term, and he subsequently moved to the Minnesota territory. When Minnesota was granted statehood in 1858, the new state had to send its first two senators to Washington. Because Shields was a former senator, there was a certain logic to his selection by Minnesota's legislature; Shields's experience in the Senate would enable him to navigate it more readily than someone without that experience might. Shields might have gone on to spend a long career in the Senate from Minnesota, but he and his fellow appointee Henry Mower Rice drew lots to see who would sit in which seat—the one with a shorter term, which would expire in just under a year, or the one with a longer term. Shields had the bad luck to receive the shorter-term seat and lost his bid for a full term the following year.[7]

Shields's third and final term came in 1879, toward the very end of his life. Following the Civil War, Shields spent several years in Wisconsin before moving to Missouri. He had become a figure of some renown among Irish Americans by this time. When Missouri's Senator Lewis Bogy died with just a few weeks left in his term, the Missouri legislature needed to appoint a replacement, and many in the state suggested that Shields be elected to this brief term as the capstone of a long career in public service that had included not just his two previous terms in the Senate but also military service during the war with Mexico and the Civil War, as well as appointed and elective offices in Oregon territory, Wisconsin, and Missouri.[8] On January 22, 1879, the Missouri legislature elected Shields to the remainder of Bogy's term; he died in June, just a few months after leaving office.[9]

Shields's obituaries noted correctly that he had represented three states in the United States Senate among his other prodigious political accomplishments. But Shields would almost certainly have preferred to serve one state for three terms than three states for one full term and two abbreviated terms. He remains the only person ever to have represented three states, and it is unlikely that anyone will ever do so again; his page on the Senate's web site hails him as the "Senator for Three States."[10] Shields's name resurfaces whenever someone who has represented one state in the Senate seeks election from a second state.

It is important to note that his feat was only possible thanks to the nature of Senate elections and American politics in the nineteenth century. Each of his elections was the decision of a small group of state legislators, not the voting population of an entire state. In Minnesota, he benefitted from the fact that the new state would profit from having an experienced legislator represent it in the Senate and that in a new state there were perhaps fewer ambitious politicians than there might have been in a more established state. It was just bad luck that Shields wound up with Minnesota's short-term seat. In Missouri, on the other hand, the brevity of the term remaining to be filled helped Shields' prospects. While other ambitious Missouri politicians would have jockeyed for consideration for a longer term, the fact that the term's length was best measured in weeks made the appointment of a popular figure as a placeholder appealing. Had a full term been at stake in 1879, the elderly Shields, in declining health at the time of his election, would likely have been passed over in favor of another option. Shields led a life characterized by a tireless dedication to public service, even aside from his Senate record, but would have had a much more difficult time getting elected from three different states outside the political context of the mid-to-late nineteenth century.

Two more examples of candidates who managed to represent two different states in Congress are similarly instructive. J. Hamilton Lewis was elected to Washington's at-large House seat just a few years after that territory became a state in 1896 but lost his campaign for re-election in 1898 and a bid for one of Washington's seats in the Senate in 1899. Lewis then moved east to Illinois, where he practiced law and was elected to the Senate by the state legislature in 1912. He was defeated in 1918, but in 1930—after the switch to direct, popular election of senators—Lewis returned to the Senate with the backing of Chicago mayor Anton Cermak's political machine and served there until his death in 1939. In Lewis's elections, as with those of Shields, the nature of American politics and Senate elections at the time help explain his ability to win in two different states. Lewis's initial service in Washington state consisted of a single, two-year House term, and, more importantly, his initial Senate election in Illinois took place at the end of the era during which state legislatures still chose US senators. As a result, Lewis did not have to persuade a statewide electorate that his past service in Washington would not be a bar to his representing the interests of Illinois when he sought election in 1912; instead, the decision was made by a much smaller group of legislators. By the time Lewis sought to return to the Senate in 1930, the Seventeenth Amendment required him to appeal directly to voters, not just legislators. But he could then point to his past service in Illinois as proof that he would be a good representative of these voters' interests. That he was backed by a powerful urban political machine in an era when such organizations wielded considerable influence did not hurt him, either.[11]

But since the popular election of senators became the norm, there are no cases in which someone managed to get elected to the Senate from two different states. The nearest equivalent would be the oddball case of Ed Foreman, who represented both New Mexico and Texas in the House of Representatives, each for a single term, in the 1960s, before moving on to a postpolitical career as a motivational speaker. Others who have tried to get elected in a second state after first holding office in another have been unsuccessful. Some of these carpetbagger candidacies will be examined in depth later in this book.

Looking only at the failures of carpetbaggers tells us only part of the story. Attention must also be paid to those carpetbaggers who, despite the formidable obstacles they faced, succeeded in their bids for office in a new state. Comparing and contrasting the successes and failures will help illuminate the circumstances in which carpetbagger candidates do and do not manage to succeed despite that label. Put another way, this will help answer the question implicit in Jim Merrill's comment about Scott Brown's New Hampshire race in 2014: What is the real difference between Hillary Clinton and Scott Brown?

This book examines the campaigns of nine carpetbagger candidates who ran for the US Senate in a new state despite a lack of ties to that state, or who returned to a state after a long absence for the sole purpose of seeking a Senate seat from that state. Three of these cases involve former senators who, having lost re-election bids in one state, sought to return to the Senate from a second state. The first is James Buckley, the conservative Republican who represented New York for one term from 1971 to 1977, lost his re-election bid, and then ran as a candidate in Connecticut in 1980. The second is Bill Brock, a Republican who, like Buckley, spent a single term in the Senate from 1971 to 1977 and lost his race for a second term. In 1994, Brock, after serving in a variety of positions in the Reagan administration and the Republican Party, ran for the Senate in Maryland. And the third, of course, is Scott Brown. Neither Buckley nor Brock, like Brown after them, succeeded.

Other carpetbaggers successfully overcame the label. In 1964, Robert F. Kennedy resigned from his position as attorney general and ran for the Senate in New York, despite his lack of immediate ties to that state. In 2000, First Lady Hillary Rodham Clinton, who like Kennedy lacked any strong ties to the state, ran for and won the same seat.

Several less famous examples will also be discussed. Scott Brown was not the first Massachusetts politician to move to New Hampshire and run for the Senate; in 1986, former Massachusetts governor Endicott Peabody lost a race against incumbent Warren Rudman. In 2004, Alan Keyes, who had twice run unsuccessfully for the Senate in Maryland, moved to Illinois to oppose a then-obscure state legislator named Barack Obama after the Illinois Republicans' initial nominee dropped out of the race. In 2010, Harold Ford Jr., who lost a 2006 Senate race in Tennessee, considered a primary challenge to newly appointed senator Kirsten Gillibrand in his new state of New York, and in 2014, Elizabeth Cheney launched and then abandoned a challenge to incumbent Mike Enzi in Wyoming.

These analyses will be informed by an exploration of existing research on the various factors that may help explain why some carpetbaggers succeed while most fail. The next chapter brings together these disparate threads—representation, the politics of localism, candidate ambition, and the role of state party actors—to develop a theoretical framework for examining carpetbaggers and their campaigns.

Chapter 2

Representation, Localism, Ambition, and Party

In 1998, the satirical website *The Onion* ran a story entitled "Free-Agent Clinton Signs Five-Year, $37 Million Deal with Argentina."[1] The story posits a world in which political leaders move from one country to another in pursuit of higher salaries and fringe benefits, receive bonuses for good performance, and deploy their readily transplantable skills in each new market for the duration of each contract term. *The Onion's* story is funny because it mashes up the world of politics, where politicians are customarily expected to remain in one place for the duration of their careers, with the world of professional sports, where (the odd Cal Ripken Jr. or Derek Jeter notwithstanding) athletes tend to move from team to team across the course of a career. The story's deadpan prose highlights the absurdity of the idea that an American president could parachute into Argentina and begin running that country on the spot in the same way that a pitcher might throw a fastball in Yankee Stadium as easily as in Camden Yards.

But the humor also comes from readers' expectations about the way American politicians behave. American political norms are such that politicians are generally tied to one state throughout their careers. Those careers may take politicians from the city council to the state legislature to Congress, but not from one state to another. The idea of politicians as globetrotting free agents is funny for the same reason that the joke about the elephant who goes to the ballet is funny: it asks its audience to imagine something absurd that does not exist in reality.

But why is it so absurd to imagine politicians moving, if not from one country to another, from one state to another? Why has no one, in the era of direct election of senators, managed to represent two different states in the Senate, and why do even prominent political figures who have never held office anywhere else face suspicion about their ambitions, motives, and capacity to serve when they move to a state with the express intention of running for the Senate there? Why are politicians whose credentials would make them, at the very least, serious contenders for higher office if they had stayed in their home state tarred, upon crossing a state border, with the label "carpetbagger"?

This chapter examines scholarly research on several interrelated aspects of carpetbaggers and their campaigns. One of these aspects is representation: How do we understand the task of representation that elected officials perform, and how do Americans link representation to the role of localism and place in American politics? Given the strength of this link, what motivates carpetbaggers to run in races that are exceptionally difficult to win—what personal, political, and career characteristics do carpetbagger candidates have in common? And finally, when do these outsiders to their new states manage to win their party's nomination and their new state's general election, and when do they fail? But this analysis must first begin with understanding the origins of the term "carpetbagger" and how it evolved from a term with a specific meaning in the context of the South during Reconstruction to an enduring entry in the American political vocabulary.

The Original Carpetbaggers

The term "carpetbagger" has its origins in the Reconstruction period that followed the Civil War. Those unfamiliar with this period may recall that Southern whites used the term to denigrate Northern Republicans who came south after the Civil War to seek positions in the newly reconstituted state governments and that the name referred to the luggage the Northerners carried: large bags rebuilt from sturdy, secondhand carpeting. But a closer examination of the origins of the term and the circumstances under which it came into common usage helps explain why it became popular in the first place and why it entered the American political lexicon in contexts beyond Reconstruction and remains in use today.

In March of 1867, Congress passed the Reconstruction Act, which, among other things, made two critical changes to the political landscape of the South: It forced Southern states to convene conventions to write new constitutions that met federal specifications, and it barred many former Confederates from holding elective office. As a result of that second requirement, both the constitutional conventions and the elected offices that they created faced a deficit of individuals willing and eligible to serve in them. Many of those who stepped into this vacuum were Northern Republicans who had moved south after the Civil War in pursuit of business, farming, or other opportunities in what many saw as a frontier equal to the American West—individuals who had already been living and working in the south for some time.[2] Others moved to the South during this period. In the view of many of the native white residents of these states, these northerners were alien interlopers and scavengers who, unable to succeed at home, were now fueling their political ambitions at the expense of their defeated countrymen. These feelings were only exacerbated by the humiliation of the South's defeat in the Civil War and the threat that the new constitutions—crafted largely by a mix of northern whites and freed blacks—could pose to the region's white supremacist order.

It was only natural that an all-purpose epithet to denounce these interstate migrants would come into use. Tunnell, however, argues that the widespread use of "carpetbagger" as such an epithet did not occur spontaneously. Rather, he finds that the term was deliberately crafted and developed in the pages of Southern newspapers, which, in the wake of the 1867 Reconstruction Act, were one of the only civic institutions in the region exclusively controlled by native whites. Tunnell's analysis of Southern newspaper editorials from this period finds that the term first came into usage in the pages of the influential Montgomery, Alabama, *Daily Mail* during that state's convention in the fall of 1867, as references to "black carpet sacks" and "carpet bag gentry" ultimately evolved into the noun "carpetbagger" by the end of November. From there, the term quickly spread throughout the Southern region to other states holding constitutional conventions, and it was picked up by the Northern press shortly thereafter. In the South, it became the preeminent shorthand slur for nonnative whites involved in government and quickly eclipsed derogatory terms like "scalawag" or the florid phrases like "radical emissaries" or "outside white" that had previously been used to denounce Northerners new to the region.[3]

The term spread so quickly and stuck so readily, Tunnell argues, for several reasons. First, it emphasized the carpetbaggers' status as outsiders. While many of those described as carpetbaggers had in fact come to the South years before the state constitutional conventions for reasons other than politics, that fact was irrelevant to the propaganda value of the term. By linking carpetbaggers' identity to the luggage they carried—luggage that they would of course not need had they been born and bred in the South—the term defined them as aliens motivated by exceptional and predatory ambition.

Second, by casting doubt on the carpetbaggers' legitimacy as representatives of the places they ostensibly acted on behalf of, the term undercut the new governments emerging from state conventions, as well as the people constituting them. A government full of carpetbaggers, in this view, could never be legitimate, because it would be composed of individuals with no real ties to the state and whose primary motive was to benefit themselves rather than the people of the state.

Additionally, "carpetbagger" had the benefit of novelty. Because it had come into use only after the conclusion of the war, it was, at least on the surface, free of the racial connotations with which existing slurs like "scalawag" were weighted. This made its use beyond the South much more palatable than any antebellum term could have been, even though the Southern editors using the term invariably linked it to the presence of freed blacks at state constitutional conventions. The term's palatability beyond the South was key to its effectiveness. Its emphasis on carpetbaggers as outsiders played on unease among some in the North about the radical reconstruction taking place in the South. "The case that northern newcomers were bogus representatives of southern localities," Tunnell writes, "resonated not just with white southerners but with white northerners too."[4] In some states, Southerners who had remained loyal to the Union throughout the Civil War found themselves unable to find an opportunity to serve in the new governments because so many positions had been filled by Northerners. Americans in other parts of the country did not need to sympathize with the Confederacy to find this situation to be, on some level, fundamentally unfair and counterproductive to the goal of reunifying North and South.

Unlike other political terminology of the late nineteenth century like "mugwump" or "greenbacker," "carpetbagger" became an enduring part of the United States' political lexicon. Even after Reconstruction ended, the term remained in use as a derogatory term to refer to any "low-class, poverty-stricken, ignorant, greedy, utterly unscrupulous adventurer and exploiter" who crossed state lines in the transparent pursuit of political success.[5] Central to this conception was the carpetbaggers' supposed rootlessness and blatant ambition. Carpetbaggers were objectionable not simply because they had moved to new states, but because, in the eyes of their critics, they had done so in naked pursuit of political power, and at the expense of the residents of these states. This pursuit of power, in turn, undercut the carpetbaggers' legitimacy as would-be representatives.

It is important to note that a number of historians have, in recent decades, argued powerfully that this is a grossly unfair mischaracterization and smear of a group that generally consisted of well-intentioned, well-educated, and successful men trying to engage in public service in the aftermath of a terrible conflict.[6] For the purposes of this book's analysis, however, the most important thing about the term is the simple fact that it stuck. It soon came to refer not just to Republicans from the North who had headed south and entered politics, but to any and all itinerant politicians whose ambition led them from one state to another in order to seek a new office. In 1880, just a few years after Reconstruction ended, the editorial page of the *New York Times* denounced outgoing New Jersey governor George McClellan, the former Union general and presidential candidate, as a carpetbagger. McClellan, it seemed, was resuming his residence in New York before the expiration of his term as governor, and he had run for governor in New Jersey while drawing a salary from the city of New York.[7]

While this editorial may have been motivated in part by partisan concerns (the *Times'* editorial page had a decided Republican lean in this era,[8] and McClellan was not just a carpetbagger, but a Democrat as well; the *Times'* editorial delights in the chance to pin the term on a Democrat), it also raised important questions and points about carpetbagging. "A due regard for the conventional usages of political society will induce [a politician] to change his abiding, as well as his voting, place as seldom as possible," the editorial clucked.[9] This illuminates a key aspect of the controversy that surrounds carpetbagging: there is, in the view of the *Times'* editorial board, something inherently improper and unseemly about a candidate so transparently ambitious as to move to another state with the open intention of running for office there. Reading between the lines of the editorial, the *Times* suggests that strong ties to a particular place help protect citizens against politicians' ambition by giving those politicians a stake in the place that will be affected by their actions once they are in office. And as we will see in subsequent chapters, the overall dismal record of carpetbaggers suggests that this attitude persists to the present day and is robust well beyond the *Times'* editorial office. The idea that someone from Ohio could represent Arkansas, is, if only to a lesser degree, generally accepted as being as absurd as the idea of Bill Clinton parachuting into Argentina to become that nation's president.

The perception that a candidate is an ambitious outsider seeking office for personal gain, rather than to represent his or her constituents, can be a damaging one. In his first campaign for Congress in Massachusetts' Eleventh

District in 1946, John F. Kennedy was confronted by a heckler who asked, "Where do you live? New York? Palm Beach? Not Boston. You're a god-damned carpetbagger."[10] Kennedy defused the heckler and his sentiments by noting his World War II service, and the strength of his family's presence in the district meant the charges gained little traction among voters.[11] In 1988, the Republican candidate for the US Senate in New Jersey was Peter Dawkins, a retired brigadier general who found the length of his residency in the state—Dawkins had moved to the state not long before he declared his candidacy—under attack throughout the fall campaign. Incumbent Democrat Frank Lautenberg's campaign mocked Dawkins's introductory ad about how much he loved New Jersey and declared that Dawkins would "move anywhere, say anything, to get elected."[12] Dawkins lost even as George H. W. Bush carried the state.

Even for longtime officeholders, a perception that one's ties to home have weakened or faded can be dangerous. In 2012, the bid of Republican senator Dick Lugar of Indiana for a seventh term fell apart when his residency came under scrutiny. Both Lugar's Republican primary challenger and Indiana Democrats pointed to the fact that Lugar owned a home in Virginia and stayed in hotels when visiting Indiana to portray the incumbent as an entrenched and out-of-touch politician.[13] A Marion County election board even ruled that Lugar was ineligible to vote in the state, though that ruling was overturned on appeal.[14] But the damage was done; Lugar lost his primary, and his seat went Democratic that fall. Two years later, in as good a year as Republicans have ever had, Senator Pat Roberts of Kansas found his re-election prospects endangered after it was revealed that he did not own a home in Kansas and listed as his state residence the home of two longtime supporters.[15]

But why is this the case? Why do we not simply view politicians who move from one state to another to seek office the same way we view people in any other profession who move from one place to another? Why is a surgeon who moves to Portland from Seattle simply bringing years of experience and expertise to a new community, while a politician making the same move would be accused of having suspect motives? To begin to answer that question, it is necessary to examine it in light of one of the key concepts that underlies electoral politics in America—the concept of representation.

Representation

Theorists of democracy have debated the meaning and implications of representation for as long as there have been representatives. Representation is, broadly speaking, the task that we elect public officials to perform; the lower house of Congress even has representation as a part of its name. Whether an elected official holds a post as grand as president of the United States or as humble as town councilor for Ward 5, that official's duties include the representation of his or her constituents. But just what is the task of representation? Much of the discussion over representation has focused on the link between representatives and those they represent. Should representatives view themselves as delegates, empowered to do precisely what their constituents sent them to do, and no more, even if the representative believes her constituents to be in error? Or do representatives owe their constituents the benefit of their independent judgment, even when that judgment conflicts with the wishes of constituents? If a representative tries to strike a middle ground, following constituents on some issues and breaking with them on others, how is that representative to decide when to follow which path?

Central to these questions is the idea of legitimacy—that there is a proper way in which a representative ought to act in order to engage in the task of representation properly. How are citizens' preferences to be translated into governmental action in a way that is consistent with those preferences? How are representatives to craft policies that are legitimate, given the preferences of citizens? Schumpeter argues that it is impossible for citizens to meaningfully resolve complex and technical policy questions on their own, and that as a result, elections are crucial to the task of representation.[16] Elections in a democracy serve the representational function of creating a space within which parties and candidates can compete to win from the citizenry the authority to resolve those questions on their own. But in her lengthy examination of representation as a concept, Pitkin notes that the fundamental function of representation is to make present—figuratively re-present—in the decisions of government constituents who cannot be physically present when those decisions are made. As a result, she proposes the idea of substantive representation, in which a representative generally follows his or her constituents' wishes while reserving the right to act on his or her own initiative. Such cases should, however, be rare, Pitkin argues, and when they do occur they must be accompanied with an explanation for the representative's actions.[17] The key to substantive representation is the idea of interest—if a representative's job is to protect and advance the interests of his or her constituents, then when those interests conflict with the constituents' wishes, the representative is justified in breaking with their wishes in order to safeguard their long-term interests. By this standard, a representative succeeds to the extent that he or she is able to discern the best interests of his or her constituents and act accordingly, even when those actions clash with the constituents' preferences.

But within that conception of representation remains a host of questions and controversies. Chief among these is the question of whose interests, exactly, are being represented by elected officials. A constituency consisting of many thousands or even millions of people will likely have only a handful of core interests that are universally shared by its members. As a result, a representative pursuing the worthy goal of representing his constituents' interests substantively might find himself having to make decisions about which of his constituents' interests will be represented at the expense of those of other constituents. What if the representative is confronted with the need to make a decision that will either benefit one group of constituents at the expense of a second or benefit the second group at the expense of the first? Few of the questions a representative will be presented with will clearly benefit all of his or her constituents equally; even the best-intentioned representative will frequently have to make trade-offs and difficult decisions about which constituents will be most meaningfully "made present again" from issue to issue.

As a further complication, consider that the right to vote is denied to those under eighteen, those in prison, and in some states to felons who have completed their prison sentences. Do elected officials represent those who are barred from voting? If we accept that an elected official represents every inhabitant of his or her district or state, then the answer must be yes. But might the logic of re-election lead elected officials to prefer to "make present again" those who can vote for them, rather than those who cannot? Even if the franchise were truly universal, would elected officials seek to represent their entire constituency or simply those who supported them in their most recent election? American voting turnout rates are notoriously low; might a representative who wants another term in office be expected to focus on the interests of those who turn out to vote rather than those who do not?

Just as all of a representative's constituents do not share all of the same interests, so too do constituents have different characteristics, backgrounds, and experiences. These differences present additional complications for understanding representation, since many of those differences have formed the basis for excluding classes of people from the political process. For much of American history, for instance, membership in Congress and the exercise of the right to vote was, by both law and custom, denied to women, African Americans, and other minority groups; well into the nineteenth century, one could even find states with religious tests for officeholders still on the books. These exclusions have a dramatic impact on the quality and the output of representative government. Mansbridge argues that one of the purposes of representative government is to ensure that deliberations about policy include the perspective of members of each group within a constituency or nation that will be affected by a policy change, and that the decisions resulting from those deliberations will have greater legitimacy if the full range of perspectives contributes to the deliberations in question.[18] But the exclusion or underrepresentation of entire classes of individuals, on the basis of the class with which they identify, leads to deliberations that are lacking in the perspectives of many of those who will be affected, and the decisions coming out of those deliberations will in turn be less legitimate than they otherwise would be.

Several types of representation have been advanced as means of addressing concerns over whom representatives will make present again in the course of their duties. Perhaps most relevant to the question of carpetbaggers and representation, for reasons that will be made clear in the next section of this chapter, is the idea of descriptive representation, which asks how much representatives resemble and reflect the shared experiences of the people they represent. This type of representation is keenly interested in the cases of historically underrepresented groups: How can the interests of women, African Americans, gay Americans, or any other group that has been at one time excluded from the political process be advanced by representatives who do not belong to these groups, have no real ties to their members, and whose knowledge of them comes secondhand at best? This question is of more than symbolic importance; increases in the numbers of women in Congress, to take just one example, have been found to lead to an increase in the numbers of bills introduced to address issues such as equal pay, sex discrimination, child care, and other concerns generally neglected in all-male legislatures.[19] The more homogenous a representative body is, the more likely it is that there will be a mismatch between the interests and preferences of diverse constituents and the interests and preferences of the members of that body. The more diverse a representative body is, by contrast, the more likely it is that the interests and preferences of representatives will encompass the interests and preferences of a greater proportion of the population at large. Who representatives are has a clear and unmistakable impact on whose interests get represented.

Discussions of descriptive representation necessarily focus on members of groups that have, historically, faced discrimination and exclusion from the political process. While it has been almost a century since the Nineteenth Amendment gave women the right to vote, and over fifty years since the civil rights bills of the 1960s, for instance, women and African Americans remain, as do members of other minority groups, underrepresented in elective office relative to their proportions of the population. For those citizens who identify with these groups, the election of people like themselves is a way to amplify their voice and advance policy in their preferred direction. And as new groups emerge onto the political landscape, they, too, seek to elect representatives who share not just their policy goals but their life experiences as well.

But descriptive representation need not be limited to considerations of race, gender, ethnicity, and other personal characteristics of voters. The next section of this chapter examines how the connection between representation and place shapes American attitudes and expectations about representation and suggests one reason for the poor success rate for modern carpetbagger candidates.

The Politics of Presence: Representation and Place

In American politics, representation is closely linked to place. Representatives are elected from specific places to advocate for and protect the interests of their constituents, and those constituents are unified by, even if nothing else, the common place they call home. The Constitution mandates that members of Congress be residents of the states from which they are elected, and, to the frustration of politicians like California's Arnold Schwarzenegger, who came to America as an adult, or Michigan's Jennifer Granholm, who moved to America with her Canadian parents as a child, that the president be a native-born citizen. Many states have similar residency requirements for those seeking or holding office. Most of the time, this linkage between representation and place is taken for granted in the same way that we take for granted that water is wet and oranges are orange—the sort of too-obvious-to-mention elemental truth that theorist of representation Andrew Rehfield describes as a "silence of the land."[20] But as Rehfield notes in his examination of constituency as a concept, this need not necessarily be so; in fact, he goes so far as to propose eliminating geographic constituencies in the House of Representatives, and instead randomly and permanently assigning each citizen, on his or her eighteenth birthday, to one of 435 nongeographic "districts." Simply reading about this audacious thought experiment triggers not just counterarguments against its practicability and desirability but also a discomfort with such a radical severing of the tie between place and representation. But that almost instinctive reaction illuminates how tightly linked location and representation are in American politics.

The work of Richard Fenno sheds additional light on the connection between representatives and their constituencies. Through his personal interviews with and observations of members of Congress, Fenno identified several critical facts about how representation works in practice that are relevant to considering how a candidate's carpetbagger status could affect a campaign.

Fenno argues that candidates do not simply consider their constituency as an undifferentiated mass of voters. Instead, candidates identify the subgroups within that constituency that are likely to support them. Fenno describes four levels of constituencies as concentric circles. The largest circle represents the geographic constituency—the total population of a district or state. Within that is the representative's re-election constituency—the people whose votes the representative has identified as necessary for his or her electoral victory. Within that constituency is nested what Fenno dubs the primary constituency—the candidate's strongest supporters among the electorate at large. And finally, the smallest circle consists of a candidate's personal constituency—his or her very closest friends, family, and supporters.[21]

What do Fenno's concentric circles of constituencies mean for carpetbaggers? A typical candidate's impressions of these constituencies will be shaped by his or her experience living in a particular place. A candidate might count her law partners or college friends among her personal constituency or view a local branch of a particular union as a key part of her primary constituency because she once belonged to it herself or a relative was once a member. However a member approaches or imagines his or her different levels of constituencies, local experience shapes those imaginings. A carpetbagger, on the other hand, starts from zero; even those close friends and supporters he or she might bring along will generally lack the sort of knowledge of a state that natives and longtime residents would possess.

Fenno also identifies representatives' decisions about how to engage in the task of representing as originating with representatives' impressions about their constituencies. Where many theoretical accounts view representatives' role in abstract terms, Fenno argues that the activity of representation is an ongoing one and that savvy politicians consider the nature of their constituency monitor their constituents' impressions and opinions of both policy questions and the member himself or herself as they asses what actions to take while in office. This activity extends beyond the realm of votes cast in Washington; Fenno calls the activities in which representatives engage their "home style." Fenno's home style includes three aspects: a member or candidate's allocation of resources; his or her explanation of their work in Washington; and, most crucially to the matter at hand, his or her presentation of self. This self-presentation, Fenno argues, is ultimately about creating a sense of trust between a representative (or would-be representative) and constituents, by convincing them that he or she is qualified, identifies with the residents of the state or district, and possesses empathy for them and for their experiences.

Fenno's work makes the challenge facing a carpetbagger clear. The carpetbagger is not merely being judged on his or her qualifications; as later chapters make clear, most of those examined here had long careers in politics, and the sorts of credentials that tend to mark a candidate as a strong, or at least plausible, one. But voters are concerned with more that just credentials and qualifications, Fenno argues; they also want candidates to demonstrate that they understand the people they seek to represent. As Fenno puts it, candidates, explicitly or implicitly, tell voters, "You can trust me because we are like each other."[22] Candidates who demonstrate shared identity and empathy for voters' lives and worldviews are going to fare better than those who cannot. Carpetbaggers, as newcomers to a state, have to clear an exceptionally high bar to win voters' trust. Voters aware of their carpetbagger status will likely be more skeptical of them and their motives than they would be of other candidates. As a further complication, Fenno identifies time as an essential ingredient in building a trusting relationship with voters. A newcomer to a state will generally have little time in which to build up such a relationship of trust, while an incumbent or a home-grown challenger will have more of the local knowledge and experience that helps build that relationship. And many candidates for office do so following careers that help them establish ties and connections that are useful in launching a campaign: law colleagues, insurance agency clients, patients, former students, and the like. But, to the extent that most carpetbaggers had precampaign careers, they had them somewhere other than the place they seek to represent.

The many difficulties a carpetbagger candidacy presents helps explain why they are so rare, and so rarely successful, in American politics. This is not the case in every representative democracy. In parliamentary systems, where parties draw lists of candidates for office and directly select which candidate will run in which constituency, it is much more common for candidates to come from a region other than the one they seek to represent. Gandy, for instance, notes that in the Parliament elected in Great Britain in 2010, the Conservative Party tended to populate its safest seats with candidates external to those constituencies and that fully half of the members of the cabinet and shadow cabinet in that Parliament were not originally from their constituencies.[23] External candidates remain a minority and are often denigrated as carpetbaggers or *parachutistes*, but they also enjoy a level and frequency of electoral success that their American equivalents do not.

Childs and Cowley argue that the aversion to external candidates, even in systems where such candidates run and win with some regularity, is not simply rooted in parochial notions of hometown pride or suspicion of the motivations of carpetbaggers. Instead, they examine this aversion from the perspective of descriptive representation. In the case of descriptive representation as applied to women, racial and ethnic minorities, and other historically excluded or disadvantaged groups, the argument for descriptive representation is not made solely on symbolic grounds—that it would be, simply, nice, or validating, or fairer to have women serving alongside men or blacks serving alongside whites. Advocates for descriptive representation argue that a representative government that excludes classes of citizens is, as a result of that exclusion, going to have poorer deliberations, and thus poorer policy making, and that the decisions made by such an exclusionary government will on a fundamental level be lacking in legitimacy. When members of excluded groups have a role in the deliberative process, on the other hand, those deliberations will be stronger thanks to the presence of a greater number of perspectives and shared experiences, and the resulting decisions will enjoy a greater level of legitimacy.

Childs and Cowley ask whether living in a parliamentary constituency can be conceived of as a criteria of historic exclusion similar to gender or racial minority status; were this to be the case, then residence such a constituency could similarly be considered as an identity that merits descriptive representation. Childs and Cowley analyze each constituency in the United Kingdom on a variety of socioeconomic metrics and conclude that at least one-quarter of those constituencies meet the criteria for being viewed as a historically excluded or disadvantaged group. In other words, for the residents of those specific constituencies, living where they do is as exclusionary, at least in terms of representation, as is belonging to any of the other groups more commonly thought of in terms of historic discrimination and exclusion.[24] Additional research in British politics has found that respondents valued having a representative with local ties as highly as they did having a representative who shared their opinions on important issues.[25]

These and other findings present powerful, empirical explanations of why localism or geography can affect voters' reactions to candidates and officeholders. Even in a political system where politicians move from one constituency to another with more frequency and success, and where parties use their safest seats as safe havens for key party leaders, having an external or outside representative is undesirable to many voters. Being a carpetbagger is seen as lessening a candidate's ability, capacity, and perhaps even willingness to be a good representative of the candidate's constituents.

In American elections, carpetbaggers face an additional hurdle resulting from the design of the United States Senate. In races for the House of Representatives, it is not unheard of for candidates to move from one district to another within a state or even for a candidate to be elected from a district other than the one he or she lives in. But the lines of a congressional district are fluid, redrawn every ten years, and possess little inherent meaning to voters; Indiana, for instance, is "the Hoosier State," while its Fifth Congressional District is something that was designed through political squabbling and deal making in the state's legislature and may look completely different in ten years, after the next round of redistricting. It is meaningful to say something about the culture of a state, whether that be New Hampshire's libertarianism or Minnesota nice, in a way that rarely applies to a congressional district.

Beyond the different perceptions of each level of government in American political culture, there is also the matter of institutional design. In the Senate, each state has two, and only two, seats, and each senator serves for six years—the longest elected term in the federal government. That makes Senate seats valuable and scarce tools for representation, and perhaps makes voters warier of electing a carpetbagger or other "outsider" candidate to one. Voters can "fix" a poor choice of a House member in just two years' time; a poor Senate choice will be around for a while. And a poor Senate choice would likewise mean a long-term cost in terms of a state's representation. Electing a carpetbagger to a state's Senate seat might imperil the quality of the state's representation in a substantive way. While members of a minority group might, if ignored by their own representative, find surrogate representation in the form of a representative from another state or district who belongs to the same minority group, it is far less likely that a senator from another state would do the same for residents of a state that elected a neglectful carpetbagger. While gender and racial identities can be fluid and cross political boundaries, state identities, in particular, are fixed and static in a way that does not lend itself to surrogate representation, and tend to endure even in the face of interstate migration. The linkage between localism and representation, particularly when it comes to the United States Senate, is sufficiently strong that question should perhaps not be why are carpetbaggers so unsuccessful as it should be why any of them bother to run in the first place.

Ambition and Party Actors

That politicians are creatures of ambition has been an axiom of American politics as long as American politics has existed; the regulation and moderation of that ambition was, to James Madison, one of the key challenges facing the new American nation.[26] But for a candidate to pull up stakes and move to a state expressly to run for office signals a level of ambition that exists on an entirely different level than one normally encounters. It goes beyond the level of ego and ambition that leads someone to announce that he or she, out of however many thousands of people live in a state, is the one, best person to hold a given office. A carpetbagger takes the additional step of implicitly telling the residents of a state that he or she is better suited to hold a particular office than literally every person who was present in the state prior to the carpetbagger's arrival. How can someone displaying such unseemly ambition—since we generally expect politicians to hide their ambitions, rather than admit to them—have even a prayer of winning a party's nomination, let alone a general election?

To answer that question, it is useful to consider the different ways in which politicians' ambition can play out in their campaigns. Schlesinger identifies three different types of ambition that can motivate a politician. A candidate driven by what Schlesinger calls discrete ambition seeks a particular office for its allotted term and nothing more. An example would be New Hampshire's John Lynch, whose first entry into electoral politics was his successful campaign for governor; since leaving office, Lynch has resisted entreaties to run for higher office. Candidates with static ambition want to make a long-term career out of holding a specific office; many members of Congress, whose power and influence increase along with their seniority, can be said to possess this type of ambition. And candidates with progressive ambition constantly aspire to higher offices than the ones they currently hold or even the ones they are currently seeking. Both Barack Obama and Marco Rubio—candidates who were considered potential presidential candidates even before they were elected to the Senate—typify this sort of ambition.[27] Motivations might vary throughout a career; a politician might have progressive ambitions, but after a losing primary campaign for president decide to focus on his or her work in Congress rather than run for president again. Or a governor might dream of becoming president when he or she is first elected but then decide that the governorship is enough public service for one lifetime.

Candidates' ambition affects not just decisions about which office to seek but also when to seek it. Candidates run not just when an office they aspire to is on the ballot but also when they think they are best able to win that election. Carpetbaggers' geographic relocation adds another dimension to the calculations involved as well as to how voters will respond to them. Many politicians with presidential ambitions have, in seeking re-election in the election year prior to a presidential election year, found themselves grappling with voters who want to know whether that politician intends to serve out a full term. This concern is a sensible one. Voters might fear that someone with an eye on the White House will govern and otherwise behave in a way that will help him or her win the presidency rather than in a way that is best for the state. In this instance, open progressive ambition can be a stumbling block that a candidate must finesse, as Bill Clinton did in first pledging to serve out his term as governor in his 1990 re-election campaign and then backtracking on that pledge in order to run in 1992.[28]

For carpetbaggers, however, the nature of their ambitions can play a different role. While progressive ambitions may be an obstacle for a normal candidate, they may turn out to help a carpetbagger. The two successful candidates examined in later chapters—Robert Kennedy and Hillary Clinton—were both viewed as potential presidential candidates at the time they ran for the Senate in their new states. And even if neither had ever run for president, their backgrounds before running for Senate had already made them national figures. As first lady, Clinton was arguably the most famous woman in politics when she decided to become a New Yorker. Kennedy had served as a cabinet secretary, where he influenced policy on a national level alongside his brother the president. For both candidates, the decision to move to a new state could be presented as the next step in a long career of public service. And their national ambitions may have presented an upside; as an exceptionally rational voter in New York said of Kennedy during the 1964 campaign, "He'll have to do a lot for this state if he wants to become president."[29] Carpetbaggers with national stature also have a head start in making themselves known to voters, which may help them establish the sense of trust Fenno identifies as so vital to successful representation.

For other carpetbaggers, like would-be two-state senators James Buckley and Bill Brock, the decision to run in a new state may have come across as not just static ambition, but static ambition to hold the office of senator regardless of what state they had to run in to win it a second time. In these cases, the reasoning that normally accompanies static ambition does not apply. When a longtime member of Congress goes home and seeks yet another term in office, part of the appeal to voters involves the benefits of that member's tenure: seniority, committee chairmanship, deep and specific knowledge of a state or district and the people who live there, an ability to both represent the area's interests well and direct federal dollars back home, and so on. In other words, the member's lengthy service in Congress benefits not just the member, who gets to enjoy holding the office and all that goes with it, but also the voters, whose interests the member can serve better than a new member would be able to. With a carpetbagger who is seeking the same office he or she once held in a new state, a voter's thinking might change; instead of a mutually beneficial relationship, the voter might see the candidate as using the voter and the voter's state as a means to the carpetbagger's own end of winning or regaining power. This is not, it bears emphasizing, necessarily any different than what any candidate does; the point of running for office is, in part, to win office. But carpetbaggers' lack of ties to a new state makes their ambition clear in a way that it is not, necessarily, for other candidates. National ambitions and national stature might make those ambitions more palatable to voters for a carpetbagger, where they might damage an ordinary candidate. For instance, in the run-up to his 2006 re-election campaign, Senator George Allen of Virginia found that his nascent plans for a presidential campaign—including visits to Iowa during the year of his re-election campaign—were making him appear distracted from and uninterested in what was going on at home.[30] It seems likely that voters would evaluate a national figure who develops state ambitions differently than a state figure who develops national ambitions.

State Characteristics

While all of the states enjoy equal representation in the Senate, the characteristics and cultures of the different states vary widely. Daniel Elazar's work found wide variation among the states in terms of what he termed their "intrastate cohesion," a general internal consensus on both the state's goals and norms and the need to protect those goals and norms in the face of pressure from other states or the federal government. These may involve specific public policy goals, defense of unique local cultural patterns, encouraging or discouraging new residents, and more. Some states, Elazar found, have very strong intrastate cohesion and as a result might be expected to be hostile or suspicious toward a would-be carpetbagger; in others, with less cohesive state political cultures, a carpetbagger might receive a warmer welcome. New York, the site of three of the campaigns studied in the chapters that follow, was among the least cohesive states in Elazar's 1965 and 1970 analyses.[31]

Subsequent research suggests that political culture helps explain different outcomes between states. Fitzpatrick and Hero found that states with what they dubbed moralistic political cultures displayed more innovative policy, more policy that emerges from party competition, and have less economic inequality, among other things, while states with traditionalistic cultures had opposite outcomes. States with individualistic cultures, on the other hand, tended to resemble states with moralistic cultures but tended to have less use of merit systems for hiring, and party competition had less of an impact on policy outcomes.[32] These findings suggest that cultural variations between states may have an impact on how carpetbaggers run for office in their new states. In traditionalist and individualist states, the support of party elites may prove more essential to a carpetbagger's hopes than they would in a state with a moralistic culture that views the everyday citizen as the most important actor in the political system. On the other hand, the strong party competition in individualistic and moralistic states might lead voters in the carpetbagger's party to be more willing to support a newcomer to their state than voters in a traditionalist state might.

Culture is not the only feature that varies between the states. States also vary dramatically in population size. States like California, New York, and Florida have populations in the tens of millions, while states like Vermont, Montana, and Wyoming have populations at or slightly below the one million mark. Variations in size can affect the way representatives engage in representation. Fenno observed that senators from small states behave more like House members, in terms of their representational activities and their relationships with constituents, than their counterparts from larger states do.[33] This finding may inform expectations about how well carpetbaggers will adapt to or fare in new states. Carpetbaggers moving to larger states might find that residents will have lower expectations of interpersonal interaction and trust, while carpetbaggers coming to smaller states may have to work harder to try to establish trusting relationships with voters.

Population size can also affect electoral outcomes. Hibbing and Brandes found, in their examination of Senate elections from 1946 to 1980, that incumbent senators from small states had an easier time getting re-elected than did incumbent senators from larger states. Hibbing and Brandes speculate that representing a larger state makes it harder for an incumbent to succeed at the sorts of activities that help other members of Congress win re-election: They do less constituency work than House members, their constituency work likely engages a smaller proportion of their constituents, they have to please more people to win re-election, and the greater heterogeneity of their constituents means there is likely to be less of a consensus within the electorate on both policy matters and partisan identification.[34]

In addition to variations in population size, there are also variations in the diversity of the populations found in each state. This could also affect how carpetbaggers approach their campaigns. Fenno contrasted "Congressman A," who represented what Fenno described as a homogeneous district, with "Congressman B," from a more heterogeneous district.[35] Congressman A's district featured a broad consensus on major issues, which meant that Congressman A's focus in his visits to the district was on interpersonal interactions through which he could reassure and remind voters that he was just like them. Congressman B, on the other hand, had to vary his interactions with constituents depending on whether he was in a rural area of the district or in the suburbs. Because of the variations between parts of his district, Congressman B could not solely present himself as one and the same with his all of his constituents. Instead, he cultivated what Fenno called a "big man on campus" persona, built on his background as a local sports hero, so that an air of likability would help him appeal to voters across the diverse parts of his district.[36]

In addition to population size, we might then expect carpetbaggers to have an easier time fitting into states with more heterogeneous populations. Heterogeneity is not the same thing as population size; one can easily imagine a small state that nevertheless has a wide range of diverse groups living within it. But as a state's population increases, it becomes more likely that that population will tend to be more heterogeneous. In these larger states, candidates' identification with voters would not be as one-note as it would have to be in Congressman A's district, and candidates would have some freedom to try to assemble a winning coalition by appealing to various segments of the electorate in a way that is not possible in more homogeneous constituencies. The more heterogeneous an electorate is, the more possibilities a candidate has in putting together enough votes to win. Fenno's Congressman A noted that there was little difference of opinion between his constituents at large and those he considered his primary constituency. In a more heterogeneous state, a carpetbagger has more options and the chance to build outward from a primary constituency—if he or she can put one together on relatively short notice.

For a carpetbagger's Senate candidacy to be taken seriously, two things are necessary. The first is that potential candidates who belong to the carpetbagger's party must either decline to run or be viewed by others in the party as much weaker candidates than the carpetbagger would be. This puts potential carpetbaggers in a precarious position. Since most candidates and would-be candidates want to win their elections, they tend to be careful to run only in those elections they think they have a good chance of winning. An absence of strong local candidates for a high-profile election is often an indicator that the race is one that will be difficult for a candidate from their party to win. So, for many carpetbaggers, the opportunity available to them in a new state may in many cases be less valuable than it might appear on the surface.

On the other hand, consider the potential carpetbagger. Someone who finds himself or herself in the position of decamping to a new state in order to run for office is unlikely to do so if he or she has better options available. Politicians are, generally, pragmatic about when they run for office and tend to run when they have their best chance of winning and retire when they are likely to lose.[37] But those chances may differ from candidate to candidate. For instance, Banks and Kiewlet found that experienced politicians tend to wait to run for open seats in Congress, while inexperienced candidates tend to challenge incumbents.[38] All things being equal, it is generally easier to win an open-seat race than it is to defeat an incumbent officeholder. But for someone without much political experience, the best chance at winning a nomination to run for Congress is often going to be against an incumbent because more experienced candidates tend to wait for an easier win in an open-seat contest. For a would-be carpetbagger, a move to a new state means closing the door on elective opportunities in the one he or she had previously been associated with. A politician who decides to become a carpetbagger is likely to be one without viable options in his or her previous state. The opportunity to run, even one that more local potential candidates have passed on as too costly or too unlikely to result in a victory, may represent the best chance a potential carpetbagger candidate is going to get. In this regard, a carpetbagger is not that different from an ambitious House member whose state's seats in the Senate are held by members of his own party who have no plans to retire any time soon and, as a result, runs for governor instead of the Senate: ambition is constrained by the opportunities available. For a candidate who finds constraints at every turn in one state, a move to another might present the best chance to satisfy electoral goals, even though that move is itself fraught with its own set of difficulties.

State party actors can help facilitate a carpetbagger's candidacy in a second way. As prominent figures with strong, existing ties to the carpetbagger's new state, they can vouch for the carpetbagger's ability to be a good representative of the state's interests, even though the carpetbagger has a short history in the state. While voters are concerned with representation, party leaders are concerned, first and foremost, with winning elections. If a carpetbagger represents a party's best chance of winning an election, party leaders will likely rush to tell voters that the carpetbagger will be a good and able representative of their state's interests. By reassuring voters that the carpetbagger has their interests at heart, these established, local figures can downplay the idea that the carpetbagger is moved solely by his or her own ambition. If, on the other hand, established figures in the state party do not support the carpetbagger's campaign, or actively take steps to oppose it, such as endorsing a rival candidate, that lack of support will hurt or even end the carpetbagger's campaign in its earliest stages. State party actors' support is most likely to be forthcoming when other potential candidates have passed on the chance to run, but party leaders still think the race is winnable, and least likely to come when the carpetbagger offers no chance of improving the party's prospects, or providing any other benefits to the party as an institution.

Candidate Characteristics

A final factor that must be considered in studying carpetbaggers is the carpetbaggers themselves. What strengths and weaknesses do they bring, as individuals and as political figures, to their campaigns? The link between locality and representation means that any carpetbagger's campaign will start at a disadvantage. That disadvantage can, in part, be ameliorated by the support of state party figures. But that support, while it might be sufficient to win a party's nomination, is not enough to help a carpetbagger win an election. That hinges on the campaign the carpetbagger runs and whether the carpetbagger can successfully convince voters that he or she is motivated by more than simply the ambition to hold office.

However, the role of that ambition should not be discounted. Fenno argues that politicians' decisions to run for office are best viewed not in isolation but in the context of their larger careers in public service.[39] In other words, candidates run for office not just when they think they will win, but when they think running and winning will help them achieve their goals. For some, these goals might mean achieving a specific policy outcome. Others may seek to move up in party leadership, to chair an important committee, or to establish themselves as leaders of important factions within their parties. Candidates also assess the risks running presents: not just the risk of loss in a given campaign, but risks posed by the impact of a loss on one's reputation, of an opponent's negative campaign, or whether running for another term is, in the candidate's view, worth it.

Viewing the decision to run for office as part of a larger career trajectory is useful when trying to understand why carpetbaggers decide to run for office. It is likely that many of them will turn out to be figures who are, for one reason or another, in need of the platform, independence, and legitimacy that elected office provides, so they can advance their views or continue (or revive) a political career. Given the complications involved in running for office in a brand-new state, it is unlikely that anyone would take such a step if any more plausible route to elected office were available. Ambitious politicians will only swim upstream against the powerful tides of localism and the carpetbagger label if doing so is their best chance for electoral success and if electoral success is necessary to realize other career ambitions. Carpetbaggers' ability to present their ambitions in terms of service to a new state, rather than service of their own interests and ends, may help explain why some are more successful than others in the electoral arena.

Another carpetbagger characteristic that may prove important is the extent of the carpetbagger's ties to another state. The stronger and more explicitly a carpetbagger is tied to another state, the more difficult it may prove to be for that carpetbagger to overcome the label. So a carpetbagger who has held elected office in another state would face a higher hurdle than a candidate who has not, for instance.

Given the representational conundrum carpetbaggers confront, why would any talented, ambitious, politician to take the step of becoming a carpetbagger? Politicians are, for the most part, rational about deciding whether to run for office. When could running in a new state and having to address the carpetbagger question, on top of all of the other headaches involved in running for office, possibly qualify as a rational decision?

In considering this question, it is important to bear in mind that one person's rational decision is another person's descent into madness. The issue is not whether the decision is, taken in isolation, purely rational on its own merits. Instead, the question is whether the decision is, from the perspective of the carpetbagger candidate, a rational one—with rationality in this case meaning simply that it represents the carpetbagger candidate's best opportunity to achieve his or her goal and that not running would represent a worse outcome than running. Viewed from this angle, the decision to become a carpetbagger becomes one that we would only expect politicians in specific circumstances to make—that the candidates who become carpetbaggers do so only because other, more conventional avenues to elected office are closed off to them. Beyond their own, individual circumstances, national trends may play a role as well; if the carpetbagger's party is expected to win seats in the Senate in a given election year, that may make the difficulties of running as a carpetbagger more worthwhile to a candidate.

When, then, should we expect carpetbaggers to be able to overcome the considerable obstacles their status puts in the way of getting nominated and elected? Here, state and national party actors, as well as the national political atmosphere more generally, play a role. The support of established figures in a state party will be crucial to any carpetbagger's success. But that support is likely to be rooted in those figures' own calculations. Support for a carpetbagger will emerge if that support is of benefit to those figures' own particular goals. If a carpetbagger represents the party's best chance to win an election, or if no other strong candidate with closer ties to the state emerges, then state party figures are likely to back a candidate from outside the state. If, on the other hand, the carpetbagger cannot win the support of state party figures, or if those figures actively oppose the carpetbagger's win, then the carpetbagger candidate is unlikely to win his or her party's nomination. These considerations likely take into account more than simply the appeal of the carpetbagger candidate; state party figures also are likely to incorporate the national political landscape in much the same way that the candidates themselves do. If potential in-state candidates have passed on a race, and a willing carpetbagger presents himself or herself, the state party's leaders might be more likely to get behind the carpetbagger's candidacy on the sensible grounds that it takes a candidate to win an election. This does not, however, necessarily mean that every carpetbagger who wins a nomination does so because state party leaders are strong supporters of the carpetbagger's candidacy. If a nomination is viewed as less than valuable, for instance because an incumbent is perceived as unbeatable, then state party actors might acquiesce to a carpetbagger's run because they see such a run as offering little benefit but unlikely to cause any harm.

The support of state actors should be a necessary, but not sufficient, condition for a carpetbagger candidate's election. Even with that support, a carpetbagger must still address the representational issues carpetbagging presents, by convincing voters that he or she will, despite being a newcomer, be able to represent the interests of the state's residents effectively.

The chapters that follow examine the candidacies of nine individuals described as carpetbaggers during their campaigns for the US Senate. Some succeeded, but most did not. All of these candidates took different approaches to their campaigns and to responding to the carpetbagger charge. In each of these analyses, particular attention will be paid to the way in which these candidates try to navigate the challenges of overcoming the carpetbagger label by addressing voters' representational concerns, downplaying their own ambitions, and casting themselves as authentically belonging to their new states.

Chapter 3

Robert Kennedy

New York, 1964

An examination of modern carpetbagger candidates must begin with Robert F. Kennedy, who ran for a Senate seat in New York in 1964, less than a year after President John F. Kennedy's assassination, and won the election despite his lack of meaningful ties to that state. His election may, in retrospect, seem like the inevitable, necessary step between his service as his brother's attorney general and his own campaign for president and tragic assassination in 1968. However, despite his family name and his rendezvous with history, neither Kennedy's victory in New York nor his decision to run there in the first place was by any means assured. Instead, they were the result of a series of stars moving into a precise alignment: Kennedy's own ambitions and the closing off of other, easier paths to their achievement; a national political environment that favored Democrats; the state of the New York Democratic Party; the behavior and interests of state and national Democratic leaders; and the vulnerabilities of Kennedy's general election opponent, Republican Kenneth Keating. In the absence of even one of these factors, it is unlikely that Kennedy would have run in or won this election.

Carpetbagging in Kennedy's Career Context

By the start of 1964, Robert Kennedy's public image was tightly tied to the memory of his brother, President John F. Kennedy. Robert Kennedy had first made a name for himself managing his brother's campaign for the United

States Senate in 1952 and then for his role as an attorney for several Senate investigative panels. But it was as the manager of his brother's 1960 campaign for president and then as his brother's attorney general that he became a household figure. As early as 1962, there was speculation that RFK might succeed JFK, and a *U.S. News and World Report* article described him as "assistant president."[1]

Whatever plans for the future the Kennedy brothers may have had were shattered when President Kennedy was assassinated in Dallas, Texas, on November 22, 1963. Robert Kennedy's prominence in the funeral ceremonies for the late president helped make him universally known to Americans and softened his image in the eyes of many. But when the mourning and ceremonies ended, Kennedy's standing within the government had diminished dramatically. Kennedy, who had spent years with unfettered access to the Oval Office and had advised his brother on decisions far outside the Department of Justice's traditional jurisdiction, was suddenly an exile within the executive branch.

Much of that stemmed from Kennedy's relationship with the new president, Lyndon Johnson. The bad blood between the two dated back to their first meeting in 1953, when Kennedy was a Senate committee staffer and Johnson was Senate Majority Leader.[2] In 1960, Robert Kennedy had objected to his brother's offer of the vice presidential slot on the Democratic ticket to Johnson and worked furiously to try to revoke the invitation.[3] While Johnson was vice president, both Kennedys ignored, diminished, and slighted Johnson on matters significant (such as rejecting his offers to coordinate legislative strategy for passing the new president's program), symbolic (such as requiring Johnson to get one of the Kennedy brothers to sign off on any authorization for Johnson to use a government airplane), and personal (excluding the vice president from social gatherings at Bobby Kennedy's Hickory Hill estate).[4]

Now that Johnson was president, however, the tables were turned. Johnson saw little need to consult the attorney general on matters beyond the immediate jurisdiction of the Department of Justice. For symbolic reasons, as well, Johnson wanted to keep the late president's brother at a distance. Johnson was keenly aware that he had become president not through the votes of the American people but thanks to an assassin's bullets, and the new president wanted to establish himself as legitimate in his own right. Keeping Bobby Kennedy in the same sort of favored position he'd previously enjoyed would undercut perceptions of Johnson's ability to function as president and imply that Johnson needed Kennedy's assistance to do the job. But as much as Johnson wanted to signal his independence, Johnson was also desperate to keep Bobby from resigning. For Johnson, keeping the "Kennedy men" around him was vital to ensuring Johnson's own legitimacy as president.[5] And no Kennedy man was more closely identified with the late president than Bobby.

Kennedy spent the months after the assassination adrift as he considered and rejected one strategy for remaining in public life after another. For a time, he considered immersing himself in the details of running the Department of Justice so deeply that he would not have the time to consider his diminished status relative to the White House.[6] He quietly pursued a shadow campaign for the vice presidency and pointedly declined to instruct the organizers of write-in campaigns in primary states to cease and desist in their efforts. He did this despite his having witnessed what a miserable position that had been for Lyndon Johnson and having helped to make Johnson's tenure so miserable. Kennedy tried to convince himself that President Johnson could not treat a vice president Kennedy the way President Kennedy had treated Vice President Johnson.[7] Johnson, who would have preferred almost literally anyone in the Democratic Party other than Bobby to be his vice president, ultimately closed that door by announcing that no members of his cabinet could be spared to run on the Democratic ticket in 1964.[8] At one point during this aimless period, Kennedy recommended himself as a replacement for Henry Cabot Lodge Jr. as ambassador to South Vietnam. Johnson demurred.[9]

If Kennedy were going to remain in public life, he would have to do it somewhere other than Lyndon Johnson's executive branch. And Kennedy desperately wanted to remain in public life. This was not just a matter of personal ambition, though Kennedy was certainly ambitious. It was also a matter of legacy. Kennedy saw himself as the keeper of his brother's memory and legacy and as the person who now bore the burden of keeping the late president's spirit and energy a vital part of American political life. Simply leaving the public stage was not an option; doing so would, in Bobby's mind, take his brother off that stage as well.

The most logical step for Kennedy to take would have been to return to Massachusetts and run for the Senate, where Kennedy would enjoy the independence and prominence that accompanies membership in that body. Kennedy would have been certain to win such an election, but an immovable obstacle blocked that path: Massachusetts already had a Senator Kennedy. Ted, the youngest Kennedy brother, had won the 1962 special election to serve the remaining two years of John F. Kennedy's Senate term. Worse yet for Bobby's ambitions, Ted was running for a full term of his own in 1964. Even if the people of Massachusetts would have been happy with being represented by two Senators Kennedy at the same time—and less than a year after Dallas, they very may well have been, if given the opportunity—there was no way for Bobby to run for that office without displacing Ted.

So, by the summer of 1964, Robert Kennedy found himself in a very strange position. In the eyes of many Americans, he was his brother's spiritual and political heir and a tangible, visible link to all that had been lost in Dallas. But at the same time that he was shut out of the corridors of power, he wanted, and needed, to stay involved in public life. To do that, he needed a platform. However, all of the most obvious and sensible options were closed off for one reason or another. If Kennedy truly wanted to find some way to continue the sort of politics his brother's campaign and presidency had represented, he would have to display some adaptability.

In June, Kennedy asked family confidant Milton Gwirtzman to evaluate two options. The first was to run for governor of Massachusetts. That position, Gwirtzman wrote in his report, had two benefits: it was far away from President Johnson, and it would be easy for Kennedy to win. But there were downsides to running for governor as well. The position was a weak one and would require constant handling of the state's legislature. Worst of all, the governorship of Massachusetts lacked the profile Kennedy desired; rather than elevating the office by holding it, the nature of the office itself—limited in power and far from national and world events—could diminish Kennedy's own stature.

The second option Gwirtzman evaluated was running for the Senate in New York. This position would put Kennedy at the center of things in Washington, with the independence and influence a senator enjoys and the opportunity to join the young liberal senators who had been elected in recent years. It was apparent by this point that Lyndon Johnson would defeat Barry Goldwater in a landslide in that fall's presidential election, which could boost the electoral fortunes of Democrats across the country. New York's incumbent, Kenneth Keating, was a Republican, so Kennedy would not be displacing anyone in his own party (or family) by running. Kennedy's standing as the spiritual and political heir of his brother's legacy would be enhanced by the prestige of the Senate, and he would gain additional stature as the senator from a state that was, in 1964, in many ways the center of American culture and media.[10] There was, however, one glaring problem with this gambit: Kennedy was not, as Article I, Section 3 of the Constitution requires, an inhabitant of the state he would be seeking to represent. Were Kennedy to choose this path, he would have to become a resident of New York. And in so doing, Kennedy would inevitably become—and have to address the baggage that goes along with being—a carpetbagger.

New York Politics in 1964

Fortunately for Kennedy, several aspects of the political landscape in New York were in many ways favorable for a Kennedy campaign. First and foremost, the seat in question was held by Kenneth Keating, a Republican seeking a second term in 1964. This meant that Kennedy could begin his campaign without raising the specter of ruthlessness by shoving aside a fellow Democrat. Keating had been elected to the Senate in 1958, as part of the Republican tide in New York that had also elected Nelson Rockefeller governor. By 1964, Rockefeller was in the middle of his second term, and Republicans were enjoying electoral success across the state. In hindsight, 1964 would turn out to be the midpoint of a period during which New York was "the seventh most Republican state in the nation and the most Republican of the ten most important states."[11] While Democrats retained an advantage in voter registration in the state throughout this period, Republicans would hold most important statewide offices throughout the rest of the decade.

The state's Democrats were divided between reformers, on the one hand, and liberals, on the other, with each side suspicious and mistrustful of the other and protective of whatever territory it still controlled. Navigating the divides within the state party had proven a persistent headache for the Kennedy campaign in 1960.[12] Worse yet for the Democrats, there were few individuals in the party who appeared interested in and capable of opposing Keating's bid for a second term. Well into 1964, the only declared candidate for the Democratic nomination was Samuel S. Stratton, an upstate congressman who had sought and lost the party's nomination for governor two years earlier and who inspired little enthusiasm among the state's Democrats.

This dismal state of affairs for New York's Democrats was, however, a favorable state of affairs for Kennedy, whose late declaration of his availability as a candidate would be seen as a lifeline to a desperate party, rather than a coup against a local candidate for the Democratic nomination. Kennedy further benefited from the fact that the New York State Democratic Party was choosing its Senate nominee through a state party convention, rather than through a primary, and that this convention was being held at the start of September rather than earlier in the year. The use of a convention, rather than a primary, meant that Kennedy needed only to target the delegates to the convention, rather than the state's Democrats at large, in making the case for his candidacy over Stratton's. Representative Stratton refused to end his own campaign, and he assailed Kennedy's campaign as "basically wrong" and denounced the "total bankruptcy of New York's Democratic leadership" for getting behind a carpetbagger.[13] But the party's choice of a convention meant that rank-and-file Democrats did not have to choose between Kennedy and Stratton. The timing of the convention also benefited Kennedy. Its late date meant that Kennedy had months to explore other options, and its timing just after the Democratic National Convention in Atlantic City meant Kennedy's enthusiastic reception there would be fresh in the state convention delegates' minds when they chose their nominee.

The political terrain in New York was, thanks to these factors, favorable for a Kennedy campaign. But Kennedy, like any carpetbagger, lacked the sort of longstanding ties to and knowledge of the state and its politics that a local candidate would have. As a result, he needed the support of party officials to smooth his path and to assure others in the party that his selection as the party's nominee would benefit people beyond Kennedy himself.

Party Actors

In the absence of a sitting governor or senator, the public leadership of the party fell by default to Mayor Robert Wagner of New York City. Wagner was resistant to the idea of a Kennedy candidacy and ultimately came around and endorsed Kennedy's campaign only after repeated lobbying by President Johnson. Johnson saw a Kennedy run in New York as a win-win: if Bobby won the election, there would be one more Democrat in the Senate, and if Bobby lost, Bobby would have lost the election. Wagner's hesitant feelings were public enough that he found it necessary to make a statement shortly before the state party's nominating convention to the effect that he did not think a Kennedy candidacy or victory would diminish Wagner's own position in the state party.[14]

Wagner, however, was not the totality of the New York Democratic Party. While some party regulars backed Kennedy's candidacy, Kennedy continued to encounter resistance from the reformists in the party, some of whom would go on to create a "Democrats for Keating" organization during the general election.[15] Therefore, the Kennedy campaign devoted considerable effort to creating the impression that the idea of Kennedy's candidacy had originated with and been encouraged by leaders of the state party. An August 16, 1964, letter and statement signed by Democratic notables like former governor Averill Harriman, former *New York Post* publisher George Backer, and prodigious Democratic fundraiser Abraham Feinberg, urged Kennedy to run, noting his experience in the executive branch with domestic and foreign affairs and his party affiliation. For good measure, the statement also ran down the list of the Kennedy family's personal and business ties to New York.[16] Another campaign statement listed the "many leading Reformers" who had urged him to become a candidate, in an effort to bring the reformist wing of the state party on board.[17]

The support of these and other figures within the New York Democratic Party benefited Kennedy in two ways. First, it signaled to other elite actors within the party that Kennedy was not simply muscling in from outside, but was making his case to party leaders that he was the party's best option for defeating Keating. Second, it conveyed to the New York electorate the impression that Kennedy's candidacy was not simply a product of Kennedy's own ambitions, but instead bolstered by invitations from many of the state's leading Democratic figures. The public appeals from these party leaders to Kennedy also previewed something of the manner in which Kennedy and his campaign would address the carpetbagger issue that cast a long shadow over his candidacy.

The Carpetbagger with Experience

Kennedy was not the first candidate to move to a state to seek office, nor was he the first candidate to be branded with the carpetbagger label. But he was an extraordinarily famous carpetbagger. Kennedy confidante Arthur Schlesinger Jr., in his biography of Kennedy, observes that the charge had the potential to be particularly damaging against Kennedy. Kennedy's position in the public mind as his brother's political heir and mourner-in-chief, after all, had only started after Dallas. Previously, Kennedy's defining characteristic in the minds of many had been his long-attributed ruthlessness; a move to New York could conceivably come across to voters as "a power grab by a madly ambitious, arrogant, opportunistic, primitive, and dangerous young man."[18] Schlesinger was not the only Kennedy insider concerned with the amount of damage the carpetbagger charge could inflict. Even before Kennedy became a candidate, he and his closest supporters took the issue seriously and spent considerable time and effort trying to address it.

One approach the candidate and his campaign took was to emphasize the ties Kennedy did have to New York. Time and again throughout his campaign, Kennedy recited a list of biographical facts that were meant to suggest that he was less a carpetbagger than a long-displaced New Yorker finally come home after years of wandering the wilderness: his family's

residences in Riverdale and Bronxville, his time attending public schools in
Bronxville in third through fifth grades, his sisters' continued residence in
the state, and his family's ongoing business presence in the state.[19] Briefing
materials prepared in advance of an October appearance on *Meet the Press*
recommended Kennedy present himself as having "lived in New York for
the first 20 years of [his] life,"[20] which elided his time spent living outside of
New York at boarding schools, as a college student, and in London during
his father's tenure as ambassador to the United Kingdom. It is worth noting
that in a televised appearance earlier in the campaign, Kennedy stated that
he had lived in New York for only twelve years;[21] as Kennedy's campaign
sought to recover from a rocky start, the candidate may have decided it was
worth counting his youthful residency in the state more generously than he
otherwise might have.

　　Not everyone inside the campaign thought an emphasis on Kennedy's
ties to the state would satisfy the critics of Kennedy's move. One unsigned
internal memo, prepared in advance of the launch of Kennedy's campaign,
argued that it would be "an unacceptable sophistry to proclaim the Attorney
General as a Bronx boy because he once lived briefly in Riverdale."[22] This
memo suggested that Kennedy instead present his decision to run as simply
seeking a chance to continue to serve the public good and emphasize that
the voters of New York would have the final say on whether he would get
that chance. The sort of "one of us" strategy Fenno observed in practice by
multiple congressional candidates, this memo argued, was not an option for
Kennedy. His time in the state as a child was long past, and he had not lived
in the state as an adult, so his claims of being a New Yorker come home at
last simply did not hold up. Everyone in the state knew that Kennedy was
not, in any way that mattered, a New Yorker. As one newspaper editorial
put it, his "slim claim" to being a New Yorker was outweighed by "the fact
that Kennedy was born in Massachusetts, attended Harvard University, was
admitted to the bar in Massachusetts, has voted there, and is unmistakably a
son of the Bay State from his Boston accent to his Cape Cod tan."[23]

　　While Kennedy never abandoned his mentions of his youthful residence in New York and his family's ties to the state, those were not the only
credentials he offered to voters. He and his supporters repeatedly used his
experience as attorney general to justify his candidacy and his ability to serve
New York. The great issues facing New York in 1964—poverty, civil rights,
housing, labor, and more—were the same great issues facing the nation at
large. Kennedy and his campaign argued that these were also the same issues
he had worked on alongside his brother. The campaign assembled a sheet

touting "Kennedy-Johnson Accomplishments for New York" in such areas as education (176,595 more students enrolled in school lunch programs than under Eisenhower; 32,778 more college students receiving educational loans), health and welfare (375,727 more people receiving surplus food), and housing ($1,447,584 in urban planning grants).[24] The August 16 letter from New York Democratic leaders urging Kennedy to run similarly cited his first-hand experience in both foreign and domestic affairs as a justification for his campaign.[25] Kennedy may have been a very new New Yorker, this argument suggested, but he would bring an unmatched level of knowledge and experience to the race. At the heart of this claim was the candidate's close relationship with his brother; while cabinet secretaries had run for office before, and would again, few could claim the kind of intimate working relationship with a president that Kennedy could. Kennedy's record in the executive branch would let him easily meet the competence threshold Fenno identifies as necessary for any candidate to have a chance of success.[26]

The campaign also cited historical and contemporary events to justify his run in New York. Kennedy frequently noted that one of New York's first senators, Rufus King, had moved to the state from Massachusetts.[27] And the Kennedy campaign prepared a memo that noted that the delegates to the Constitutional Convention had rejected fixed state residency requirements for federal candidates in favor of simply requiring that candidates be inhabitants of a state at the time of their election.[28] Another campaign document noted that eighteen of one hundred sitting senators had been born in a state other than the one they represented.[29]

These tactics all sought to downplay the spectacle of Kennedy's arrival in New York as an instant candidate and instead make a case that New York would benefit from his election. But while they may have helped establish Kennedy's qualifications, they did not by themselves help establish the trust between candidate and constituent that is crucial to electoral success. The Kennedy campaign therefore employed additional tactics to convince voters that Kennedy was not just qualified but also a good "fit" with the people of the state of New York.

A Democratic Electorate in a Republican State

One of these tactics involved emphasizing New York's longstanding ties to the Democratic Party. While Republicans were enjoying a very good run in New York throughout the 1960s, they did so in spite of the statewide electorate's pronounced Democratic tilt; many New Yorkers cast their ballots for Republicans like Rockefeller and Keating without themselves becoming Republicans. In the absence of an electoral realignment toward the GOP beyond the ballot box, the identification of a large segment of the electorate with the Democratic Party presented Kennedy's campaign with an opportunity.

Kennedy took advantage of this opportunity by presenting himself as a candidate in the tradition of New York's Democratic Party. He did this with particular emphasis on two Democrats who had represented the state in the Senate: Robert Wagner (father of the then-mayor of New York City) and Herbert Lehman. Throughout the campaign, Kennedy would return to Wagner and Lehman as examples of the sort of senator he promised New Yorkers he would be. He quoted Lehman in his acceptance speech at the state Democratic convention: "The fight to maintain progressive government is one without end. The effort to carry on must never cease."[30] This fight, Kennedy argued, was one he had helped wage as part of his brother's administration and one he would continue to fight if he were elected to the Senate. Kennedy did more than just invoke the names of Wagner and Lehman; he also pointed to their best-known accomplishments. When Kennedy spoke of Wagner, he often referenced the Wagner Act of 1935 and its importance in labor relations.[31] When Kennedy spoke of Lehman, he brought up Lehman's leading role in housing legislation and his unofficial position as what Kennedy called the conscience of the Senate.[32] In these and other areas, Kennedy said he would distinguish himself by being a leader, much as Wagner and Lehman had been. This approach smartly recast the meaning of "New Yorker" in Kennedy's favor. Being one of New York's senators meant more than simply being from the state; it also meant being a leader worthy of the state's place in American history. This also had the benefit of taking Kennedy's status as a national Democratic figure—a former "assistant president" who still might run for the presidency in his own right someday—and presenting it as an asset that he brought to the table, rather than a reason to question his motives. New York Democrats might have found many of Keating's positions admirable, but Kennedy argued that it was not enough to vote in a certain way; New York needed a senator who would lead as well.

There was another very good reason for Kennedy to place himself squarely in New York's Democratic tradition: 1964 was a presidential election year, and Lyndon Johnson was the clear favorite to win. Helping Johnson's prospects was the GOP's nominee, Senator Barry Goldwater of Arizona, whose conservative record and rhetoric doomed his candidacy in New York. Whatever animosity there was between Lyndon Johnson and Bobby Kennedy, each knew that the other's success would redound to his own benefit as well. Were Goldwater to become president, there would be little to no progress on any of the policy priorities Kennedy was placing at the center of his campaign. And, for Johnson, having a liberal Democrat in the Senate was preferable to having another liberal Republican. Kennedy frequently presented a Democratic victory in the fall as a foregone conclusion, telling audiences that it was certain that after the election there would be a Democratic president, a Democratic majority in the Senate, and a Democratic majority in the House. In light of the Democrats' coming sweep, Kennedy argued, did it not make sense for New York to send a Democratic senator to Washington? In case this seemed a bit too self-serving a justification, Kennedy deployed a letter from former president Harry Truman to support his case.[33]

After several weeks early in the campaign in which his lead appeared to be slipping, Kennedy linked his campaign to that of President Johnson and Johnson's running mate, Hubert Humphrey. Flyers and signs urged voters to cast their ballot for the "Johnson-Humphrey-Kennedy" ticket, and both Humphrey and Johnson came to New York to campaign alongside Kennedy. At a late rally at Madison Square Garden, Kennedy praised Johnson's performance as president and told voters he looked forward to having the chance to help Johnson build his Great Society.[34]

This approach was additionally helpful because Goldwater was particularly unpopular in New York. Goldwater's extremism put a liberal Republican like Kenneth Keating in a bind: Embracing Goldwater would alienate the Democratic-identifying voters who had helped elect Keating in 1958, and without whose support Keating could not win in 1964, while denouncing him would alienate a percentage of the Republican-leaning voters who were his base of support, none of whose votes Keating could afford to lose. Either course of action would cost him votes that he needed. *New York Post* columnist Max Lerner wrote that a Keating win would require him to win the support of "a crossover of Democrats who want to reward a liberal Senatorial record and show that an anti-Goldwater Republican can get re-elected."[35] So Keating spent the campaign trying to avoid saying whether or not he supported Goldwater, would endorse Goldwater, or planned to vote for Goldwater. Unsurprisingly, this approach satisfied absolutely no one. Kennedy, of course, had no such problems with the head of his ticket. And by repeatedly linking himself to the state's tradition of Democratic leaders and to President Johnson, Kennedy reminded New York's Democratic voters of their own ties to their party, and perhaps made their party identification one of their uppermost considerations in deciding which candidate to vote for. If Kennedy was not "one of us" as a New Yorker, he could still be "one of us" for those New Yorkers who considered themselves Democrats.

Bobby Kennedy's New York

In addition to tying himself to New York's liberal tradition and its voters' Democratic identification, Kennedy also presented voters with a carefully crafted view of New York's role in the political process. Throughout his campaign against Keating, Kennedy would describe New York as the nation's "touchstone" or "first state" in much the same way that New York City was, in 1964, the nation's first city.[36] When it came to the issues facing the United States in the 1960s, Kennedy argued, it was only logical that New York should lead the way. Implicit in these appeals, of course, was the claim that Kennedy himself was the candidate best able to help New York do so from a seat in the United States Senate. In making this appeal, Kennedy sought to flatter New Yorkers: New York was a state unlike any other; it was not Pennsylvania or Illinois or Texas, and it was certainly not that upstart California, which had only recently eclipsed New York in population size. New York, alone among the states, had a critical role to play in leading the nation. In addition to flattering New Yorkers, this appeal justified his candidacy: those other states were not ones where a national figure would go to get elected, but New York, because it was New York, was.

This vision of New York's role in American political life also allowed Kennedy to attack Keating's record as a senator despite the fact that Keating's record was, on many of the issues Kennedy was campaigning on, quite liberal. But voting, Kennedy argued, wasn't enough; instead, he told voters, "the way a Senator from New York speaks and acts and votes, should symbolize the response of America to the needs and aspirations of the people of the world."[37] Keating may have been a reliable vote on education and housing and labor and other liberal concerns, but Kennedy charged that this was not the same thing as leading on these issues and that Keating's failure to do so was especially galling given that he represented America's first state.

Kennedy painted a second picture of New York that benefited his campaign. He and his supporters often described New York as a state that had thrived in no small part because of an ongoing influx of newcomers. Whether these were immigrants coming to New York from other nations, Americans seeking a fame or fortune on Broadway, or simply people seeking a new start in a new state, one of the things that defined New York was that it welcomed these newcomers with open arms. In accepting the Democratic nomination, Kennedy noted that for every New Yorker who had been born in the state, "there is one who is a New Yorker by choice, or whose parents were."[38] The letter from reform Democrats urging Kennedy to run paused to note that New York was a state that "has welcomed millions from every country of the world."[39] By reminding New Yorkers of their state's history of embracing newcomers, Kennedy presented himself not as a carpetbagger, but simply as a very prominent example of a phenomenon that, he argued, helped define the state and set it apart from others. At least one voter found this persuasive and was recorded as saying "I came from Philadelphia, so we're *all* carpetbaggers."[40] A state full of newcomers, this line of argument went, could not very well judge someone else for being a newcomer himself.

The Keating Record

The incumbent, Kenneth Keating, was a Republican first elected statewide in 1958. As a first-term senator seeking re-election in a state the size of New York, Keating was more vulnerable to a challenge than one might expect. Fenno has found that senators from large states do not have the same opportunity to engage in the sort of constituency service and relations that members of the House of Representatives do, and the six years between a senator's first election and his or her pursuit of a second term can provide ample opportunity for voters with short memories to forget why they voted for the incumbent in the first place, or even who the incumbent is. The size of New York's population did Keating no favors, either; voters seeking help from a member of Congress were more likely to seek out their House member than one of their more distant senators. A senator who can win a second term has a strong chance of remaining in office for a third term and beyond, but winning that second term can be a formidable challenge.

In addition to his first-term status, Keating also had the worst possible companion at the top of the Republican ticket. Had the Republicans nominated a more moderate candidate like New York's own Nelson Rockefeller, Governor William Scranton of Pennsylvania, or Governor George Romney of Michigan, Keating would not have had to contort himself in the way that he did in the face of repeated questions about whether Keating supported Goldwater. Keating would likely have downplayed his support for Scranton, Romney, or even Rockefeller in the face of a looming Johnson landslide, but he would probably have been able to express that support publicly without alienating the Democrats whose votes he needed to win a second term. With Goldwater atop the Republican ticket, however, Keating was forced into a defensive posture that, in practice, afforded him little protection. Keating's Republican affiliation placed him in the party of Goldwater, and he could not explicitly support or renounce either Goldwater or Johnson without losing part of his precarious re-election constituency. As a Republican in a Democratic state, running in a year in which a Democratic president was cruising to a landslide, against one of the most famous Democrats in the country, Keating had no electoral margin for error and could not afford to alienate a single voter. Even after casting his ballot on election day, Keating refused to say for whom he'd voted and told reporters (in what the *Times* described as a "slightly gravelly" voice), "I said I'd leave it to my conscience, and this I've done."[41]

Had the little-known Samuel Stratton been the Democratic candidate, Keating may have been able to navigate these challenges and win a second term. But Kennedy was not simply better known than Stratton; he came into the campaign carrying the mantle of his slain brother. If not for President Kennedy's assassination, Robert Kennedy's campaign would never have happened. But the fact of the president's death made Kennedy the inheritor and incarnation of his brother's politics, and this, in turn, made it difficult for Keating to attack Kennedy simply for being from out of state. Instead, Keating used the carpetbagger issue to cast doubt on Robert Kennedy's motives, suggesting that his true goal had been to run for vice president and that he had only decided to run in New York after that door had been definitively closed. Keating argued that New Yorkers were being asked to get rid of an able incumbent for the sake of Kennedy's ambitions and that his ambition to serve in the Senate was nothing more than a consolation prize to salve Kennedy's wounded ego. And just as Kennedy pointed to the support of Mayor Wagner and placed himself in the tradition of the elder Wagner and Lehman, Keating deployed familiar faces from the moderate wing of New York's Republican Party to speak on his behalf.

For instance, Thomas E. Dewey, the former governor who had twice been the Republican nominee for president, defended Keating as a "tremendously able and hard-working man" who "can do more for the people of New York in the next six years than any other possible candidate." Without naming Kennedy, Dewey declared that Keating "loves the people of our State all the year 'round, not just as a visitor in October. He is one of us."[42] In Dewey's framing of things, Kennedy's carpetbagger status undercut his claims that he would be a better senator than Keating had been; how could he be, Dewey asked, without the sort of knowledge that comes from really living in a place? Kennedy's experiences in the executive branch could not make up for his lack of meaningful ties to and knowledge of the state.

New York's other Republican senator, Jacob Javits, used similar language to defend Keating and criticize Kennedy. In a televised appeal to voters, Javits sounded incredulous at the fact of Kennedy's running, saying, "[S]uddenly out of the blue comes a young man, with a glamorous name and a glamorous reputation, and says, throw him out, throw out Ken Keating, take me, because I want that job. Why? What are the qualifications? What is the reason? Do we serve the people better? Not at all. Just throw him out, because I want it."[43] Javits also took pains to note that Keating was supported by the vast majority of New York's newspapers and by many liberal magazines thanks to his progressive record. In that same broadcast, Keating echoed Javits' arguments and said that he was "appealing to the people of New York to vindicate my record, my principles, and my reputation, and to reject for all time the notion that a man with a ruthless ambition and a private fortune can destroy whoever stands in his way."[44] The argument Keating and Javits made did not solely focus on Kennedy's carpetbagger status; instead, it contrasted that status with Keating's record and length of service in the House of Representatives and the Senate. That Kennedy was a carpetbagger was bad enough; what was worse was that this carpetbagger was pushing aside a dedicated and experienced public servant just to win a consolation prize. But this argument played into the Kennedy campaign's hands, since Kennedy was charging that Keating's long tenure—ten years in the House and six in the Senate—had little to distinguish it. Instead, Keating's appeal seemed almost to be based on asking voters to consider the impact losing to Kennedy would have on Keating's feelings and personal dignity.

Keating supporters also tried to depict Kennedy's ambition as leading him to arrogantly assume voters would simply fall in line and support him. A flyer by Democrats for Keating, Johnson, and Humphrey, for instance, targeted Kennedy's support among black voters. The flyer depicted a cartoon RFK proclaiming, "I have the NEGRO vote in my bag!" while three African-American men, also cartoons, say, "Later for Kennedy, man! WE have KEATING'S vote in our bag!"[45] The same flyer included a page recounting Keating's support for civil rights during his tenure in Congress and featured photos of Keating with Thurgood Marshall, Sidney Poitier, Jackie Robinson, and other African American leaders. This was an attempt to retain support for Keating among black voters without directly attacking Kennedy on policy grounds. But while Kennedy's civil rights record has certainly come under criticism in the years since his death, in 1964 he was running on the same ballot line as the president who had signed the Civil Rights Act of 1964. Keating, on the other hand, shared his ticket with a presidential nominee who had voted against it.

While Keating's campaign attacked Kennedy as a carpetbagger, Kennedy's campaign took aim at Keating on ideological grounds. To the extent that Keating enjoyed crossover support from Democratic voters, he did so because they perceived him as an example of the liberal wing of the Republican Party. Without that crossover support, Keating's chances in the general election would fall to zero. The Kennedy campaign therefore called Keating's liberalism into question. One Kennedy flyer assailed Keating for his high rating from the "ultra-conservative, right wing" group Americans for Constitutional Action—a high rating he had maintained, the flyer noted ominously, "until this election year."[46] Keating had also received an award from the group in 1961, along with Strom Thurmond, Harry Byrd, and both Barry Goldwater and his running mate, William Miller.

Kennedy's repeated invocations of Robert Wagner and Herbert Lehman did more than just cast Kennedy as their political heir. Kennedy also used these figures from New York's past to help him criticize Keating. Wagner and Lehman, Kennedy argued, were political giants, figures who not only cast votes in the Senate but also led New York and the nation on the important issues of their day. Keating, in Kennedy's telling, came up short in comparison. Keating did not let this criticism go unanswered; throughout the fall campaign, Keating and his supporters would defend his record on civil rights and other issues; Thomas Dewey's televised address even argued that Keating had been unusually prescient about the threat of Russian nuclear missiles being based in Cuba.[47] But the nature of Kennedy's charge was such that attempts to respond to it tended to confirm or strengthen it. Since Kennedy's attack was not on specific votes Keating had cast or positions Keating had taken, Keating did himself little good by pointing to the details of his record in office. Kennedy did not even deny that Keating had cast some good votes, but he argued that leadership consisted of more than just good votes. Good votes might be enough for a senator from Indiana or Idaho, but not for a senator from New York. Leadership was something more, something ineffable, and whatever it was, Kennedy's campaign argued, Keating was not doing it. Instead, Kennedy said again and again, "On the gravest problems facing New York it has been Senators from other states who have been taking the lead."[48]

Analyzing the Results

Ultimately, the voters of New York came down on Kennedy's side; he won 53.5 percent of the vote to Keating's 43.4 percent, a margin of more than 720,000 votes.[49] This was both a landslide, by any reasonable definition, and much less of a landslide than Lyndon Johnson's over Barry Goldwater; Johnson received almost 2 million more votes than Goldwater. Keating, after the election, said that he thought he could have won had Johnson's margin been under 1 million votes and that he would have won if the Republican presidential nominee had been anyone other than Goldwater.[50] It is tough to imagine that every single one of the 720,000 votes that separated Kennedy from Keating was swayed solely by the way Kennedy linked his campaign to Johnson's. But even this top-level comparison indicates that many New Yorkers voted for Johnson for president and Keating for Senate. This suggests that the carpetbagger issue was in fact a drag on Kennedy's candidacy and cost him votes even though it did not cost him the election.

Robert Kennedy's successful campaign holds several lessons for the study of other carpetbagger candidates. In looking back at events from the perspective of a half-century or more, it can be tempting to see those events as the natural progression of things. Another temptation is to view events as way stations in the biographies of historical figures: *of course* Robert Kennedy defeated Kenneth Keating! Kennedy is a major historical figure, and Keating is a forgotten backbencher! How could things have *possibly* gone any differently? But such thinking obscures the fact that events unfolded as they did for particular reasons, and not just because the grand sweep of history demanded that they happen. Considering the reasons why Kennedy ran and won will inform the analysis of other carpetbagger candidates in the remaining chapters of this book.

Candidates for office are almost always strategic in their decision to run, in that they run when they want to hold office and when think they have a chance to win. But different candidates assess their odds differently. Outsiders and first-time candidates are more likely to mount campaigns against incumbents, for instance, because waiting to run in an open-seat contest would mean facing better-known and better-funded primary candidates who were waiting to run until a given seat was open and their chances of winning the general election would be improved. Depending on who you are, you may actually have better luck running when the odds are longer.

Robert Kennedy's decision to run in New York reflects this. Viewed in absolute terms, the decision to move to a new state to run for the Senate appears bafflingly strange. But viewed relative to this particular candidate's particular circumstances, the decision to become a carpetbagger makes more sense. Kennedy would rather have been vice president or, failing that, senator from Massachusetts. But with those options closed off by Lyndon Johnson and Kennedy's younger brother, Ted, running in New York became more appealing. And as Kennedy's reaction to Milton Gwirtzman's memo shows, he judged it better for his ambitions to run for the Senate in New York than to pursue an almost certain victory running for governor of Massachusetts. That decision, however, hinged upon on the state of play in New York, where a potentially vulnerable Republican was seeking re-election and the only home-grown Democrat in the running had little support. Had Keating been a Democrat, or someone with the stature of Mayor Wagner been seeking the Democratic nomination, Kennedy would probably have pursued yet another option. Other political figures who make the decision to become carpetbaggers likely do so because they, like Kennedy, have the ambition of being involved in public life and, importantly, do not have any more sensible options available to them. In other words, they will make the decision to carpetbag because even with the long odds carpetbaggers face, doing so is the best option they have available.

Kennedy had several advantages that helped him succeed in running in a new state. Most carpetbaggers as we imagine them are likely to start off at a disadvantage: as newcomers to a state, they tend to lack the sorts of connections to local movers and shakers and name recognition a local candidate possesses. That was clearly not the case for Robert Kennedy, however. To begin with, he had just served as attorney general. And while many attorneys general are not terribly well known among the general public, Kennedy was exceptionally prominent thanks to the fact that he was also the president's brother. On top of that, Kennedy had stood beside Jacqueline Kennedy throughout the public memorials for President Kennedy. By the time he announced his campaign in New York, days after he had received a twenty-two-minute ovation at the Democratic National Convention, Kennedy enjoyed a level of name recognition that most candidates would envy.

However, it would be a mistake to say that Kennedy's name alone made him a viable candidate. Another Kennedy relative who had never been involved in politics in an official capacity, or who had done so quietly behind the scenes, would probably not have been as strong a candidate. It was the combination of Kennedy's name with his service as attorney general that made him a credible candidate and acceptable to leading New York Democrats. We should therefore expect that the strongest carpetbagger candidates will be nationally known individuals who also can also lay claim to serious experience in government. To use the case that will be covered in the next chapter for the sake of example, we would expect that Hillary Clinton would be considered a more serious candidate than would Bill Clinton's brother, Roger, despite the fact that both Hillary and Roger have the same last name. It is not enough to be nationally known; instead, a carpetbagger will ideally already be nationally known for his or her serious involvement in public affairs.

The Kennedy campaign is also instructive in illustrating how carpetbaggers and their opponents address the carpetbagger issue. Kennedy did emphasize the slender ties he had to the state of New York, but more important to his success was the image of the state of New York that he created in his rhetoric. Politicians often create idealized images of the communities they seek to lead, of course; in this case, Kennedy appealed to New York's history as a state that was welcoming of newcomers and New Yorkers' vanity about the importance of their state. He then linked this to his own vision of a New York senator's ability to lead in the Senate, which he contrasted with the record of his Republican opponent. Kennedy's success raises interesting questions about how carpetbaggers negotiate the politics of place: Was Kennedy successful because New York lent itself so well to the image of the state he was putting forth? The same rhetorical strategy would not have lent itself to many other states. Is New York simply fertile ground for carpetbaggers and other newcomers? Do carpetbagger candidates in other states try to project an electorally advantageous image of their new states, and how do they go about doing so?

National and state party actors were likewise instrumental in clearing Kennedy's path to the nomination and vouching for him as a candidate despite his carpetbagger status. In examining other carpetbagger races, it will be worth focusing on the role of equivalent figures. What happens if a carpetbagger charges in without the support of state party leaders? Do carpetbaggers only run when they can say state figures are inviting them into a state to run?

Chapter 4 examines the candidacy of Hillary Clinton, who, like Robert Kennedy, possessed a famous political name and decided to run for Senate in her own right by relocating to New York.

Chapter 4

Hillary Rodham Clinton

New York, 2000

In many ways, the Senate candidacy of Hillary Clinton in New York in 2000 bears a striking resemblance to that of Bobby Kennedy in 1964. Clinton, like Kennedy, had no meaningful ties to New York when she first began to explore the idea of running. Clinton also had in common with Kennedy the fact that she had a famous political name as the wife of Bill Clinton, whose second and final term as president was ending as her campaign began and, despite his recent impeachment, enjoyed high levels of public support. And like Kennedy, Clinton won her election in spite of the carpetbagger issue. And like Kennedy's, Clinton's case offers important insights into the relationships among representation, place, and campaign strategy and tactics.

The New York Campaign in Clinton's Career Context

Clinton's decision to run must be viewed in the context of her larger career in public life. As the 2000 campaign cycle warmed up, Clinton found herself in a place where a Senate race, even one begun under the burden of the carpetbagger label, represented her best available opportunity for continuing her career in public life. By 1998, Clinton found herself in a frustrating position for multiple reasons. First and foremost was the revelation of her husband's affair with a young White House staffer; after months of public denials from the president, and her own public defenses of him, President Clinton acknowledged the affair that August. Worse, the affair led to the president's impeachment in December and his Senate trial and acquittal the following February. Despite the scandal, many Americans found the impeachment unwarranted, and President Clinton's job approval ratings—already high thanks to a booming economy and a world at relative peace—only increased throughout the impeachment drama.[1] The scandal boosted Hillary Clinton's approval ratings as well; surveys found that Americans generally sympathized with her and felt that she had been wronged by her husband's bad behavior.[2]

Clinton's elevated standing with the public came at a point when she had stepped back from the active policy engagement of her husband's early years in office. Clinton's role in her husband's political life had been controversial even before he was elected president. During his first term as governor of Arkansas, she had continued to go by her maiden name, Hillary Rodham. When Bill ran for governor in 1982 after losing his 1980 re-election bid, she had conspicuously changed her name to "Hillary Clinton," and commentators breathlessly noted during Bill's 1993 inauguration that she was announced as "Hillary Rodham Clinton." Even when Clinton was running for president in 2016 after nearly forty years in the public eye, media outlets devoted time and energy to determining by which of Clinton's names to refer to her, and explaining their decisions to their readers.[3] During 1992, the Clinton campaign presented her as an asset and someone who would have a leading role in a Clinton presidency, and she and Bill were sometimes described as a "two-for-one" deal. But many critics found Mrs. Clinton to be overly involved in politics and policy for someone who had no official position and was only in the White House by virtue of marriage. Others saw the Clintons as representing the 1960s counterculture run amok and a threat to more traditional conceptions of the appropriate role of presidential wives or, indeed, of wives in general. An April 1992 poll found 67 percent of respondents disliked the idea of Clinton holding a major position in the White House.[4] Trent and Short-Thompson catalogue the many terms, positive and negative, that were used to describe Clinton during her years as first lady: "saint, sinner, co-president, pathbreaker, power-seeker, victim, doctrinaire liberal, she-devil, symbol of baby-boomer womanhood, icon, international activist and defender of women and children, congenital liar, the president's closest political advisor, and a disgrace to the role of first lady."[5] Once Bill became president, he appointed Hillary to chair the president's Task Force on Health Care Reform and to serve as the public face of the effort. After the health plan's failure, Clinton withdrew from a formal policy-making role while continuing to speak out on issues that concerned her, particularly "education, health care, human rights, and children."[6]

Hillary Clinton's newfound popularity during the impeachment drama made her an in-demand figure during the 1998 midterm elections, in which Democrats defied expectations and historical precedent by gaining seats in the House and losing none in the Senate. She made multiple trips to New York to campaign for Chuck Schumer, the Democratic congressman from Brooklyn running for the Senate against Al D'Amato, the Republican incumbent. Clinton also visited New York several times in 1998 in her capacity as first lady to support a White House preservation initiative aimed at historical buildings, landmarks, and other sites.[7] These trips further boosted Clinton's profile in the state, and her performance impressed local Democratic leaders.

Thanks to these activities, when New York's Senator Daniel Patrick Moynihan announced, shortly after the 1998 elections, that he would not seek a fifth term in 2000, prominent Democrats included Clinton's name in the mix of potential candidates alongside people like Andrew Cuomo, the Housing and Urban Development secretary and son of former governor Mario Cuomo, state comptroller Carl McCall, United States Representative Nita Lowey, and Health and Human Services Secretary Donna Shalala.[8] While national audiences might have dismissed the suggestion, the prospect of a Clinton campaign in New York appealed to many leaders of the state party. There was, however, the same complication that Bobby Kennedy had faced in 1964: Mrs. Clinton, who was raised in Illinois and had spent over a decade as the first lady of Arkansas, was not a resident of New York and lacked even the tenuous childhood ties to the state that Robert Kennedy had used to bolster his Senate campaign in 1964.

Many asked why Clinton would choose to run in New York, instead of one of the other states she had lived in at various points in her life: Illinois, where she had spent most of her youth; Arkansas, where she had practiced law and been first lady for a dozen years; or even Pennsylvania, where her family had roots and she had spent time when she was growing up. While New York was not the only possible place she could have run in, it did in many ways present a better opportunity for her than these states to which she had stronger ties. Arkansas' next Senate election would not take place until 2002, and if that state's attorney general, Mark Pryor, were to run, Clinton would have to defeat an established figure from a family that had been part of state politics since before Bill Clinton had ever been elected governor. If Clinton had decided to return to Illinois, the next Senate race in which she could run—assuming incumbent Democrat Dick Durbin ran again in 2002—would not take place until 2004. Running in Pennsylvania would have meant taking on an incumbent Republican in either 2000 or 2004 in a state that had not elected a Democrat to a full Senate term since 1962. In comparison, New York's open seat was a better chance and a better option. In any state, Clinton would face the carpetbagger charge. Despite her ties to states like Arkansas and Illinois, she could expect to be described, accurately, as having been away for years and only returning to run for office; in Arkansas and Pennsylvania, she would also face attacks for not being from the state originally. She would also have to defeat strong opponents in general and possible primary elections. Those arguing that Clinton should run in another state also had their causal relationships reversed: they assumed that Clinton's interest in the Senate preceded her decision to explore a campaign in New York, when it was New York Democrats' interest that led Clinton to consider running there. And in none of the other states could the state's Democrats clear the decks for Clinton. New York, in comparison, presented Clinton with a certain path to the Democratic nomination and an open-seat contest in the general election. Victory was not assured, but that would have been the case in any state, and it was more likely in New York than anywhere else.

New York was also an immediate opportunity. Running in Arkansas, Illinois, or Pennsylvania would have meant waiting until 2002 or 2004, when Clinton would no longer be the first lady. Running in New York in 2000 would let her run while her standing in the eyes of the public was as high as it had ever been. In another two or four years, the political landscape could very well change in ways that were not amenable to a Clinton candidacy: her public image might erode, public sentiment might turn against the Democratic Party, or ambitious local candidates might emerge in these other states. Running in 2000 would also allow her to enter the race with the full apparatus of her position as first lady, including access to the resources of the White House and Secret Service protection, at her disposal. While there were downsides to this—audiences hoping to see Clinton on the campaign trail would learn to show up hours early for her events in order to get through security—the considerable benefits that Clinton enjoyed as the sitting first lady would end when her husband left office at noon on January 20, 2001.

Some intimates and observers were baffled by Clinton's interest in the Senate; an NBC News report suggested that moving from the White House to the Senate—where her years as first lady would not count toward her seniority—could only be seen as a demotion.[9] And more than once, she was asked why, after being first lady, she would ever want to be just one among a hundred, and a very junior one among those hundred to boot. The answer she gave to David Axelrod, whose consulting firm worked on her campaign, when he asked her this question is instructive: "I think it's important to have a platform."[10] Clinton confidante Harold Ickes's recollection echoes Axelrod's account; Ickes reported that Clinton had told him "she could have a tremendous impact on shaping policy" as a senator in a way that she could not have through a foundation or a nonprofit organization.[11] These recollections indicate that Clinton was motivated at least in part by progressive ambition—a desire to move up the rungs of the political ladder. For Hillary Clinton, the Senate offered a chance to influence public policy directly in her own right, rather than in her unofficial, indirect capacity as the spouse of the president. In this regard, her position was not dissimilar to that of Robert Kennedy, who saw a New York Senate seat—the same New York Senate seat, to be exact—as an escape hatch from his impossible position in Lyndon Johnson's cabinet.

However, Clinton began her campaign from a different place than her predecessor in carpetbagging. Robert Kennedy was the brother of a slain president; Clinton was the spouse of an impeached one. Both positions evoked public sympathy, but the latter did not quite compare to the former. Kennedy was also aided by the fact that he represented a tie to the image of the Kennedy White House that had already, by the time he began moving toward running during the summer of 1964, begun to be memorialized in the public memory as a mythical Camelot. Clinton, on the other hand, represented a tie to a presidency that was approaching its natural end and had perhaps been dramatic and exhausting enough that many New Yorkers might not want more of the same, even though they had twice voted for Bill Clinton by wide margins.

As had been the case with Kennedy, when Clinton began her campaign, many wondered if she was using New York as a stepping stone to the presidency. In this regard, the critics of each candidate took their public perceptions as a starting point for their anxiety, and each candidate took steps to combat those perceptions. Just as Robert Kennedy and his advisers had worried about perceptions of ruthlessness, Clinton had to contend with perceptions of her as so overwhelmingly ambitious and calculating that she would up and move to a new state just so that she could stay in public life. Kennedy had been mentioned as a potential president even before his brother's assassination, and his cabinet position and close working relationship with President Kennedy may very well have made Bobby a plausible future candidate even if his brother had served a full two terms. In contrast, the idea of Hillary Clinton running for president had, until she became interested in New York's Senate seat, previously been limited to the fever swamps of conspiracy-minded Clinton-haters. But once she expressed interest in New York's Senate seat, many observers (sympathetic or otherwise) speculated that her campaign was at least in part about acquiring a credential that would make her a credible presidential candidate in 2004 or 2008—and, in fact, a reporter asked Clinton about a possible 2004 candidacy during a press conference the day after the election, even before the Supreme Court finally resolved the disputed election between George W. Bush and Al Gore.[12]

As Clinton considered entering the race, she faced several early challenges: first, establishing residency in New York; second, winning the Democratic nomination, and third (and perhaps most importantly), addressing the carpetbagger issue. Doing so would require her to successfully navigate the complex web of geographical and demographic concerns, rivalries, and history that characterize politics in New York state. And all of these challenges needed to be handled well in advance of the general election, if she didn't want her Republican opponent—whoever that might turn out to be—to have a potentially potent weapon to use against her.

State Party Actors

State party actors did more than provide crucial support for the idea of a Clinton campaign; they also helped persuade Clinton to become a candidate in the first place. In 1964, Robert Kennedy had worked hard to create the impression that leaders of the New York Democratic Party had invited him to run. In Hillary Clinton's case, the reality of her decision to run resembled the image Kennedy sought to project. Some party leaders had been kicking around the prospect of a Clinton run for office in New York even before Pat Moynihan had announced his retirement. Clinton also benefited from several complications facing the New York Democrats.

The first of these was the party's demoralized state in the years following its back-to-back defeats in 1993, when New York City mayor David Dinkins lost his re-election bid to Rudy Giuliani, and 1994, when Governor Mario Cuomo lost to George Pataki. In the aftermath of the 1998 elections, the first in years to have any bright spots at all for New York Democrats, party leaders were first and foremost interested in racking up more wins, and they were willing to think unconventionally in order to do so.

The Democrats' hunger for victory, however, ran afoul of a strange paradox of New York Democratic politics: many Democratic politicians in New York are simply uninterested in going to Washington and would rather hold office in New York City or elsewhere in the state or serve as governor or in another capacity in the state government in Albany. For Democrats who get elected to the House of Representatives, it can be difficult for members elected from the city to appeal to more moderate voters upstate and for moderates from upstate to appeal to more liberal voters in the city. And to many New York Democrats, the nation's capital is a provincial backwater that simply cannot compare to anything New York—city or state—has to offer. But the same Democrats who do not, themselves, want to go to Washington nonetheless want to send someone important to Washington—someone who can credibly be listed in the same company as Robert Wagner and Herbert Lehman and Bobby Kennedy and Pat Moynihan.[13] A Clinton candidacy would satisfy both concerns. Both Clinton and the New York Democratic Party would benefit from the association, and, importantly, no one with an eye on the governor's mansion (like Andrew Cuomo or Carl McCall) or a secure elected position elsewhere in the state (such as Representative Nita Lowey, who said she would run if and only if Clinton did not) would have to endanger either their current positions or their dreams for the future in a statewide race for the Senate.

Clinton's support from state party figures included that of Daniel Patrick Moynihan. Moynihan's relationship with Bill Clinton's White House had been a rocky one, so the extent of his support for Hillary Clinton surprised many. But Moynihan extended support to Clinton throughout her campaign. She announced her candidacy alongside Senator Moynihan at his farmhouse in Pindars Corners, New York. Moynihan helped Clinton navigate local norms by gently correcting her when she called on a Washington-based reporter, rather than a reporter from a New York news outlet, at a press event after the announcement.[14] Later in the campaign, Moynihan forcefully criticized a television ad aired by Clinton's opponent, Rick Lazio, for inaccurately implying that Lazio and Moynihan had been close collaborators in Congress.[15]

Geography and Demography

Clinton needed to address the geographic mismatch at the heart of her candidacy. She had never lived in the state and now sought to convince voters that she was the one person in the state best able to represent its interests. She also had to contend with the different geographic regions of the state; New York is not an undifferentiated mass of voters but is generally seen by political observers as a state that consists of the five boroughs of New York City, the five suburban counties often referred to simply as "the suburbs," and "upstate," the collective term for the rest of the state.[16] Each of these areas has its own particular political leanings and presents different challenges for candidates. Throughout the twentieth century, statewide candidates grappled with the limitations each party's base of support imposed upon their candidacies. In the 1990s, Republicans were the majority party in the suburbs and in most of the upstate region, while Democrats had as their base of support New York City and a handful of urban upstate areas. The divisions between the city and the rest of the state date back to the beginnings of the steady influx of immigrants into New York City during the 1800s, which rendered the city, as Stonecash puts it, "different" from the rest of the state in the eyes of upstaters.[17] This tension between the city and the rest of the state defined New York state politics for generations. It obligated Democrats running for statewide offices to find or create paths to victory that built on the New York City vote by incorporating votes from elsewhere in the state into a winning coalition and for Republicans to cut into the vote in the city in order to have a chance at victory.

As a result of this dynamic, candidates "from the city" are at particular risk of self-inflected wounds when they venture upstate in search of a majority. A classic example of such political self-immolation took place in 1982, when New York City mayor Ed Koch ran in the Democratic primary for governor. In an interview during the campaign, Koch described life beyond the city as "wasting time in a pickup truck when you have to drive 20 miles to buy a gingham dress or a Sears Roebuck suit."[18] The resulting backlash from upstaters and upstate media helped Koch lose the region and the primary, and upstate columnists were still using Koch's "gingham dress" gaffe as political shorthand decades later.[19] Many expected Clinton, whose unofficial campaign start preceded her actually becoming a resident of New York and whose primary base of support was widely expected to be the city, to make a similar gaffe: Surely, the first lady was more at home in Manhattan than she could ever be in Utica or Oneida or the smaller cities and towns upstate.

Clinton also faced the complex web of racial and ethnic political communities in the state. Native New York politicians who want to survive in politics acquire a certain familiarity with the policy priorities, spokespeople, leaders, and controversies specific to each of these groups, from African Americans to Jewish voters to the various Catholics ethnicities to gays and more, simply by virtue of living and working in the state before they seek office. Navigating this minefield did not come as naturally to Clinton, thanks to her carpetbagger status and her attendant lack of firsthand knowledge of these intricacies. For instance, early in her campaign Clinton was asked if she would march in New York City's St. Patrick's Day parade. To someone unfamiliar with the longstanding controversies regarding that parade's exclusion of gay marchers—someone like Hillary Clinton, for instance—her ready expression of excitement at marching in the parade may have come across as a well-meant enthusiasm at participating in a fun civic ritual. But for the gay activists whose support Clinton would need in the general election, her participation in the parade was a blunder for which she had to atone. In 2001, as a freshman senator, Clinton did not march in the parade thanks to what her staff called a scheduling conflict.[20]

Clinton's position as first lady sometimes put her in situations that caused difficulty for her campaign. In November of 1999, Clinton appeared in Ramallah at an event also attended by Suha Arafat, the wife of Palestinian Authority president Yasir Arafat. Mrs. Arafat, in her remarks, accused Israel of using poison gas on Palestinian civilians. Afterward, Clinton gave Mrs. Arafat a "polite, salutary kiss" on the cheek before leaving.[21] The kiss caused a firestorm of controversy in New York, and the *New York Post* asked if Clinton agreed with Arafat's remarks.[22] Clinton argued that the kiss had been as socially cursory as a handshake and an obligation imposed by her position as first lady; she also said the instant translation of Arafat's remarks on her earpiece was less inflammatory than the later, more careful translation. Kissing Mrs. Arafat was a blunder no native New York politician would have made, and it was a blunder only someone in a position like first lady could have been able to make in the first place; anyone else would have been able to make their own judgment about how to interact with Mrs. Arafat after her remarks and would very likely not have been present at such an event in the first place. But Clinton was not a free agent. As first lady, she represented both her husband's administration and the United States, and thus she had little choice but to interact with Mrs. Arafat—even in a perfunctory way—at the event. The incident and the resulting controversy thus doubly advertised her carpetbagger status. Nor was this the only such hiccup Clinton's campaign encountered. Even after almost a year in the state, Clinton found herself somewhat at sea in the wake of the acquittal of four New York police officers tried for the shooting death of Amadou Diallou.[23]

Clinton also faced demographic challenges unique to her candidacy. An ongoing frustration for the Clinton campaign was the resistance to her candidacy among suburban women—women who, in many ways, had a great deal in common with the first lady. By the beginning of 2000, public opinion surveys showed Clinton tied with or barely leading New York City mayor Rudy Giuliani, then her likely general election opponent, among women voters.[24] For a Democrat running in a northeastern, Democratic-leaning state, their hesitation was potentially deadly.

Overcoming the Carpetbagger Label

Hillary Clinton was not a New Yorker when leaders of that state's Democratic Party started reaching out to her as a potential candidate. Fortunately,
Moynihan had announced his retirement far enough in advance that Clinton
could make a go of becoming enough of one by Election Day 2000 to be
a plausible candidate.[25] Bobby Kennedy's campaign had begun barely two
months before the 1964 election; almost two years passed from the first trial
balloon suggesting a Clinton candidacy to Election Day 2000.

At the start of the campaign, Clinton wore her newcomer status on her
sleeve. In July of 1999, she embarked on what she called a "listening tour"
of upstate New York; the tour would ultimately take her to all sixty-two
counties in the state before she formally began her campaign on February
7, 2000.[26] These events, in which Clinton met with small groups of voters
but made no prepared remarks, proved crucial to Clinton's campaign. They
familiarized Clinton with parts of the state she had not encountered while
campaigning for her husband or other Democrats and gave her an opportunity
to learn, firsthand, from voters about the issues they were concerned with.
It also helped that these were voters and communities that, in the words of
Clinton pollster Mark Penn, felt "underlistened to" by other, more established
New York politicians.[27] These events' relentless focus on policy had the side
benefits, for the Clinton campaign, of winning prominent and favorable
coverage from local newspapers and television stations while simultaneously
boring downstate and national media. When a first lady visits a small town
in upstate New York, it is a big news story. And when that first lady has a
lengthy conversation with local residents about the issues they are concerned
about, she generally receives favorable notices. The extent of the listening tour
and Clinton's subsequent focus on upstate meant that, by the time the general
election campaign began in earnest in the fall of 2000, she had made so many
trips to so many small cities and towns upstate that many voters there came
to accept Clinton's presence as a regular part of their political landscape.

The listening tour was also savvy from a geographic perspective. New
York City was the natural center of gravity for an out-of-state political celebrity. And many might have expected that Clinton, like many other New York
Democrats running statewide during the 1990s, would have difficulty winning
votes upstate. But Clinton's rootlessness gave her a degree of flexibility that a
local candidate would have lacked. Since Clinton was from nowhere in New
York, she could choose where in New York to be "from." By focusing her
attention in the earliest stages of her campaign on upstate New York, tradi-

tionally a weak spot for Democrats, Clinton could begin the representational negotiation that is particularly difficult and delicate for a carpetbagger in a region and on terms that would eventually pay off for her. Voters like Mike Campisi of Tupper Lake might have asked, not without justification, "What the hell does she know about New York State?" when Clinton began her tour.[28] But the point of the listening tour was not what Clinton knew when it began; the point of the listening tour was to enable her to put her lack of knowledge of New York behind her by first putting it front and center. As Clinton put it at the start of her tour, she was there to "listen and learn from the people of New York and demonstrate that what I'm for is maybe as important, if not more important, than where I'm from."[29] The listening tour was a first step in Clinton's negotiation with voters over how she would represent them if she were to win the election.

The Opposition

Clinton and her campaign expected that Rudy Giuliani would be her general election opponent. While a Giuliani candidacy would have made the race into even more of a political spectacle than Clinton's own campaign already had, the Clinton campaign believed that the controversial mayor's candidacy would help them by boosting turnout among African American voters and winning over suburban women among whom Clinton was doing poorly in early polling of the race. But Giuliani ultimately passed on running on May 19, 2000, after the double whammy of the messy and public revelation of his relationship with Judith Nathan while he was still married to his second wife, Donna Hanover, and his diagnosis with prostate cancer.[30] With Giuliani out of the race, New York's Republicans turned to four-term representative Rick Lazio of Long Island. Lazio, lacking Giuliani's abrasiveness and contentious record as mayor, potentially threatened to win support from or depress turnout among many of the constituencies Clinton needed to win. Clinton and her campaign worried that African American voters in the city, for instance, might not turn out to vote against Lazio at the same rate that they would have to vote against Giuliani, during whose tenure racial tensions in the city had repeatedly flared up. And they feared that Lazio's suburban base of support and relative youth could cut into Clinton's support among women.

Lazio made Clinton's carpetbagger status the central theme of his campaign. He referred to himself, accurately, as the only candidate to have ever paid New York state income taxes, criticized the amount of New Yorkers' federal taxes going to southern states like Arkansas, to remind voters of Clinton's out of state origins, and argued that the health plan Clinton had developed early in President Clinton's first term would have harmed New York's many teaching hospitals. Lazio always pointed out that no New Yorker would ever have been foolish enough to make such a proposal, given how important these hospitals were to the economies of many upstate cities and towns. But Lazio did not follow this critique with substantive reasons to vote for him. Instead, Lazio made the carpetbagger attacks in a vacuum, without connecting them to reasons why his home-grown status would make him a better representative.

Lazio's critiques were poorly timed, among other problems. Anderson notes that the news coverage of the carpetbagger issue that so dominated the early months of Clinton's campaign had largely run its course by the time Lazio entered the race.[31] Scharrer's analysis of newspaper coverage of the campaign found that, even before Clinton became a formal candidate in February of 2000, her carpetbagger status was only the fifth-most common criticism levied at Clinton.[32] Scharrer also found that the most common source of criticisms of Clinton in newspaper reporting was not residents of New York but reporters themselves—which suggests that they were more concerned with the carpetbagger issue than many New Yorkers were. While Clinton's slow and methodical series of trips through each and every county in upstate New York had turned the spectacle of the first lady moving to New York to become a senator into something more or less routine and unremarkable; Lazio continued to hit on a theme that was old news to many voters. By the final weeks of the campaign, Clinton had gone from a candidate whose profession of youthful Yankee fandom was received with skepticism[33] to one who could comfortably wear a Yankees cap during the 2000 World Series, even as Lazio was pronouncing her a "Dodger," rather than a Met or a Yankee.[34]

Polling about Clinton's candidacy conducted throughout the campaign illustrates why Lazio's focus on carpetbagging was a poor tactic. Throughout the campaign, the Marist College Institute for Public Opinion's surveys of registered voters in New York asked whether voters were "concerned a great deal, somewhat, not very much, or not at all, about the fact that Hillary Rodham Clinton is not from New York State."[35] Figure 4.1 features the responses to this question from early 1999 to just before the election in 2000. The rise and fall of voters' concerns about Clinton's carpetbagger status is instructive. Initially, a majority of voters said they were "not very much" or "not at all" concerned. Over time, that number fell as Clinton's campaign became a reality

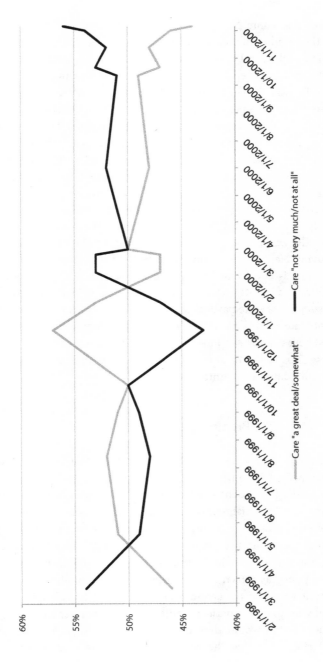

Figure 4.1. "Are You Concerned a Great Deal, Somewhat, Not Very Much, or Not at All, about the Fact That Hillary Rodham Clinton Is Not from New York State?

and Republicans and some New York media outlets criticized Clinton as a carpetbagger; the number of voters saying they were "a great deal" or "somewhat" concerned peaked in December. By the time Clinton became a formal candidate, and Rick Lazio stepped into the void Giuliani's withdrawal created, voters' partisan loyalties began to come into play and Clinton's carpetbagger status over time became less important than her partisan affiliation (and that of her opponent). By Marist's final survey on the Sunday and Monday before the election, 57 percent of respondents said they did not care much or at all about the carpetbagger issue, while 43 percent said it mattered a great deal or somewhat. Those percentages are almost exactly in line with the final outcome of the election. The effect of the Clinton campaign was not to make all voters forget the carpetbagger issue but rather to convince enough voters—particularly Democrats and Democratic-leaning voters—that other issues mattered more. The Lazio campaign's continued focus on the issue overlooked the fact that many New Yorkers came to accept Clinton over the course of the campaign. This is consistent with the idea that one of the functions of campaigns is to communicate information to voters and activate their partisan leanings. The support of state party elites helped convince enough voters that Clinton's out-of-state origins did not matter, and the Clinton campaign drew a stark contrast between the candidates along partisan lines, in order to make a Lazio victory unpalatable to any Democrats who might have preferred a locally grown candidate over Clinton.

Proximity to Power

Like Robert Kennedy, Clinton used her time in the White House to her advantage. Unlike Kennedy, Clinton had not had a formal role in policy making since her stint leading President Clinton's unsuccessful task force on health care reform. But she had maintained an active public profile in which she frequently spoke about or drew attention to issues that were important to her or to the administration, and she had an unquestionable claim to proximity to President Clinton and his administration. While she could not claim to have influenced policy as directly as Kennedy had, she nonetheless was able to present herself to voters as having a familiarity and knowledge of issue that was virtually unique in American politics. Throughout her campaign, on issue after issue, Clinton would align herself with her husband's administration, noting or suggesting that she was involved with or aware of his work on that issue, and then, crucially, argue that her proximity to power during her years in the White House meant that she could do more to address these issues than anyone else could. Clinton presented herself to voters as a knowledgeable insider whose experience meant that she knew which person or which office to call, that she knew which arms to twist, and that she had seen similar issues dealt with successfully in the White House, in a way that Lazio did not. Instead of the sheets full of facts and figures that the Kennedy campaign had circulated in 1964, Clinton claimed a more subtle and ineffable influence on and proximity to her husband's administration and its accomplishments.[36]

New York States of Mind

As in the Kennedy-Keating contest in 1964, both Clinton and her Republican opponents presented voters with very different imaginings of what being a "New Yorker" truly means. Fenno argues that political campaigns are, in part, negotiations between candidates and voters for voters' trust that a candidate will represent their interests if he or she is elected. Cos and Snee find, in their analysis of the campaign rhetoric of Hillary Clinton and Rick Lazio, that identity as well as trust was being negotiated in New York in 2000. Lazio's campaign rhetoric was about emphasizing his own credentials as a New Yorker through self-aware references to his Long Island accent, his Mets fandom, his family vacations at Montauk, and his family's ties to the state. In the strongest part of his pitch, and one which directly challenged Clinton's credibility as a candidate, he said that "New York isn't just a place I represent; it is my home."[37] To hear Lazio describe it, New York was about a set of fixed boundaries, and being a New Yorker consisted of being born within those boundaries or having deep and abiding personal ties to the state—two things, not coincidentally, to which Lazio could credibly lay claim and Hillary Clinton could not.

Clinton's rhetoric offered voters a different imagining of what being a New Yorker meant. She presented a vision of New York as a place defined more by inclusiveness—by its willingness to accept and embrace newcomers—than by physical boundaries. In this regard, her language had much in common with that of Robert Kennedy and his supporters in 1964. As a newcomer, Clinton lacked the sorts of strong ties to the state that Lazio so strongly valued and deployed on his campaign's behalf. But through her listening tour she was able to present herself as a newcomer who was forthright about the fact that she had much to learn and was willing to do the hard and unglamorous work of doing it. Clinton further presented a unity message—arguing, when she accepted the Democratic nomination in May of 2000, that "there is no upstate or downstate or rural, suburban, or urban or black or white or brown but just one New York."[38] Obviously, her campaign did not actually view voters as a homogenous mass. But the idea that the distinctions between New Yorkers were less meaningful than the fact that they were New Yorkers created rhetorical support for the idea that she was as legitimate a New Yorker as anyone else in the state and served as a counterweight to Lazio's suggestion that one was either born a New Yorker or was now and forever somebody from somewhere else.

National Trends

Clinton also benefited from the fact that she was running in a presidential election year and from shifts in national politics that took place over the course of her husband's presidency. If New York had never quite been a presidential swing state in recent years, it had been a state that Republicans could carry in a very good Republican year like 1972 or 1984. But in the wake of the Republicans' rightward turn in and after the 1994 election, the state was becoming more and more reliably Democratic at the presidential level, even while the governorship and mayor's office in New York City remained in the hands of Pataki and Giuliani.[39] The sorts of Rockefeller Republicans the state had once tended to produce became increasingly unwelcome in the national Republican Party. In 2000, there was never any real question of how New York's electoral votes would go, and George W. Bush's presidential campaign made no significant effort in the state. Instead, the real questions the presidential race posed for New York's Senate race were, first, how wide Al Gore's margin of victory in the state would be, and, second, how many Gore voters would split their ticket to vote for Clinton's Republican opponent, whether that was Giuliani (as everyone initially expected) or Lazio (as ultimately was the case).

While the Gore campaign devoted few resources to New York, one of Gore's decisions still managed to help Clinton's campaign. Thanks to the Suha Arafat kiss, the Clinton campaign was worried about alienating Jewish voters in New York. But Gore's choice of Senator Joe Lieberman of Connecticut—the first Jewish nominee for vice president—as his running mate further increased Gore's support in New York and by extension forced Lazio to need to win that many more ticket-splitters' votes. Later, Lieberman also campaigned alongside Clinton, giving her an additional boost.

Analyzing the Results

The closely watched, hard-fought race between Clinton and Lazio ended in anticlimax. For all of the media attention, endless serial and concurrent controversies, and personal drama throughout the race, the final result was not even close: Clinton won 55 percent of the vote to Lazio's 43 percent,[40] and television networks called the race for Clinton by 9:00 p.m.[41] Clinton ran behind the Gore-Lieberman ticket's 60 percent of the vote, and Lazio ahead of George W. Bush's 35 percent,[42] but, as in 1964, the ticket-splitters were too few in number to make much of a difference in the final result.

Lazio also misread his voters in his attacks against both Hillary and Bill Clinton. In many ways, he tried to make the race a referendum on the Clintons, but he was doing this in a state where both Bill and Hillary were popular.[43] Throughout the campaign, Lazio proved unable or unwilling to define his campaign beyond Hillary Clinton. He criticized her for carpetbagging, and he ran against the caricature that had grown around her during eight years on the national stage. Even when he did present himself in terms of positives, he did so in contrast to Clinton. Lazio wasn't simply saying he was from Long Island, for instance; he was also noting that Clinton was not from Long Island or anywhere else in New York. This proved limiting. While these attacks were music to the ears of those in and beyond New York who had spent years hating the Clintons, they did little to address the problem at the heart of Lazio's campaign: how to win statewide as a Republican in a presidential election year in Democratic New York. Attacking Clinton for being Hillary Clinton was not a strategy that was ever going to draw support from that many people who were also voting for Al Gore for president.

This is not to suggest that the carpetbagger issue did not matter. It dominated the early discussion of the race and forced Clinton's campaign to expend time and effort on developing a plan to address it. That was the impetus behind Clinton's listening tour: to acknowledge that she was a newcomer and to demonstrate that she was willing to work to get to know her new neighbors and would-be constituents. The error that the Giuliani and then Lazio campaigns made was to assume that nothing Clinton did could ever change the perception of her as an interloper.

Discussion

Hillary Clinton, like Bobby Kennedy before her, benefitted from a favorable set of circumstances without which she would never have become one of New York's senators. Pat Moynihan's retirement created an opportunity that otherwise would not have existed. Had Moynihan sought another term, Clinton would not have had an opening to run in New York. Republicans' success in New York throughout the 1990s meant there were fewer alternatives to Clinton in the state Democratic Party. And as their predecessors had done for Kennedy, leaders of the state party helped pave the way for her candidacy.

Clinton, like Kennedy, also brought to the campaign a famous political name. Both Kennedy and Clinton already had the sorts of credentials and experience that could have made them, in the abstract, viable candidates for federal elected office in their own right no matter what their last names were. Their credentials and experience alone, however, might not have made them appealing as carpetbaggers, rather than as candidates in states to which they had stronger ties. Instead, their political family ties enhanced their viability as candidates because of what those ties represented. In addition to personal background, these candidates had access to experienced campaign staffers and to formidable fundraising capabilities, and their political celebrity held the potential to draw the attention and support of voters. In this regard, Kennedy and Clinton were similar to other legacy politicians whose entry into the political sphere is smoothed in part by their name or family ties. Kennedy's and Clinton's political fame helped them make up the information deficit one would otherwise expect a carpetbagger to face in a new state; in fact, in each case, one could argue that the carpetbagger candidate was better known at the start of the general election campaign than his or her opponent. This in turn suggests a new variation on the findings that candidates run when they think it is advantageous to their ambitions to do so, and that different candidates' perceptions of their moment of maximum opportunity are shaped by those candidates' personal characteristics. Prior research in this area has focused on questions like how first-time candidates and past officeholders assess their opportunities differently from each other.

But the experiences of Kennedy and Clinton suggest that candidates with national profiles may have the ability to turn an opportunity others would pass up into an advantageous one. While Clinton and Kennedy were not from New York, they were not exactly from anywhere else, either. Clinton had been first lady of Arkansas only by virtue of her marriage to Bill, and her Arkansas days were eight years in the past by the time she became a candidate in New York. Kennedy's family was from Massachusetts, but he had lived in or around Washington, DC during his cabinet tenure and other federal positions. Even more crucially, perhaps, neither of these carpetbaggers had ever been elected to office anywhere else. As a result, they came to their new states without the baggage of having once sworn an oath to represent the citizens of another state.

Kennedy and Clinton also had the good luck to have begun their carpetbagger campaigns after attaining national stature and serving, officially or unofficially, in the executive branch in Washington, DC. This fact affected the nature of the carpetbagger charge; both of these candidates could point to their experience in government as an asset that would make them better able to represent New York. But only Kennedy faced questions about whether his carpetbagger status would lead him to take office with divided loyalties; when asked what he would do in a situation where New York's interests conflicted with those of Massachusetts, he said he would put New York first. For Clinton, her opponents had a hard time pointing to anywhere else that her loyalties might lie in a way that stuck. Even as Rick Lazio was urging audiences to shout "Arkansas!" as part of a call-and-response in his stump speech, Clinton was methodically making her way through one upstate town after another. And their lack of previous elected office helped them avoid the charge that they were using their new states simply to get back a status or a position that they had once enjoyed.

Kennedy's and Clinton's national stature at the time they became Senate candidates may have helped them manage the issue of their carpetbagger status more easily than they otherwise might have—making them "national carpetbaggers" who pledged to use their experience acting on behalf of the nation as a whole in the service of a new state. Rather than hopping state lines, they were moving down to the state level from the national stage in order to return to Washington and continue long and varied careers in an unusual spin on the progressive ambition Schlesinger described. Chapter 5 will consider the cases of two public servants who had, in fact, represented one state in the Senate before seeking to return to that body from another. For these two "interstate carpetbaggers," their campaigns for the Senate did not go as well as those of Kennedy and Clinton did.

Chapter 5

Two Would-Be Two-State Senators

For Robert Kennedy and Hillary Clinton, political celebrity somewhat obscured the fact that each turned to carpetbagging out of necessity. Each was in a high-profile position that had either become untenable (in Kennedy's case) or was drawing to a natural close (in Clinton's). Each used his or her status as a national political figure to help present carpetbagging as the next step in an ongoing political career, and the fact that they both sought to represent one of the most cosmopolitan states in the nation helped make their status as newcomers more palatable to voters. This chapter examines two carpetbagger candidates who lacked the celebrity of Kennedy and Clinton but had previously represented another state in the United States Senate. In both cases, those explicit representational ties to another state, along with their relative obscurity and poor partisan fit with their new states doomed their campaigns.

James L. Buckley: Connecticut, 1980

Like Kennedy and Clinton, James L. Buckley's first foray into elective politics took place in New York, in spite of his roots in another state, and as a result of the political activity of a family member. Buckley was born in Connecticut and attended Yale for college and law school, and practiced law in New Haven until he began to work for the Buckley family's Catawba Corporation in New York.[1] In 1965, he managed the campaign of his brother, *National Review* founder and *Firing Line* host William F. Buckley Jr., for mayor of New York on the Conservative Party line. Three years later, Buckley found himself on the ballot as the Conservatives' "sacrificial lamb" against Republican Jacob Javits; Buckley himself later said he had no expectations of winning, but entreaties from his brother led him to become a candidate.[2] He received just 17 percent of the vote that year. In 1970, Buckley ran again on the Conservative line, but this time the political environment and the idiosyncrasies of the year interacted in his favor. The incumbent Republican was Charles W. Goodell, appointed by Governor Nelson Rockefeller in 1968 after the assassination of Robert Kennedy. Goodell was a moderate disliked by both movement conservatives and the Nixon White House, and who won the endorsement of New York's Liberal Party as well as the GOP nomination. The Democratic nominee, Representative Richard Ottinger, split the center-left vote with Goodell, allowing Buckley to slip into office with just under 39 percent of the vote on a platform that emphasized crime and campus unrest.[3]

Even in 1970, Buckley had faced charges of carpetbagging; his family was famously associated with Connecticut, and Buckley himself lived in New York only part-time while working at his family's corporate offices in New York. But in 1970, Buckley had never held office in another state, and his emphasis on his residence and business and political ties to the state were enough to help him win a race with three major candidates. Six years later, however, after a term that saw him win the hearts of movement conservatives, successfully challenge parts of the post-Watergate campaign finance reforms at the Supreme Court, and take positions against public transit funding, the federal rescue of New York City, and other bread-and-butter New York issues, Buckley was defeated by Democrat Daniel Patrick Moynihan.

After the 1976 loss, Buckley returned to the family's business interests and a position on Wall Street;[4] he also explored converting the Buckley estate in Sharon, Connecticut, into a retirement community. But the political bug had not left him entirely, and, as the 1980 election drew near, many speculated that Buckley would run for the Senate again—in either New York or Connecticut. In many regards, then, Buckley was not unlike the carpetbaggers considered in earlier chapters. He was a politically engaged figure lacking a platform from which to engage in public affairs; had Gerald Ford won the 1976 election, he might well have offered Buckley a position in order to court favor with conservative activists in the Republican Party. In the absence of such an opportunity, however, Buckley was at political loose ends. Fortunately for his electoral prospects, one of the two states he had ties to was home to a Republican Party in need of a candidate.

Connecticut's Republicans in Need

As the 1980 electoral cycle began, Republicans were optimistic about their chances. President Jimmy Carter's low approval ratings, stemming in part from a poor economy, inflation, gas lines, the Iranian hostage crisis, and other woes of the late 1970s led Republicans to think they might reclaim the White House after just four years in the wilderness. Democratic prospects were so bleak that Republicans—correctly, it would turn out—believed they had the chance to retake control of the US Senate for the first time since 1954 as well.[5] Given this environment, Republicans wanted to put forward the best candidates available in as many states as possible. Buckley's status as a well-known former senator whose ties to the conservative movement gave him access to a nationwide fundraising network made him an obvious focus of speculation. But it was the sorry state of the Connecticut Republican Party that truly made many Republicans want him to run there in 1980.

In 1978, the state's Republicans had expected that they would have a banner year, in part because it was the midterm election of a Democratic presidency, and in part because they viewed incumbent Democratic governor Ella Grasso as eminently beatable. But on Election Day, Grasso won re-election by over two hundred thousand votes, and the GOP held just one of the state's six seats in the House of Representatives and lost seats in both houses of the legislature. The lone Republican statewide officeholder left standing was the state's maverick Republican US senator, Lowell Weicker.[6] As a result of the party's 1978 drubbing, Connecticut's Republicans had few viable options when Abraham Ribicoff, the state's three-term Democratic senator, announced that he would not seek re-election in 1980.[7] While Democrats quickly lined up behind Christopher Dodd, a three-term congressman and son of the late former governor and longtime US Senator Thomas Dodd, the initial speculation about Republican candidates focused on the party's unsuccessful candidates for governor and lieutenant governor in 1974 and 1978.[8]

As a result of this paucity of potential candidates, Frederick K. Biebel, the state party chair, began to look at unconventional options who might run well against the well-known, well-liked Dodd. Biebel met with Henry Kissinger, the former secretary of state, as well as with James Buckley. While both were officially residents of New York state at the time Biebel sounded them out, Biebel believed that Kissinger's political celebrity would allow him to hop the state border easily.[9] In Buckley's case, his family's long ties to Connecticut could similarly ease him back into Connecticut politics. Both

Kissinger and Buckley initially rejected Biebel's overtures, and as late as June of 1979 Buckley described New York, rather than Connecticut, as his political base;[10] he maintained his New York voting registration and an apartment in New York City even while making the family compound in Sharon, Connecticut, his primary residence after his 1976 loss.[11] But some of the state's Republicans refused to take Buckley's no as final. John Harney, chair of the Republican Party in Salisbury, launched an effort to convince Buckley to run.[12] This slow-motion courtship eventually persuaded Buckley to enter the race.

Why was the Connecticut GOP so invested in recruiting a candidate who had never won more than 45 percent of the vote in any of three statewide contests, none of which took place in Connecticut? In the absence of a more traditional candidate—someone who had served Connecticut as governor or in the state legislature or in Congress—Buckley had several qualities that appealed to leading Connecticut Republicans. He had run for office, successfully, in a nearby state, making him well known to voters; he had access to his personal and family fortunes; and his status as a favorite of the conservative movement then ascendant within the Republican Party meant he was capable of raising large amounts of money for his campaign.[13] None of this made him an ideal candidate, and his status as a former officeholder in New York gave many Connecticut Republicans pause. But elite party actors were not comparing Buckley to an ideal candidate; they were comparing Buckley to the likes of failed candidates for lieutenant governor. By that metric, many—though not all—leading Republicans found the case for a Buckley candidacy compelling. John Harney's efforts led to the creation of a "Committee of 100" consisting of prominent Republican officeholders and fundraisers, whose activities included buying "Draft Buckley" ads in the newspapers in and around Sharon, site of the Buckley family estate.[14]

All of this attention slowly drew Buckley into a candidacy. In August of 1979, he switched his voter registration from New York to Connecticut, not, he said, because he planned to run, but because the time he was spending in the state made it "the natural thing" to do.[15] The move overjoyed Buckley backers, since it closed the door on a Buckley challenge to Jacob Javits; Buckley could now either run in Connecticut or not run at all. Buckley soon began to act like a candidate, with a schedule of speeches and fundraisers for the state GOP.[16] After several months of candidatelike behavior, toward the end of which Buckley declared that he was "willing to seriously consider the possibility of becoming a candidate,"[17] Buckley officially launched his candidacy on December 12, 1979, at an event in his home in Sharon.

While Buckley had, in the run-up to his formal declaration of candidacy, dismissed the carpetbagger issue as unimportant, his campaign kickoff showed a clear recognition that it was a potential problem for his candidacy. Locating the event in Buckley's home, rather than at a state landmark, meant that news coverage would remind voters that Buckley was now a resident of Connecticut, despite his prior term as one of New York's senators. In his remarks, he said questions about why he was running in Connecticut were fair ones, and he helpfully answered them in advance. He emphasized that he had grown up in Sharon and returned there after his senate term "with my wife to make our home and raise our children"[18]—language that suggested he had something in common with Connecticut voters who might have lived in New York when they started their careers but moved to Connecticut as they became parents. He also said he would bring his legislative experience to the job and that in his previous term he "did [his] homework and was able to be persuasive."[19] That experience would benefit both Connecticut and the United States as a whole, Buckley argued, since the country faced "unprecedented challengers" and danger around the world.[20] The return of experienced hands to public office would help steer the nation through what Buckley foretold would be "the most dangerous decade in our history," with the ongoing hostage crisis in Iran merely a sign of things to come.[21] For good measure, the press kit his campaign distributed at the announcement event noted that Senator Lowell Weicker, Representative Stewart McKinney, and Henry Parker, the state's treasurer, had all been born out of state, and Harney of the draft committee noted to reporters that the wine served at the event was from Connecticut, not New York.[22]

In other words, Buckley treated his carpetbagger status the way many candidates before and since have treated inconvenient facts about their lives or records: acknowledge the problem, explain that it is not actually a problem, and then try to change the subject. With the enthusiastic support of so many leaders of the Connecticut Republican Party, Buckley may have expected that his candidacy would play out much like that of Robert Kennedy had in 1964, where the carpetbagger issue did not fade away completely but also did not cost Kennedy the election. However, Buckley's opponents, first in the contest for the Republican nomination and then in the general election, ensured that voters would be reminded of Buckley's status as a carpetbagger throughout the campaign.

Securing the Nomination

For many Connecticut Republicans, Buckley's fame, experience, and fundraising capacity made him a prize recruit. But that sentiment was not shared universally. Among those who objected to Buckley's candidacy was Senator

Lowell Weicker, the state's most prominent Republican officeholder after the party's disastrous 1978 showing. Weicker had publicly criticized the state party's overtures to Buckley and Kissinger,[23] and he had blamed the party's leadership for its dismal showing in 1978.[24] Seeking outsider candidates, in Weicker's view, was poor party building. Weicker also believed that Buckley was too conservative to win in Connecticut.[25] And most damaging for Buckley, Weicker had absolutely no compunctions about airing his concerns and reservations in public.[26]

The concerns of Weicker and other Republicans similarly wary of Buckley meant there was an opportunity for an alternative candidate. And one came forward; while Buckley was telling voters he had no intention of playing Hamlet, Richard Bozzuto, the GOP leader in the state senate, declared his candidacy in August, months before Buckley did.[27] Bozzuto cast himself as speaking for other members of his party when he said that "there is a strong feeling among Connecticut Republicans that we should have a candidate who knows Connecticut people" and "their needs and concerns."[28] Bozzuto's pitch to the party delegates who would choose between him and Buckley had several prongs. In addition to criticizing Buckley as a carpetbagger, Bozzuto—despite his generally conservative record and reputation as a legislator—presented himself as steering a moderate course between Buckley on the right and Dodd on the left.[29] He also sounded a populist note, presenting himself as an "old grocer" who, like so many voters, worried about paying the mortgage, sending his kids to college, and covering the bills each month.[30] This set up another stark contrast with the wealthy Buckley and the dynastic Dodd.

Unlike Robert Kennedy and Hillary Clinton, Buckley did not have the benefit of a state party unified behind his candidacy. In addition to Weicker's support, Bozzuto found a receptive audience among those Republicans who viewed Buckley "as an interloper who is too conservative for Connecticut."[31] There was, it turned out, "some backlash" against Buckley's rediscovery of his Connecticut roots.[32] Bozzuto declared that he would be "Connecticut's full-time Senator"[33] and frequently noted that Buckley's most recent campaign had been both in another state and unsuccessful.[34] When the state legislative session ended, some state legislators gave Bozzuto a t-shirt "that said on the front: 'Buckley for Senate,' but on the back 'in New York.' "[35] Bozzuto's attacks on this front were aided by the fact that Buckley had represented a different state just four years earlier and been considering a run in that state just a few months prior to becoming a candidate in Connecticut. For all of Buckley's efforts at establishing (or re-establishing) his Connecticut ties, some

Republicans agreed with Bozzuto when he said voters "are not going to buy someone who shops around for a U.S. Senate seat like a Christmas gift."[36]

And if Buckley was an ambitious politician whose wandering eye had alighted on Connecticut for the time being, Bozzuto presented himself as an experienced representative who knew the state and its voters. He argued that he had "a better understanding of Connecticut's problems, a better understanding of Connecticut's people, a record of close association and working with those problems."[37] Buckley's campaign, he charged, was run by party big shots from Washington, DC, and New York, while Bozzuto's was "a Connecticut campaign with volunteers from Connecticut."[38] And he suggested that Buckley's loss in 1976 was not just the result of facing a "formidable" opponent, as Buckley described Daniel Patrick Moynihan,[39] but the result of Buckley running down ideological blind alleys at the expense of what Bozzuto called "his responsibility back to his constituency."[40]

Bozzuto's campaign and its reminders of Buckley's carpetbagger status kept the issue alive; because the attacks came from an established Republican and were amplified by the state's leading Republican officeholder, Republicans in Connecticut did not automatically dismiss them as partisan hackery the way they likely would have had they come from the Dodd campaign. Buckley responded to these concerns by emphasizing the length and depth of his ties to the state. His campaign speeches were peppered with references to his studies at Yale and what he called his "emotional roots in Connecticut," and he described himself as "delighted to have a chance to represent the people I've grown up with and known all my life."[41] He presented the carpetbagger question as one that had already been asked and answered; he may have served New York for a term, but his roots and, no doubt, his heart had always been in Connecticut, and that was why he had returned after his loss in New York. Looking ahead to the general election, he and his supporters often noted that even with his sojourn in New York, Buckley had lived in Connecticut for more years than Chris Dodd (who turned thirty-six during the campaign) had been alive.[42]

For some Connecticut Republicans, this was persuasive. For people like the Buckleys' neighbors in Sharon, his term representing New York was no deal breaker; Buckleys, in their eyes, "always belonged to Connecticut."[43] Bozzuto, on the other hand, presented himself as the candidate who could appeal to ethnic Catholics, a key constituency in Connecticut in this era, and who might be less understanding of Buckley's years in New York politics.[44] Weicker further pressed the issue and argued that only Bozzuto stood a chance of beating Dodd and charged that Buckley had been an absentee senator "too busy traipsing around the countryside" to represent New Yorkers' interests well—attacking both the experience card Buckley was emphasizing in his campaign and reminding voters of his past service representing another state.[45]

Bozzuto turned the nomination contest into a genuine nail-biter; at the Connecticut GOP's nominating convention, Buckley won the party's endorsement for the nomination by just fifteen votes,[46] and only after deploying well-known figures like his brother, William F. Buckley Jr., and Alexander Haig to impress delegates to the party's convention. Buckley may also have been harmed by his campaign's late realization of the central role of conventions in Connecticut politics—an error a candidate with political roots in Connecticut would never have made.[47] While Buckley did prevail, the narrow margin of victory meant that Bozzuto could and did, under the party's nomination rules, force a primary election to determine the party's nominee. Bozzuto's decision did Buckley no favors; while Buckley won the primary easily, the primary campaign gave Bozzuto additional weeks in which to repeat his attacks on Buckley as a wealthy, out-of-touch, elitist carpetbagger. Buckley, eager to avoid alienating the Bozzuto voters whose support he would need to win the general election, pledged at the convention that his primary campaign would "leave no scars and the party united behind whoever was the winner of that contest."[48] He presented himself as the party's nominee-in-waiting and suggested that Weicker was an outsider to the party who had enticed Bozzuto to join him on the fringe.[49] But, for the most part, Buckley's primary campaign focused on the Democratic candidate, Chris Dodd. Once Buckley finally won the primary and the nomination, the carpetbagger issue had not been laid to rest. Instead, it continued to factor into a general election that became personal and testy by election day.

The General Election

Buckley began the general election at a disadvantage. While Connecticut was, in 1980, in the middle of a period when it was considered a swing state that had gone Republican in the previous three presidential elections, it was also a state that generally rewarded moderate candidates rather than ideologues.[50] Buckley's strong ties to the conservative movement meant that he could not reposition himself at the center of the political spectrum, and he had no interest in doing so even if he could have. Dodd, on the other hand, presented himself to voters as "a newer kind of Democrat" who was not beholden to New Deal liberalism and could steer a middle path between the state party's establishment and progressive activists;[51] in this regard, he was similar to many of the other Democrats first elected to Congress, like Dodd, as part of the Watergate class of 1974 who tried to distance themselves from the party's liberal tradition.

Dodd also benefitted from his family name. His father, Thomas Dodd, had served the state both as governor and for three terms in the US Senate. The elder Dodd's tenure as a senator did not end well; he was censured for the personal use of campaign money in 1967, denied renomination by Connecticut's Democrats in 1970, ran as an independent, and lost the general election to Lowell Weicker.[52] But, by 1980, few voters remembered or dwelt on the sins of the father, and their affection for Tom Dodd carried over to his son. One attendee at a Dodd fundraiser said he was there "because I loved Tom Dodd and I'll do whatever I can to help his son get elected."[53] Dodd did not point to his family name as a reason for voters to choose him over Buckley; he repeatedly said, throughout the campaign, that he was his own man and had built his own reputation among voters during his three terms in the House of Representatives. But every such statement reminded voters that he was Thomas Dodd's son.

Finally, the state's Democratic tendencies favored Dodd. Connecticut politics had long been dominated by a Democratic Party machine that was a shadow of its former self by the time Buckley ran against Dodd, but even so, in 1980, Connecticut was still a state where "Republicans don't win statewide elections . . . unless the Democrat blows it."[54] Dodd began the race as the prohibitive favorite to hold Ribicoff's seat for the Democrats and enjoyed support across both the rank and file of the Connecticut Democrats and its elite actors (including the "enthusiastic support" of Ribicoff himself).[55] Nevertheless, the likelihood that 1980 would be a good year for Republicans generally and Dodd's inability to compete with Buckley's fundraising meant that the campaign was hard fought on both sides.

For Buckley, victory would require building out from the base of Republican-identifying voters to include what he called "the so-called ethnic, blue-collar, work-oriented, family value-oriented" voters.[56] These traditionally Democratic voters, added to a unified GOP, could have been enough to deliver the election to Buckley with an assist from Ronald Reagan at the top of the ticket. But Buckley's attempt to win these voters by allying himself with the memory of Thomas Dodd backfired badly. A radio ad in which an announcer declared, "I sure wish Chris Dodd voted like his father" on defense issues provoked a rapid backlash and forced Buckley to promise to avoid similar comparisons for the rest of the campaign.[57]

Buckley attacked Dodd for his youth and his liberalism, both of which Buckley argued made him a poor choice for Connecticut. Dodd, Buckley charged, would use federal housing policy to engage in social engineering and "surrender control of your beaches and neighborhoods to government bureaucrats."[58] Buckley also tried to link Dodd to the unpopular incumbent president; in one debate at Wesleyan University, Buckley referenced "the Carter-Dodd inflation, the Carter-Dodd recession, the Carter-Dodd military policy that has weakened the United States."[59] And in a continuation of his campaign theme that a dangerous world needed experienced leadership, Buckley argued that Dodd was weak on defense and endangered both national security and Connecticut jobs in the defense industry.[60]

But this approach did little to close the gap between Dodd and Buckley; Dodd's name and party affiliation and Connecticut's down-ticket Democratic lean all meant he started the race at an advantage over Buckley, and the general dynamic of the race did not change between the Republican primary and Election Day. Further complicating matters was the fact that, after the bruising Republican nomination contest, Lowell Weicker remained conspicuously silent throughout the general election campaign, while Dodd enjoyed united Democratic support.[61] Dodd was also a skilled enough campaigner to parry Buckley's attacks; for instance, he noted that he had always voted for increased spending for submarines built in Connecticut.[62]

Dodd did not make the carpetbagger issue the centerpiece of his campaign, but neither was he reluctant to remind Connecticut's voters that Buckley had once represented New York. When Buckley announced his campaign in December of 1979, Dodd's response was to ask "What state did he announce in?"[63] Dodd's critique of Buckley was not just about the fact of his carpetbagger status; he also noted that Buckley had been defeated in his 1976 re-election bid in New York. This doubly reminded voters of Buckley's border hopping; had he prevailed in his run against Daniel Patrick Moynihan, Buckley would have spent 1980 laying groundwork for a 1982 re-election campaign in New York. Buckley, Dodd charged, "has no Connecticut record whatsoever," and he predicted that "Connecticut voters will see what made their neighbors in New York vote him out of office."[64] In one debate, Dodd professed to be confused as to whether New York's voters "had retired" Buckley to New York or to Connecticut.[65]

The carpetbagger issue was almost certainly not decisive in Dodd's victory over Buckley; Dodd received over 56 percent of the vote, while Buckley won just under 43 percent.[66] But it was also a cloud out from under which Buckley's campaign could never crawl.[67] Where Kennedy and Clinton had been able to present themselves to New York voters as national figures beginning new chapters in their political lives, Buckley was unable to do the same in Connecticut.

Bill Brock: Maryland, 1994

In 1962, Bill Brock won his first campaign for Tennessee's Third Congressional District and became the first Republican in forty years to hold that seat. In 1970, he defeated three-term incumbent Albert Gore Sr. in a heated Senate campaign. Brock's victory signaled that Howard Baker's election two years prior had been no fluke and that Tennessee was now a two-party state with a rising Republican Party.[68] Brock made enough of a splash as a young, up-and-coming senator that he was one of the finalists in Gerald Ford's vice presidential selection process in 1976.[69] However, Brock's term was also beset by controversies, and in 1976 he was defeated by Democrat James Sasser. After leaving the Senate, Brock served as chairman of the Republican National Committee, and President Reagan appointed him first as US Trade Representative and then as Secretary of Labor. In 1987, Brock left the Labor Department to manage Bob Dole's 1988 presidential campaign.[70] Had Dole won, Brock would have received a high-level position in Dole's administration. But President George H. W. Bush showed little interest in appointing Brock to a position in his administration, and Bill Clinton's election in 1992 definitively closed the door on another executive branch appointment for Brock.

By the early 1990s, after years of serious public service, Brock found himself on the outside with few obvious prospects available to him. And as he surveyed the political landscape after Bill Clinton's election, Maryland likely seemed to be a better bet for a political future than the state he had once represented. As a newly elected congressman, Brock had moved his family to the Maryland suburbs of Washington DC. While many members of Congress in the twenty-first century take pride in spending as little time in Washington as possible, with some going so far as to sleep in their offices rather than rent a home or an apartment, in the early 1960s many members brought their families with them to the nation's capital. As a party official and political appointee after his 1976 defeat, Brock continued to live and spend much of his time in Maryland. By 1986, he had bought a home in Annapolis, and in 1990 he began paying income taxes in the state.[71] By 1993, Brock's interest in seeking office in Maryland was widely known, and after flirting with a bid for governor, he began to lay groundwork for a Senate run.[72]

Brock was able to do this in part because the Maryland GOP was a party in decline; since the election of Charles Mathias to his final term in 1980, Maryland had not elected a Republican to the US Senate, and Democrats had held the governorship for a quarter of a century as the 1994 election season opened. The state Republicans were stuck in a negative feedback loop. Their lack of success made it hard to recruit and develop talented candidates, which led them to lose elections, which made it harder to recruit talented candidates, which led them to lose more elections. The state party's woes made Brock appealing to Maryland Republicans in a way he otherwise might not have been. As a *Baltimore Sun* columnist wrote, Brock's opportunity was the result of the party's failure to develop "enough talent to make an outsider's ambition seem more cheeky than altruistic,"[73] and an editorial hoped Brock's candidacy would energize the party at least enough for it to develop "strong candidates with deep roots here."[74]

Brock's opponent in the 1994 election was Paul Sarbanes, a three-term incumbent Democrat born in Salisbury. Sarbanes was a low-key, low-profile senator; despite his many years in office, a July 1994 survey showed him with a fairly low level of name recognition among Maryland voters.[75] Deposing a long-time incumbent in a deeply Democratic state would be a tall order, but Brock had done it before in 1970. The national context may also have played a role in Sarbanes's decision: With a Democratic president in the White House, the 1994 midterms were likely to (and did) bring Republican gains in both houses of Congress, and Clinton's unpopularity at the start of the election year might have further encouraged Brock to think an upset was possible in his second state.

A Weak State Party, Divided

When Robert Kennedy and Hillary Clinton moved to New York to run for the Senate, they benefited from the fact that the state's Democratic Party chose its nominees through a party convention and that they faced minimal or no opposition at those conventions. James Buckley, running in Connecticut, ran afoul of an opponent who held his margin at that state's Republican convention low enough to force a primary election from which he emerged bruised and damaged. In Maryland, Brock would have to win his state's primary in order to face off against Sarbanes in the general election. But the weakness of the state party meant that there were no leaders or power brokers to help clear Brock's path to the nomination. He faced several primary opponents;

most of these were little-known figures or perennial candidates like Dr. Ross Z. Pierpont, who had sought many offices unsuccessfully for many years.[76]

The largest threat to Brock came from Ruthann Aron, a member of the Montgomery County Planning Board. While Aron was a political newcomer who had been on the board for just two years before launching her Senate campaign, she did not hesitate to attack Brock for his Tennessee origins. During her announcement speeches throughout the state, she called Brock "a defeated senator from Tennessee" and asked why Marylanders should vote for someone when "the people of his home state, Tennessee, turned him out."[77] An Aron commercial also alleged that Brock, during a 1991 visit to Nashville, had expressed interest in running for governor of Tennessee, a charge Brock disputed.[78] Whether it was true or not, Aron's ad suggested that Brock, for all his years in Maryland, had only settled on Maryland after some state shopping, and would have gladly gone back to Tennessee had his prospects there looked brighter.

These attacks demonstrate the difficult position carpetbaggers with strong ties to another state face. Brock had not been a full-time resident of Tennessee since his 1962 election to the House of Representatives. He owned a home and paid state income taxes in Maryland, and he had been involved in state Republican politics for years before running for office. As someone who had spent years living in Maryland and commuting to work in Washington, DC, Brock had much in common with Maryland's many federal employees and contractors. Of all the carpetbaggers considered in this book, Brock has the single strongest claim to having become a genuine resident of his second state before seeking office there. When former cabinet members run for the Senate, their executive experience is usually presented to, and viewed by, voters as a positive feature. But Brock's past experience in Congress, rather than adding value to the rest of his resume, was attacked by Aron as a drawback: as someone who had once represented another state, Brock's motives had to be suspect, and as someone who had lost an election in another state, Brock's effectiveness had to be minimal.

Despite her lack of elected experience, on paper, Aron appealed to many Republican primary voters and party actors. One supporter in the state legislature noted that she possessed the twin virtues of coming from Maryland's largest county by population and was a woman, both of which could help make a statewide race competitive.[79] In practice, however, her campaign largely consisted of unrelentingly negative attacks on Brock. In addition to attacking him as a carpetbagger, she also attacked him for opposing term limits for members of Congress, for having voted to increase congressional salaries, and for voting to raise taxes in order to fund an increase in Social Security benefits.[80] When Brock finally responded to Aron's attacks, she cried foul and spent several years unsuccessfully suing him for defamation.[81]

The unending negativity of Aron's attacks on Brock hurt her more than they hurt him, at least as far as the primary went. One survey, taken in July, found that her unfavorable ratings had risen from 2 percent to 16 percent over the course of the primary campaign, while Brock's had barely moved from 7 percent to 10 percent. The same survey, however, found that Brock generally had low name recognition and was only leading his opponents by a small margin.[82] This was an especially poor omen for Brock's chances since he had spent over $800,000 by that point in the campaign.[83] In the September 13 primary, Brock won with just 39 percent of the vote. And once Brock was officially the nominee, his campaign still had difficulty attracting the visible support of Maryland's few prominent Republicans. When Brock held a press conference on women's health, for instance, Congresswoman Connie Morella, a popular Republican moderate, was notably absent. Brock explained that she "physically could not be" at the event, but Morella was, in fact, just a few blocks away in her district office.[84] Brock's difficulty in shaking the carpetbagger label and responding to Aron's attacks made Maryland Republicans less willing to support him publicly.

The General Election

With the primary behind him, Brock turned his attention to the incumbent, Paul Sarbanes. The three-term incumbent had a reputation as a quietly effective legislator who attended to the state's business without drawing attention to himself; some described him as a "stealth senator,"[85] and others as "an intellectual and something of an introvert."[86] One focus group of seven voters, none of whom could identify a specific accomplishment with Sarbanes, unanimously chose Sarbanes over Brock, with one member describing the incumbent as having "probably done an adequate job."[87] During a debate with Brock, Sarbanes reminded voters of his work on issues of importance to Marylanders, including Washington-area mass transit, the Chesapeake Bay cleanup, and attracting federal agencies to populous Montgomery County.[88] Sarbanes made his low-key manner a virtue and said, "[Y]ou don't want a lot of fanfare" when trying to help one state in a legislative body full of representatives from the other forty-nine.[89] And he argued that his seniority in the Senate was part of why he was able to do so much for Maryland.[90]

While Sarbanes's representational style was in many ways low key, that did not mean he was unwilling to attack Brock. Throughout the campaign, Sarbanes argued that Brock's carpetbagger status was disqualifying. Sarbanes argued to a reporter that there was no "sense that Brock comes out of this state or out of the people."[91] Sarbanes, by contrast, was a Maryland native who had held a series of elected positions since 1966.

Brock's past service representing Tennessee did more than just allow Sarbanes to brand him as an outsider; it also provided Sarbanes with plenty of fodder for attacks. As a conservative Republican elected from a southern state, Brock had amassed a conservative voting record on a host of issues. Sarbanes repeatedly attacked Brock for his vote against the Civil Rights Act of 1964; while Brock said he had come to regret his vote and viewed it as a mistake, this attack was particularly effective in Maryland, with its large and reliably Democratic African American population. This is a dramatic example of the representational disadvantage at which carpetbaggers who have held office in a previous state can find themselves. Had Brock served in office continuously in Tennessee or sought to return to office there rather than in Maryland, his vote against the Civil Rights Act might well have been less of an issue; certainly, it had not harmed him in unseating Albert Gore Sr. in 1970. Had Brock's vote become controversial in a subsequent race in Tennessee, he would have been arguing his case to voters with whom he had a long and consistent history and the shared experience of living in that state. But as a transplant to Maryland—even one who had lived there at least part-time for decades before he ran for office there—he lacked that sort of shared history with the state's voters. His vote against the Civil Rights Act was, perhaps, the second thing many Maryland voters learned about Brock during the campaign, and it was tightly bound to the fact that he had previously held office in Tennessee. Brock pointed to his outreach efforts to minority voters as chairman of the Republican National Committee and his attempts to hire more minorities as part of the Reagan administration, but as a carpetbagger he lacked a context within which to situate his claims.

That vote against the Civil Rights Act was not the only aspect of Brock's previous congressional service that Sarbanes attacked. Sarbanes criticized Brock's votes against the Clean Air Act and Medicare,[92] called the 20 percent of roll call votes Brock had missed "an absolute dereliction of duty," and attacked Brock's 1970 campaign against Albert Gore Sr. "despicable."[93] As with the Civil Rights Act vote, Brock had to respond without the benefit of a history with Maryland voters. A candidate familiar to voters might have been able to get away with responding to a critique of his attendance record in the Senate by saying, as Brock did, "I felt badly about it then, and I've felt badly about it ever since."[94] But, from a newcomer, such a response gave voters little reason to take it seriously; there was no pre-existing relationship to lend weight to Brock's declaration.

Voter disinterest in the Senate campaign was a further drag on Brock's chances. After his weak showing in the primary, his campaign took a low profile for several weeks.[95] While the Republican nominee for governor, Ellen Sauerbrey, drew attention for her stronger-than-expected poll numbers and her sharp focus on taxes, many state Republicans criticized Brock for lacking focus and a clear message.[96] By the final month of the campaign, Brock was following the lead of many Republican candidates across the country, attacking Sarbanes as a big-government liberal who supported President Clinton and was soft on crime.[97] But this had little impact. Sarbanes' liberalism made him a good fit for the state and was not something the incumbent had ever hidden or run away from. And for many Maryland residents, the federal government was then, as it is now, a direct or indirect employer; Brock's warnings against a growing government, as a result, fell flat.

Brock tried to address the carpetbagger issue at various points in the campaign. During one debate with Sarbanes, Brock declared that he had "a commitment to this state that is absolute and requires me to serve it better than it's being served."[98] But he had little to offer to demonstrate that commitment, and the fact of his carpetbagger status, reinforced by Ruthann Aron in the primary and Paul Sarbanes in the general election campaign, dogged him. When Sarbanes visited a diner toward the end of the campaign, when polls showed him trailing Sarbanes badly, a voter asked Brock, "Are you the one from Tennessee?" "Used to be," the former senator replied.[99]

Voter disinterest and Brock's carpetbagger status dogged his campaign to the finish. While the Republican candidate for governor, Ellen Sauerbrey, lost her race, by the end of October, she was trailing her Democratic opponent by just seven points; Brock, in the same survey, trailed Sarbanes by twenty-three.[100] By Election Day, polling had the governor's race within the margin of error, and the Democratic nominee, Parris Glendenning, won by just under six thousand votes.[101] The races for governor and US Senate are not directly comparable. Sauerbrey was running for governor in an open-seat race, not for a Senate seat held by a three-term incumbent, but her showing suggests that a Republican in liberal Maryland in 1994 could still be a competitive candidate. However, Brock was not that candidate. On Election Day, Sarbanes was easily re-elected with 59 percent of the vote to Brock's 41 percent. The closeness of the governor's race suggests that Brock's timing was not off. But the gap between Brock's performance and Sauerbrey's is a large one. To what extent might Brock's carpetbagger status explain the size of his loss?

While Brock never ran for any other office in Maryland, Sarbanes ran for the Senate a total of five times. A look at Sarbanes's vote totals shows a remarkably consistent performance across the years, with 1994's 59.1 percent marking Sarbanes' lowest vote share and 63.5 percent in 1982 marking his best performance. If anything, Brock performed slightly better than Sarbanes's other general election opponents. That is not to say that his carpetbagger status made no difference to his campaign; in such a good year for Republicans, perhaps another candidate whose roots in the state were clear and unambiguous would have won a few more percentage points of the final vote total. But against a well-regarded, quietly effective incumbent, it is tough to say that such a candidate would have been guaranteed to defeat Brock.

The absence of such a candidate is telling and illustrates the conundrum faced by carpetbaggers and the parties that need them. Had such a candidate been available to run, Brock would likely have passed on the race or lost the primary. But Sarbanes's strengths as an incumbent had deterred any such candidate from entering the race. There was an opportunity for Brock to run precisely because that opportunity presented whoever took advantage of it with little chance to win. Nevertheless, for Brock, this opportunity was the best one available to continue a meaningful role in public life.

Discussion

Robert Kennedy and Hillary Clinton faced formidable obstacles in their carpetbag campaigns, but they overcame these obstacles in a way that neither Buckley nor Brock was able to. Several factors help explain the different outcomes each pair of candidates experienced.

Both Buckley and Brock were hurt by their state party's nominating processes. Kennedy and Clinton had little or no competition within their own party. Kennedy faced only a challenge from Samuel Stratton, who had aroused little enthusiasm among New York Democrats even before Kennedy entered the race. Potential challengers to Clinton did not run once she became a candidate. And in both races, the nomination was decided at a party convention rather than a primary election. This meant that the support of party leaders in New York was enough for them to claim their party's nomination with minimal criticism of their carpetbagger status from their fellow Democrats. As a result, carpetbagger attacks against them came almost exclusively from

Republicans, and this turned the attacks into partisan attacks that Democrats would filter through their own partisan lenses and ignore or dismiss.

Neither Buckley nor Brock was so lucky. Buckley could not win his nomination outright at the state party convention. This forced him into a bruising primary fight in which his carpetbagger status became an issue raised not just by another Republican, but by the popular Republican senator Lowell Weicker as well. For Brock, the only route to the nomination was via primary. And while no major opponents emerged to challenge him, Ruthann Aron nonetheless made Brock's carpetbagger status the focus of many of her attacks on him during the primary campaign. Brock's dismal primary win with just 39 percent of the vote suggests that these attacks were at least somewhat effective and left him in a poor position to begin his general election campaign. A clearer field to the nomination would have benefitted each candidate.

Their primary battles also highlighted their carpetbagger status, and that status differed in a key way from that of Kennedy and Clinton. Kennedy and Clinton were national figures who came to New York to seek election to the Senate. While their carpetbagger status was an issue in each of their concerns, that status was not tied, in a formal way, to another state; Kennedy was of course linked to Massachusetts, and Clinton, to Arkansas, but neither had ever held elected or appointed office there. As a result, Kennedy and Clinton could more or less forthrightly present their decisions to run in New York as next steps in their careers in public service. But for both Buckley and Brock, the fact of their having represented other states in the Senate helped the carpetbagger charge stick, as both found themselves having to defend their past votes in Congress to new electorates. In many ways they experienced the worst of both worlds. They received all of the negatives of past congressional service that an incumbent member of Congress faces—such as attention to past votes and voting records—and none of the benefits—such as a shared history with voters or the constituent services and other activities that members of Congress engage in to get re-elected.

As national figures, Kennedy and Clinton did not have to be introduced to voters; New Yorkers were well aware of the late president's brother and the first lady before they became candidates. Buckley and Brock were far less well known to their second states' voters and had to introduce themselves during their campaigns. But news coverage of their campaigns invariably discussed the fact that they were carpetbaggers, and this information put them at a disadvantage with voters. Not only were these candidates relatively unknown to voters in their second states, but the first thing many voters were learning about them was the fact that they had once represented another state. As a result, not only did these two carpetbaggers have to introduce themselves to new voters, but they had to explain their past to those voters at the same time. Doing this took up precious time and effort and often led to a renewed focus on their carpetbagger status.

Chapter 6

Four Lesser-Known Carpetbaggers

Robert Kennedy and Hillary Clinton were able to overcome the carpetbagger stigma by winning the early support of state party actors and identifying themselves with their popular family members' presidential tenures. Both also ran in years when their party did well across the country in Senate races and ran in New York, a state whose social and political culture lent itself well to appeals from newcomers to put ideology and experience before length of residency. James Buckley and Bill Brock each served one term in the Senate, lost a re-election campaign, and then mounted a comeback attempt in a second state. In neither case was the comeback attempt successful, despite running in years when Republicans won control of the Senate. Buckley ran against a well-known opponent whose father had been an institution in Connecticut politics, in a state where Democrats tended to win downticket races. Brock similarly chose poorly in his choice of race. Even in the Republican wave year of 1994, there was little chance of any Republican, let alone one who had once represented a different state, defeating a veteran Democratic incumbent in solidly Democratic Maryland.

These four cases are well-known examples of Senate carpetbaggers. But nationally known presidential kin and former senators are not the only people who have tried to run for the Senate from a new state. This chapter considers four additional, less known carpetbaggers: Endicott Peabody, the former Massachusetts governor who ran for the Senate in New Hampshire in 1986; Alan Keyes, the former Maryland senate candidate and presidential longshot whom Illinois Republicans recruited to run against Barack Obama in 2004; Harold Ford Jr., the former Tennessee congressman who considered a run against appointed incumbent Kirsten Gillibrand in New York in 2010; and Elizabeth Cheney, who attempted a primary challenge to Wyoming's three-term Republican incumbent, Mike Enzi, in 2014. Each of these unsuccessful candidacies demonstrates the importance of key ingredients in running as a carpetbagger: the support of state actors, favorable political terrain, and political circumstances that make a longshot carpetbagger candidacy the best course of action available for the candidate.

Peabody and Keyes demonstrate how even a weak candidate can gain a major party's nomination for the Senate when a state's political party and its leaders stand behind him. Ford and Cheney show what happens when a candidate seeks to run in a new state not just with minimal support from important actors in the state party but against an incumbent of the same party.

Endicott Peabody: New Hampshire, 1986

Most candidates run for office because they want to win, and parties field and support candidates because they hope to win elections. In some cases, however, candidates and parties may have motives other than winning a general election. The 1986 Senate race in New Hampshire was one of these cases. While most other carpetbaggers run for office because they want to win and because carpetbagging is the best option available to them, the Democratic former governor of Massachusetts, Endicott "Chub" Peabody, was recruited to run to prevent the state party's nomination from being hijacked by an undesirable candidate.

As 1986 began, New Hampshire's Democrats were unable to find a credible candidate to run against first-term Republican Warren Rudman. In and of itself, the Democrats' situation was suboptimal but not disastrous; every two years there are states where incumbent senators face minimal or no opposition from the other party. The failure to field a credible candidate says nothing good about the health of a state party but rarely exacerbates an already-poor situation. However, while no acceptable candidate was willing to run, one unacceptable candidate was already running. The first declared candidate for the nomination was Robert A. Patton, a supporter of Lyndon LaRouche. LaRouche was equal parts cult leader, conspiracy theorist, and political troublemaker; he had himself run for president three times by 1986, and that same year two of his supporters won the Democratic nominations for lieutenant governor and secretary of state in Illinois, a move which helped keep Democrat Adlai Stevenson III from winning the general election for governor.[1] Failing to field a credible candidate would be one thing. Having the nomination seized by a LaRouche supporter was another. Not only would Patton's presence on the ballot as the Democratic nominee for Senate be mortifying; it would also damage the prospects of every other Democrat on the ballot and provide ready fodder for their state's Republicans. Fortunately for the leadership of the New Hampshire state party, they were able to find in Endicott Peabody a former statewide officeholder who was willing to run for the nomination. Unfortunately, the state where he had previously held office was Massachusetts.

1986 in the Context of Peabody's Quixotic Career

Previous cases demonstrate that running for office in one state after holding office in or being identified with another is a daunting task for any politician. Fortunately for New Hampshire's Democrats, Peabody's career up to 1986 was one that demonstrated both a desire to serve the public, without much concern about which office was at stake, and a willingness to pursue quixotic campaigns with little chance of success.

Peabody's political career began traditionally enough. Born to an old New England family, he attended the Groton School and Harvard. After serving in the navy in World War II, he attended law school, again at Harvard, and then practiced law in Boston. In 1954, he was elected to the Massachusetts Executive Council. In 1956 and 1958, he lost the Democratic primary for attorney general, and in 1960 he lost the Democratic primary for governor. In 1962, he was narrowly elected governor of Massachusetts over the incumbent Republican, John Volpe. In 1964, Peabody lost his bid for renomination to his own lieutenant governor, Francis Bellotti,[2] who proceeded to lose the general election to Volpe. In 1966, Peabody was the Democratic nominee for the US Senate in a race he lost to Edward Brooke, the Republican who became the first African American directly elected to the Senate. Despite his loss, Peabody "seemed genuinely pleased" at Brooke's election. After this loss, Peabody decamped to Washington, where served as assistant director of the Office of Emergency Planning and then opened a law firm once Lyndon Johnson left office.[3]

Peabody made his first political foray into New Hampshire in 1972, when he ran in the New Hampshire vice presidential primary. He ran partly in reaction to Richard Nixon's selection of Spiro Agnew in 1968 and argued that the vice presidency was too important an office not to be elected by the American people.[4] Peabody ran on the idea of expanding the vice president's

duties to include acting as a congressional liaison, serving as the president's
"eyes and ears" around the country, and playing a larger role in meetings of
the cabinet and National Security Council.[5] Given Agnew's eventual disgrace,
Peabody may have had a point, but after receiving just under thirty-eight
thousand votes,[6] he found little interest beyond New Hampshire in his campaign or his platform. Peabody moved to Hollis, New Hampshire, in 1982
and started a law firm.[7] In 1984, he was elected to the New Hampshire constitutional convention, where he pushed for the state's attorney general to be
elected rather than appointed by the governor.[8] Later that year, he ran for a
seat in New Hampshire's state legislature and lost.

Peabody represents an unusual sort of political ambition. His early
campaigns for higher and higher office—from executive council to attorney
general to governor to senator—follow a fairly standard arc. Following his
1966 loss to Edward Brooke, however, his ambitions become more eccentric
and display a certain amount of faith that arcane procedural questions—how
vice presidents are selected, whether the attorney general of a state he has
lived in for roughly two years should be elected or appointed—could some-
how provoke a groundswell of support from the public. Peabody also appears
to have stopped worrying about moving higher up the political ladder and
freely mixed campaigns for state representative and constitutional convention
delegate among his runs for the US Senate and the vice presidency. Nor did
his repeated failures deter him from any of these races.

By 1986, then, Peabody's unorthodox career and willingness to champion
obscure and hopeless causes made him receptive to the overtures of New
Hampshire's Democrats. When a delegation of party leaders led by state party
chair George Bruno visited him to recruit him into the race, Peabody had
little political future to risk by saying yes. And the campaign would give him
a platform from which to speak out about the issues he considered important.
For the state party, Peabody's campaign gave them a legitimate candidate
around whom to rally and thus avoid the moral and electoral catastrophe of
a LaRouchite supporter as the Democrats' standard bearer.

Aiding Bruno and the Democrats was a full-court press in support of
a Peabody campaign from such quarters as the editorial page of the *Nashua
Telegraph*. An editorial declared that "there is a higher responsibility than
simply winning elections; that the integrity of the process must be maintained
if the process itself is to have any meaning."[9] James Donchess, the mayor of
Nashua, similarly suggested that finding an alternative to Patton was necessary to preserve the two-party system and avoid abuses of power,[10] and other
party leaders circulated a petition asking Peabody to run.[11] These entreaties

from within and beyond the Democratic Party of New Hampshire convinced Peabody to become a candidate, and by May he was telling local reporters that while he had never contemplated running until he was approached, he also "never considered the possibility of being out of politics."[12]

The Primary

Peabody did not have a clear path to the Democratic nomination; in addition to Robert Patton's LaRouchite campaign, a former alderman from Nashua named Robert Dupay became a candidate. However, Dupay, who had placed a distant third in the 1984 primary for governor,[13] was of little interest to the party leaders who had recruited Peabody. State Democratic chair George Bruno, for instance, said that he knew of Dupay's intention to run but was "unaware of any political organization that he has."[14] Dupay's fundraising reflected this lack of organization; his final filing before the September primary showed that he had raised just $75 from three donors and borrowed another $4,500 to fund his campaign.[15]

Dupay was quick to play the carpetbagger card against Peabody. He told the *Nashua Telegraph* that he did not think "that the people of New Hampshire will ever elect a former Massachusetts governor."[16] In another statement, Dupay put Peabody's carpetbagging on the same level as nuclear power and Peabody's lobbying for the government of Haiti in terms of issues Democrats should consider in making their primary choice.[17] Dupay himself was a native of East Boston, but unlike Peabody, he had never been elected to statewide office in Massachusetts.

However, the state Democratic Party's leaders worked hard to push Peabody as the official candidate, even though both state parties in New Hampshire in this era had traditionally remained neutral in primaries and rarely recruited candidates to run.[18] The high-profile, public effort to recruit Peabody helped make the state's Democratic voters aware of him, and Bruno presented Peabody's tenure in Massachusetts as an asset: "[A]ny time you're talking to a former governor of an important region of our country, you're talking about a person of high stature."[19] Bruno notably spoke in terms of New England as a region, rather than New Hampshire, to suggest that Peabody's Massachusetts experience was relevant to a New Hampshire context. National Democrats lent support as well. Illinois senator Paul Simon—soon to become a candidate for president in 1988—phoned into a press conference Bruno held to warn New Hampshire Democrats not to be complacent about Patton's candidacy and cited his Illinois Democrats' painful experience earlier that year as a worst-case scenario New Hampshire could avoid if its Democrats turned out to support Peabody.[20] Democrats also helped Peabody with fund-raising, his distaste for which he had specifically cited as an obstacle to his candidacy.

This institutional press from state and national Democrats had its intended effect; Peabody won the primary with over 61 percent of the vote. Patton, whose candidacy prompted Peabody's recruitment, finished a distant third behind Dupay with just over 11 percent of the vote.[21] But the support that carried Peabody to victory among the state's Democratic primary voters did him little good in the general election against Warren Rudman.

The General Election

In his first term, Warren Rudman made a name for himself as a key architect of the Gramm-Rudman-Hollings Act, which cemented his bona fides as a fiscal conservative. Rudman himself did not think Peabody presented much of a challenge; in Rudman's memoir, he writes that the main obstacle he faced in the 1986 election was not his opponent, but his own ambivalence about seeking a second term.[22] Rudman also had a massive fundraising advantage over Peabody; shortly before the start of the general election campaign, Peabody had just $93,769 on hand, compared to Rudman's $623,215.[23] The eventual fate of Peabody's campaign could be divined from the entrails of his own fundraising reports. Peabody reported contributions of over $200 from just sixty-one individuals; only three of these people were New Hampshire residents. Most of the rest came from residents of New York, Washington, DC, and Massachusetts.[24] For a candidate who had held office in another state, this was not a strong sign that Peabody had made the sort of connections to life in New Hampshire that a native would have. The revelation that Peabody was maintaining a campaign office on Beacon Hill in Boston did not help matters.

Peabody gamely tried to present himself as more in touch with the people of New Hampshire than Rudman was. On issues like nuclear power and the debate over a freeze on nuclear weapons, Peabody argued that Rudman did not truly represent the beliefs and preferences of Granite Staters, while Peabody himself did. He also attacked Rudman for the bill which bore his name, and charged that Gramm-Rudman was a "dangerous" abdication of Congress's authority.[25] Peabody further complained that Rudman's workload in the Senate was keeping him from participating in debates.[26] This was a novel inversion of the customary charge that an incumbent is neglecting his or her duties in order to campaign.

Rudman's campaign went after Peabody as a carpetbagger. Campaign buttons urged voters to "Scrub Taxachusetts Chub," both reminding them of

Peabody's state of origin and playing on Granite Staters' aversion to sales and income taxes. A Rudman campaign ad featured a Peabody impersonator who called New Hampshire the "Green Mountain State" and considered running in Rhode Island and in Maine. For added measure, the faux Peabody called the Maine campaign as one for Ed Muskie's seat—even though Muskie left the Senate in 1980.[27] The ad thus served two strategic ends for Rudman. The reference to Muskie suggested that Peabody—who had last held office in the 1960s—was an out-of-touch figure who had been hauled out of mothballs to run against Rudman. The references to other New England states reminded voters of Peabody's carpetbagger status and suggested that he had run in New Hampshire for cynical reasons rooted in his ambition to win a Senate seat. These charges were not entirely fair; Peabody had lived in New Hampshire for several years before his 1986 campaign. But campaign attacks are not meant to be fair; they are meant to heighten an opponent's weakness, and Peabody's carpetbagger status was an irresistible point of attack. While Peabody tried to align himself with New Hampshire voters by claiming to be closer to their views on the issues of the day, Rudman undercut Peabody's efforts by pointing out his carpetbagging.

The year 1986 was very good for Democrats running for the Senate, and Democrats won back the majority they'd lost in 1980's Reagan landslide. But even as their emerging good fortune became clear during the fall campaign, no one thought there was a chance of a New Hampshire upset. One analysis of "sleeper" races that might have unexpected outcomes concluded there was no chance that Rudman could lose to Peabody.[28] On Election Day, Rudman won in a landslide, with nearly 63 percent of the vote to Peabody's 32 percent.[29] A quirky, out-of-state ex-governor was no match for a popular incumbent with long ties to the state and a major piece of legislation bearing his name. But to what extent did Peabody's carpetbagger status affect the outcome of the race? It is unlikely that any Democrat, native to New Hampshire or not, could have defeated Rudman in 1986. Rudman's strength as a candidate led the few local options the state's Democrats had to decline to run and created an opportunity for Peabody to win the nomination. This lack of interest by home-grown Democrats was what gave the LaRouchite candidate a shot at winning the nomination in the first place, which in turn prompted the Democrats' effort to recruit Peabody.

What is most noteworthy about Peabody's campaign is this recruitment campaign. Once these trusted party actors signaled to Democratic primary voters that Peabody was their preferred candidate, rank-and-file Democrats turned out in sufficient numbers to end the LaRouchite candidate's chances. The party actors who made the pilgrimage to Hollis, New Hampshire, to ask

Peabody to run were motivated not by a desire to win the general election, but to prevent their weakened party from having an unacceptable candidate hijack its nomination. Peabody's 1986 campaign is a reminder that candidates and parties alike can have motives other than simple electoral victory.

Alan Keyes: Illinois, 2004

The circumstances that led Illinois Republicans to ask Alan Keyes to run in their state against Barack Obama in 2004 in some ways mirror those that led to Endicott Peabody's campaign in 1986: a weakened party in need of a candidate reached out across state lines to avoid embarrassment. In New Hampshire in 1986, the embarrassment would have come in the form of a nomination won by a candidate antithetical to the party; in Illinois eighteen years later, the embarrassment came from a series of party and candidate scandals.

Illinois Republicans entered the 2004 election cycle in poor shape. Democrats had won all but one statewide office and both houses of the state legislature in 2002, thanks in large part to scandals surrounding then-governor George Ryan; Ryan was indicted and convicted on corruption charges after leaving office.[30] Adding to the state party's woes, US Senator Peter Fitzgerald announced in 2003 that he would not seek a second term. This concerned national Republicans as well; with a bare majority of fifty-one seats in the Senate, there was little margin for error in their efforts to retain control of the chamber. The 2004 primary was won by Jack Ryan (no relation to the former governor), a forty-five-year-old investment banker who had left the financial sector to teach at a Catholic high school in Chicago.[31] As a young political newcomer with an intriguing life story and the capacity to fund his own campaign, many Republican leaders found Ryan appealing. As a fresh face, Ryan also sidestepped the ongoing conflict between moderates and conservatives in the state party. Some party officials were concerned over rumors that damaging information lurked in the sealed records of Ryan's divorce from *Star Trek: Voyager* actress Jeri Ryan, but Ryan assured them that the records contained nothing damaging and had been sealed only to protect his ex-wife's privacy from a fan-turned-stalker.[32]

Ryan won the primary,[33] but the *Chicago Tribune* and Chicago's WLS television station filed suit to unseal the Ryans' divorce records. The records revealed that during their divorce, Jeri Ryan had charged Jack with taking her to sex clubs in New York and Paris, where he had tried to pressure her into performing sex acts with him while other guests at these clubs watched.[34] Ryan denied the claims and said he had merely taken Jeri to "avant-garde clubs," but many in the state party felt that the charges made Ryan too radioactive to stay on the ballot. Representative Ray LaHood, for instance, did not think Ryan's denial would play in his hometown of Peoria, and he argued that "there's no way the people of Illinois are going to countenance this type of behavior from a Senate candidate from the Republican Party."[35] Ryan was also mocked and criticized by late-night comics and Illinois newspapers and talk-radio shows, and House Speaker Dennis Hastert canceled an appearance at a Ryan fund-raiser.[36] Pressure from Hastert and other members of the Illinois Republican State Central Committee quickly led Ryan to resign from the ticket,[37] which solved the problem of how to handle a candidate like Ryan but left the party with the new problem of finding a replacement.[38]

However, there was no obvious replacement for Ryan; and Ryan had been badly trailing Barack Obama even before the details of his divorce went public.[39] James Thompson and Jim Edgar, two well-regarded Republican former governors, had no interest in a campaign likely to end in defeat; neither did state treasurer and party chair Judy Baar Topinka or outgoing senator Peter Fitzgerald.[40] The candidates who had lost the primary to Ryan all presented complications of their own. Second-place-finisher Jim Oberweis was wealthy but too stridently anti-immigration for the moderates in the party, and third-place-finisher state senator Steven Rauschenberger had suburban appeal but a demonstrated inability to raise enough money to compete against Obama.[41] Rauschenberger soon took his name out of the running,[42] as did Ron Gidwitz, former chair of the state's board of education.[43] Al Salvi, who had previously run for the Senate, announced he would not run unless personally asked to do so by President George W. Bush.[44] Bush did not ask. Things became so dire that a boomlet for the candidacy of former Chicago Bears coach, Mike Ditka, started to gain steam,[45] until Ditka took himself out of consideration, in no small part because running for federal office would have meant giving up multiple profitable revenue streams.[46]

While the state Republicans flailed, the Democratic candidate's star continued to rise. Obama smartly kept himself above the fray of Ryan's scandal and the GOP's search for a replacement.[47] After his keynote address at the Democratic National Convention, Obama became such a national political phenomenon that outgoing Senator Fitzgerald called the Republican nomination "akin to accepting a cancer transplant."[48] Whoever ran against Obama not only would be very likely to lose, but to lose under the national spotlight that now shone on the Democratic nominee.

Illinois Republicans' ongoing search for a candidate was by this point drawing national attention of its own and earning comparisons to a three-ring circus,[49] the Bay of Pigs invasion,[50] and *The Gong Show*.[51] When the state committee finally met early in August to pick Ryan's replacement, their final choices were surprising to many. From an initial list of fourteen candidates, they narrowed the list down to two, and then one. The two were Andrea Grubb Barthwell, a deputy drug czar in the George W. Bush administration, and Alan Keyes, who had served as an ambassador to the United Nations under Ronald Reagan and run for president in 1996 and 2000.[52] Neither candidate was without baggage. Barthwell had been reprimanded for making sexually explicit comments to a subordinate and had donated to Democratic campaigns in the past, while Keyes was not a resident of Illinois and had already unsuccessfully run for the Senate twice in his home state of Maryland. That both candidates were, like Obama, African American likely played a role in the committee's thinking.

After a heated, closed-door meeting during which reporters outside heard shouting,[53] the state party committee chose to offer the nomination to Keyes.[54] Keyes was the candidate favored by the conservative wing of the party; state Senator Dave Syverson also argued to his colleagues that "we need a name" to compete with Obama.[55] This reasoning may have been persuasive enough for the state party committee to decide to give Keyes the nomination, but it did not help Keyes in the general election campaign.

The Campaign in Keyes's Career Context

Just as the Illinois Republicans' search for a candidate resembled a funhouse mirror reflection of the New Hampshire Democrats' dilemma in 1986, so too did Keyes's decision to run resemble a bizarre spin on Endicott Peabody's. Like Peabody, Keyes was a perennial candidate for office. He had unsuccessfully run for the Senate in Maryland in 1988 and 1992, and he had sought the Republican presidential nomination in 1996 and 2000. In neither campaign did Keyes meet with much electoral success; the high point of his presidential runs was, arguably, diving into a mosh pit just before the 2000 Iowa caucus in order to win the endorsement of political provocateur Michael Moore's television series, *The Awful Truth*.[56]

His campaigns had, however, raised his profile among conservative activists, and in 2002 MSNBC hired him to host a nightly series, *Alan Keyes Is Making Sense*. Like so many shows in MSNBC's early years, Keyes's lasted only a few months.[57] With an incumbent president certain to win the Republican nomination, Keyes did not seek the Republican nomination in 2004. The summer of 2004 found Keyes without a platform from which to preach his particular brand of conservativism. But while Peabody was a serial office seeker who had settled in New Hampshire and previously sought office there, Keyes was new to Illinois. In this regard, he was little different from Hillary Clinton, but he was coming to the state just three months before the election. Not helping matters was the fact that he had in 2000 criticized Clinton for her campaign in New York.[58]

As many of the cases examined in this book demonstrate, however, politicians are very creative when it comes to justifying the decision to run in a new state. Keyes and some Illinois Republicans argued that the Democrats, by turning Barack Obama into a national political star, had thereby turned the Illinois senate race into a national contest. In that case, they argued, it only made sense to bring in a well-known figure from out of state.[59] Keyes himself declared that the Democrats had "thrown down a gauntlet of national challenge" with Obama's candidacy.[60] Keyes acknowledged that he had reservations about parachuting into the state but said, rather grandiosely, that he had asked himself, "Are we in a position where if I do nothing the principles of national union will be sacrificed?"[61] Like Hillary Clinton, at the start of her campaign in New York, Keyes was up-front about being a newcomer, telling a crowd of Republicans in his first appearance as a candidate, "There's a lot I don't know yet about Illinois." But, unlike Clinton, he did not announce a plan to learn about his new state. Instead, he placed the burden on the people of Illinois and declared that if they "still stand together on the American creed, still assert their right of self-government, still have the sense of responsible citizenship, then I believe I know their spirit and their conscience and their heart."[62]

State party chair Judy Baar Topinka suggested that Keyes was no different than any other American seeking a new start in Illinois. She said that "anytime you can get some really good people as Illinoisians, we're there."[63] But this did not carry the same heft as the similar statements Robert Kennedy and Hillary Clinton had made in New York. And while Baar Topinka sought to put a good face on the campaign, two moderate Republican state legislators introduced a bill to require parties to fill future vacancies with the primary's second-place finisher.[64]

In New Hampshire, in 1986, newspaper editorials applauded the state's Democrats for reaching out to Endicott Peabody in order to protect their party from political extremism. In Illinois, in 2004, the reaction to Keyes' recruitment was scathing. One incredulous editorial asked, "Shouldn't [an Illinois candidate] know where Centralia and Edwardsville are? Shouldn't he know what issues matter to people in Peoria and Prospect Heights? Should he not have more than a passing knowledge of the state's people?"[65] Another snarked that Keyes, in coming to the aid of the hopeless Illinois GOP, was acting "in the noble tradition of the Marquis de Lafayette, the Seven Samurai, Mighty Mouse, and Obi-Wan Kenobi."[66] And the *Chicago Tribune*, after noting that Keyes represented a dramatic break from decades of pragmatic Republicanism in the state, advised him on the proper pronunciation of Cairo, Illinois.[67]

Keyes, however, showed little interest in learning about his new state. Instead of working to get up to speed on local issues, Keyes declined opportunities to speak to Illinois' delegation to the Republican National Convention. His emphasis on social issues courted controversy; a satellite radio interview in which he denounced homosexuality as "selfish hedonsism" and Vice President Cheney's daughter Mary as a "selfish hedonist" managed the neat trick in 2004 of angering and alienating both gays and Republicans.[68] His remarks about Mary Cheney also drew rebukes from the Bush-Cheney campaign and Senator John McCain. These and similar comments condemning abortion and abortion providers may have been catnip to social conservative activists across the country, but they did little to build bridges in a large and diverse state whose Republicans had, for a generation, been pragmatic conservatives who worked to win support from moderate voters. By October, Keyes's relations with the state party had so badly deteriorated that he was left off of their glossy pre-election flyer,[69] and the Bush campaign kept Keyes at a very long arm's length.[70] Former governor James Thompson said of Keyes, "It certainly seems like the party made a mistake, didn't it?"[71]

Keyes did make some gestures toward the state; when he moved into a Calumet City apartment, he emphasized that the diverse town was "almost a microcosm of Chicago but also of Illinois."[72] But at the same time, he noted that the accommodations were temporary and that a permanent residence would come only if he won the election.

Obama greeted Keyes in terms that emphasized his carpetbagger status. In a statement welcoming Keyes to the campaign, Obama presented himself as speaking for the people of Illinois, who wanted "a Senate candidate who will attack the problems they and their families face" and not each other.[73] But, for the most part, with a wide lead in polls and a reputation as a candidate seeking a different kind of politics, Obama's attacks on Keyes were few and tended to focus on the stark policy differences between the two. In some cases, Obama linked Keyes's positions on issues with his carpetbagger status, as when, in their second debate, Obama said that "millions of people all across this state . . . are having a tough time," and neither Washington, DC, nor Keyes was listening to them.[74] But, for Keyes, the point of his campaign was speaking much more than listening. In September, Keyes told donors he planned to make "inflammatory" remarks until Election Day, and he kept this promise.[75] Obama, in contrast, conducted an energetic and optimistic campaign that largely ignored Keyes's rhetorical bomb tossing, even when Keyes announced that Jesus Christ would not vote for Obama because of Obama's position on abortion.[76]

On November 2, Illinois voters chose Barack Obama over Alan Keyes by a forty-three-point margin. Obama won among voters of every race, age, gender, religion, and income bracket and in every region in the state.[77] Keyes's only successes occurred in ten small, rural counties characterized by cultural conservatism and economic distress.[78] Given the collapse of the Illinois Republican Party, the Jack Ryan scandal, the partisan composition of the state's electorate, and the crowning of Obama as a political rock star and a potential future president during the summer, it is hard to say that Keyes's carpetbagger status was the decisive factor in his loss and Obama's victory. But it is also hard to argue that Keyes did not provide Obama with an easier path to election than Ryan, absent his sex scandal, would have. Keyes's fiery campaign rhetoric left him unable to carry any but the most ancestrally Republican parts of the state. Ryan might have run more toward the center and lost by a smaller margin, but in either case, the outcome would almost certainly have been the same.

Alan Keyes's Illinois sojourn, like Endicott Peabody's 1986 campaign in New Hampshire, demonstrates the limits of party leaders' support. When party leaders support a carpetbagger, they can deliver a nomination in a primary or an emergency party meeting. But their support does not automatically translate into general election votes from the party's rank and file. And while elite commentary on the Peabody campaign praised him for coming to the aid of a party in need, Keyes was generally seen as a carpetbagger in the most opportunistic sense of the word. Neither the presence nor the absence of this goodwill helped either candidate convince voters that he was the better candidate than his opponent.

Harold Ford Jr.: New York, 2010

Harold Ford Jr., the former congressman from Tennessee, briefly considered a campaign for the Senate in New York in 2010. As is typical for carpetbaggers, Ford had few other political avenues available to him by that point in his career. He had first won election to Congress in 1996 at age twenty-six; helping him considerably was the fact that he ran to succeed his father, Harold Ford Sr., who had held the seat for eleven terms and was the patriarch of the Ford political family. In 2000, Ford was the keynote speaker at the Democratic National Convention, and his performance touched off chatter of a bright future in national politics, potentially culminating in becoming the first African American president. In 2006, Ford ran for the United States Senate seat vacated by the retirement of Senate majority leader Bill Frist. But after a difficult campaign, Ford narrowly lost to Chattanooga mayor Bob Corker despite the blue tide that swept Democrats into control of the Senate.[79]

In the wake of this loss, and perhaps in recognition of the difficulties an African American candidate faces when seeking statewide office in Tennessee, Ford's next steps took him out of the elective politics realm. He became the leader of the centrist Democratic Leadership Council, went to work on Wall Street as a vice chairman of Merrill Lynch, and became a paid political analyst, first with Fox and then with NBC. But Ford's interest in seeking elective office remained, even as he slipped into a new life based largely in Manhattan. In April of 2009, he considered, but did not undertake, a campaign for governor of Tennessee, and promised supporters that there would be another campaign in his future.[80] By the end of 2009, it appeared that Ford's next campaign would be another run for the Senate, this time in New York rather than Tennessee. Ford's opportunity stemmed from a complicated series of political dominoes that fell in 2007 and 2008.

The first was the inauguration of Eliot Spitzer as governor of New York and David Paterson as lieutenant governor in 2007, which ended twelve years of Republican administration in Albany. The next was Spitzer's resignation in the wake of a prostitution scandal in March of 2008, which elevated Paterson to the governorship.[81] The third was President-elect Barack Obama's decision to appoint Hillary Clinton to serve as secretary of state; this required her to resign her Senate seat and Paterson to name a replacement.[82] (Ironically, at the start of Clinton's 2008 campaign, some had speculated that Spitzer would name Paterson to replace her should she be elected president.) The fourth was Paterson's hapless and unsuccessful effort to recruit Caroline Kennedy, the daughter of the late president, who had been active in the Obama presidential campaign, to the seat Clinton was vacating.[83] And the fifth was Paterson's ultimate decision, shortly after Kennedy withdrew her name from consideration, to appoint Representative Kirsten Gillibrand to the seat.[84]

Gillibrand's appointment made strategic and political sense. It was important to Paterson to replace Clinton—New York's first female senator—with
another woman. Gillibrand lacked Caroline Kennedy's star power but fit the
bill on the gender equity front. Paterson's motives were not entirely altruistic;
he planned to seek election to a term of his own in 2010, and his appointee
would be running that year to be elected to the final two years of Clinton's
term. Picking the right person to fill the vacancy, Paterson reasoned, could
help boost his own electoral prospects as well.[85] Since Paterson had not been
elected to the governorship and had less than a full term in which to build a
record and introduce himself to New York's voters, these factors mattered to
Paterson in a way they might not have to another governor. Gillibrand also
brought geographic benefits to the 2010 race. She had first been elected to
the House of Representatives in 2006 from New York's Twentieth Congressional District, when she defeated a four-term Republican incumbent in a
heated contest and had room to move left where she needed to in order to
win election to the remaining two years of Clinton's term in 2010.

But as an appointed incumbent who had never run for office outside
of her district, Gillibrand was unknown to most of New York's voters, and
the liberalization of her policy positions that her upstate roots made both
possible and necessary also opened her to charges of inauthenticity. As 2010
opened with Scott Brown's upset in Massachusetts and Republicans became
giddy about the prospects of massive gains in the midterm elections, Harold
Ford Jr. began to float his name as a potential challenger to Gillibrand for
the Democratic nomination. He was not the only Democrat in New York to
consider a challenge to the newly appointed incumbent, but the fact that he
became the last one standing illustrates both the persistent difficulties carpetbaggers face in a new state and how a lack of other, better options generally
characterizes carpetbaggers.

Gillibrand's record in the House of Representatives and the positions
she had held in order to win in her upstate district put her out of step with
many New York Democrats, and made her potentially vulnerable to a challenge
from her left in a low-turnout primary. Given New York's overwhelmingly
Democratic electorate by 2010, winning the primary would not necessarily
be a guarantee of victory in the general election, but it would put whoever
won it at a distinct advantage over a Republican opponent. It was not hard
to imagine a more liberal challenger raising money from the liberal netroots
activists who had, by 2010, become formidable in Democratic politics. That
same year, for instance, online activists had rallied around the candidacy of

Arkansas' lieutenant governor, Bill Halter, in a primary challenge to incumbent senator Blanche Lincoln, whom they saw as too moderate on too many issues.[86]

Harold Ford Jr., however, was poorly suited to make such a challenge. As a Tennessee Democrat with statewide ambitions, he had amassed the same sort of moderate positions and voting record Gillibrand had during her House tenure. In his 2006 race, he had opposed abortion, same-sex marriage, and a withdrawal from Iraq and supported George W. Bush's tax cuts.[87] Gillibrand, in 2006 and 2008, had identified herself as part of the Democratic "blue dog" caucus, whose members—almost all of whom represented swing or Republican-leaning districts—tacked toward the center right on many cultural and social issues and distanced themselves from more liberal leaders of the party like Nancy Pelosi. Gillibrand had received the endorsement of the National Rifle Association as a candidate, and a 100 percent score from that organization as a lawmaker.[88]

As a result, Gillibrand's appointment was not greeted warmly by everyone in her party. Several Democratic officeholders considered challenging her. Perhaps the most noteworthy of these was Carolyn McCarthy, the Nassau County congresswoman who entered politics after her husband was killed by a gunman on the Long Island Rail Road. McCarthy, in an appearance on *Hardball*, accused Gillibrand of "working for the NRA" in Congress[89] and told National Public Radio that Gillibrand would be a "poster child" for the group in the Senate.[90] Other elected Democrats who considered challenges included Representatives Steve Israel, Carolyn Maloney, and Jose Serrano, and Jon Cooper, the majority leader of the Suffolk County legislature.[91] But each of these potential challengers ultimately decided not to run.

Gillibrand, as aware as any of her potential challengers that she was vulnerable to a challenge from her left and that New York as a whole would not only tolerate but embrace a senator who was more liberal than she had been willing to be as a representative from an upstate district, fended these challengers off through her savvy maneuvering. In her first months in office, Gillibrand hustled to reposition herself for her statewide campaign in 2010. She embarked on a listening tour of her own that began in Harlem and gave her the chance to lay the groundwork for a newfound openness to gun control.[92] As a representative, Gillibrand had taken a conservative line on immigration; as a new senator, she became a supporter of the DREAM Act and met with Hispanic elected officials, interest groups, and leaders.[93] She also courted New York's gay activist community. Shortly after her appointment, she came out in favor of same-sex marriage rights, a shift from her previous position in favor of civil unions for gay couples.[94] She defended the president's $787 billion stimulus package and the Obama economic team.[95] By the summer of 2009, she had emerged as a leader in the fight to repeal the military's "Don't Ask, Don't Tell" policy regarding gay servicemembers, which put her to the left of the Obama administration, which was moving too cautiously, in the eyes of the gay activists who had supported Obama in 2008.[96] And she positioned herself in ways meant to assuage online activists. At the start of 2010, Gillibrand was one of the first senators to urge Senate Majority Leader Harry Reid to press forward on health care reform even after the Massachusetts special election that elected Scott Brown and ended the Democrats' brief filibuster-proof majority.[97] Despite these moves to the left, Gillibrand did not neglect her upstate roots. She received a seat on the Senate Agriculture Committee, where she could advocate for the interests of the state's farmers, and brought a "folksy and earnest" style to town meetings with farmers and other upstaters.[98]

Gillibrand also enjoyed considerable support from within her party's elite leadership. President Obama offered public praise for Paterson's selection of Gillibrand, and both he and his chief of staff, Rahm Emanuel, made clear that they would support Gillibrand over any of her would-be challengers.[99] New York's senior senator, Chuck Schumer, had a relationship with Gillibrand that dated back to her initial consideration of a campaign for Congress in 2005. Now that she was in the Senate, Schumer helped mentor her and introduce her to at-times skeptical Democratic constituencies, in no small part because he had concluded that avoiding a primary battle was key to keeping the seat out of Republican hands.[100]

In addition to her support from the White House and Schumer, Gillibrand rolled up one endorsement after another early in her term. Before she had been in office for a month, she received the endorsement of EMILY's List, and NARAL endorsed her in June.[101] State labor unions like CSEA and the Public Employees Federation also supported her.[102] She won the support of the Human Rights Campaign and Reverend Al Sharpton.[103] And she announced a steady stream of endorsements from Democrats representing New York in Congress and in the state assembly.[104]

Gillibrand's maneuvers and institutional backing deterred not only most Democratic challengers, but arguably her best-known potential Republican opponents. Representative Peter King opted not to run after winning a seat on the House Intelligence Committee, recruitment appeals from New York Republicans to former New York mayor Rudy Giuliani went unheard, and former Governor George Pataki did not run despite polls indicating that he would start a race with a slight advantage over Gillibrand.[105]

But the tactics that cleared other potential challengers from the field—appeals to the good of the Democratic Party, to favorable polling numbers, to avoiding the wrath of the Obama White House and Rahm Emanuel, to the wisdom of not giving up a safe House seat for an uncertain challenge to an incumbent—had little effect on Harold Ford. As is so often the case for carpetbaggers, he found himself contemplating a campaign as a carpetbagger in large part because he had no better options and little to lose. But he eventually concluded, like other potential challengers to Gillibrand, that there was no upside for him in becoming a candidate. Why did Ford's nascent carpetbagger campaign fall apart before it really started? Much of that comes down to geography and Ford's relationship to his new state.

Gillibrand, a native of the Albany area, had represented the upstate town of Hudson as a member of the House of Representatives and worked as a lawyer in Manhattan. She was thus well prepared as a result of her own lived experiences as a New Yorker to navigate the differences among the city, the suburbs, and upstate. Ford, on the other hand, had made his new home in New York in Manhattan. And he lived his new life in a very rarefied slice of Manhattan. One profile described his days this way:

> NBC sends a black car to whisk him to 30 Rock for *Morning Joe*. He breakfasts at the Regency, favorite haunt of senior bankers. His favorite 'hangout,' a close friend said, is the Waverly Inn, the exclusive, clubby restaurant run by Vanity Fair Editor and scene-maker Graydon Carter. After that, it's Grey Goose vodka at the 35th-floor bar at the Mandarin Oriental, one of the city's most expensive hotels.[106]

In an interview with the *New York Times*, Ford noted that he rarely rode the subway, except for those rare occasions in the winter when he was unable to hail a cab.[107] When asked if he preferred the Jets or the Giants, he chose the Giants, not because of a particular affinity for the team, its players, or its history, but because the team's owner was a friend.[108] Ford was not just a Tennesseean-turned-New Yorker, nor even merely a Tennesseean-turned-Manhattanite. He was a Tennesseean who had become a very particular species of wealthy, high-rolling Manhattanite and who lived a life utterly removed from those of almost all of his would-be constituents. Ford further came across as oblivious to the general necessity for wealthy candidates for high office to try to relate to their constituents. Some wealthy candidates promise to apply the skills that helped build their fortunes to help their state, some say that their wealth obliges them to try to help others through public service, some listen to country music and eat pork rinds. Ford, instead, ran as an unabashed advocate for Wall Street, displaying the same tin political ear that led him, as a candidate for statewide office in a socially conservative state, to attend a Super Bowl party thrown by *Playboy* magazine.[109] It is possible that Ford simply had a very poor idea of what being a New Yorker meant. But journalist Peter Beinart went further and suggested that Ford's ambitions were utterly disconnected from geography. Ford, Beinart argued, sought to represent not New York, but "the American overclass, a large chunk of which happens to reside in the Empire State."[110] New York was simply, in this view, a convenient platform from which to do this. In this regard, Ford was not particularly distinct from any other carpetbagger in need of a place from which to run. But he was, perhaps, the only carpetbagger in this volume whose personal ambitions encompassed representing a particular economic interest.

At the same time, Ford's residency in New York was less than clear-cut. He had voted in Tennessee in 2008 and only registered in New York late in 2009, and told one audience that he had been a New Yorker "off and on" for several years before becoming a full-time resident just in time to think about running for the Senate.[111] His gradual acclimation to his new state meant that he did not file his first New York state tax return until 2010, though the gossip site *Gawker* theorized that this indicated that before becoming a full-time New Yorker Ford had been careful to spend fewer than 184 days each year in New York in order to claim Tennessee, which has no income tax, as his primary state of residence and thus avoid paying New York taxes on all of his income.[112]

In addition to his questionable commitment to actually living in New York, Ford had to address the positions he had taken back when he was a Democrat with ambitions of winning statewide office in Tennessee. His opposition to same-sex marriage and abortion did him little harm in Tennessee. But in New York, they doubly weighed him down. First, they required him to distance himself from himself in order to have any hope of winning a primary challenge to Gillibrand. Second, they hampered his capacity to use Gillibrand's own blue dog record against her. While Gillibrand had moved left so sharply that Chuck Schumer warned her to take it easy,[113] Ford was a poor messenger for the clearest line of attack on Gillibrand—that her newly liberal positions were expediently adopted and would last no longer than midnight on election night. Thus, Ford found himself repeatedly tripping over his past positions on social issues, for instance, trying to portray himself as "personally pro-choice and legislatively pro-choice" despite his past record as an opponent of legal abortion.[114] Exacerbating matters was Ford's lack of an office or other platform of his own; while Gillibrand was positioning herself as an advocate for gay rights and the Obama stimulus, Ford could point to no concrete actions that demonstrated the evolution of his own viewpoints. He instead attacked Gillibrand on economic issues. This was a potentially potent tactic in the aftermath of the 2008 economic crisis. But Ford's proposed remedies—including corporate tax cuts, taxpayer bailouts of the financial industry he was part of, and opposition to Obama's health care reform efforts—were not ones that would set off an uprising to Gillibrand's left.[115]

Ford also attacked Gillibrand as lacking independence, and instead doing the bidding of Democratic leaders in the Senate. He tried to cast his opposition to, and Gillibrand's support for, health care reform as an example of Gillibrand putting party loyalty ahead of the interests of New York and New Yorkers. Much like his attack on Gillibrand on economic issues, this was a potentially effective message from the wrong messenger; as a carpetbagger, Ford was particularly vulnerable to criticisms that he simply did not understand New York. As Ford's not-quite-campaign continued, Gillibrand did not hesitate to play the carpetbagger card by suggesting that Ford's positions were "right for Tennessee" but not for his new state.[116] And while Hillary Clinton had spent months touring upstate New York early in her candidacy, by January of 2010 Ford had just started to venture out beyond New York City. Even then, his only visit to Staten Island had been as part of a helicopter tour of the city with other financial executives.[117] Ironically, one of the key concerns of Staten Island residents—those without helicopter access, at least—was increasing transit options to and from the island.[118]

Ford also lacked a base of support within the leadership of the New York Democratic Party. While Gillibrand was working hard to build bridges to important party leaders and Democratic constituencies, Ford instead relied on a motley assortment of figures with little standing among the voters who would be voting in a Democratic primary. Peter Beinart, in his jeremiad against Ford, argued that Ford's candidacy was brought about by "rich donors who went searching" for a challenger to Gillibrand.[119] Ford also appeared to have some support from New York City mayor Michael Bloomberg, and several of Bloomberg's top aides signed on with Ford.[120] But Bloomberg had begun his tenure as a nominal Republican and had become an independent in 2007.[121] While many of the Democrats in New York had voted for Bloomberg for mayor—the city's overwhelmingly Democratic electorate made it impossible for anyone, of any party, to be elected mayor without some Democratic votes—that did not necessarily mean those voters would follow Bloomberg's lead in a primary contest, particularly when any Bloomberg support was tacit, rather than overt.

If party leaders were cool to Ford's campaign, were there elements of the party rank and file who might welcome his candidacy? Ford and those close to him thought that his race could provide him with a base of support; one postmortem of his noncampaign claimed that "Ford's advisers thought he had a chance to win 80 percent of the black vote."[122] But running against so much of what Barack Obama was doing in 2009 and 2010 did little to endear Ford to New York's African American voters. And even among his hoped-for base of support, Ford was playing catchup; Gillibrand had started reaching out to African American leaders within days of taking office. Worse yet for Ford, Gillibrand had won the active support of women and gay activists and taken active steps in office to prove herself to them and distance herself from her more centrist past positions. Ford could say he'd changed his mind on gay marriage, abortion, and similar issues, but he lacked Gillibrand's ability to support his changes of heart with concrete, visible votes and actions.

After two months of intense press coverage and speculation, Ford ultimately opted not to run. In the *New York Times*, Ford wrote that he feared that his campaign would lead to a "brutal and highly negative Democratic primary . . . where the winner emerges weakened and the Republican strengthened."[123] More important than either candidate's ambitions, or what he saw as arm twisting and bullying by party leaders, he argued, was keeping Gillibrand's seat in Democratic hands. In ending his campaign, Ford cast himself as an independent public servant acting for the good of his party and, by extension, the good of New York. Afterward, one commentator remarked that it took ending his campaign for Ford to start sounding like a senator.[124]

Elizabeth Cheney: Wyoming, 2014

The final case this chapter considers is that of Elizabeth Cheney, who moved to Wyoming in 2012 in order to run for the Senate in 2014. Her family name and credentials would ordinarily have made her a strong candidate, and in other circumstances her return to Wyoming might have been viewed as more of a homecoming than an act of carpetbagging. But her decision to challenge incumbent Republican Mike Enzi proved to be a fatal miscalculation—a high-risk, high-reward gambit that failed spectacularly, in large part because Cheney's campaign ran counter to established norms of politics in Wyoming.

Like Bobby Kennedy, Hillary Clinton, and Harold Ford, Cheney came from a political family. The daughter of Vice President Dick Cheney, she had served in the State Department during the George W. Bush administration, and she subsequently organized a group called Keep America Safe to promote the neoconservative foreign policy views that had characterized the Bush administration's approach to international relations.[125] Following President Obama's re-election in 2012, Cheney and her family moved back to Wyoming, the state her father had represented in the House of Representatives between his service in the Ford and first Bush administrations, and began appearing at political and community events throughout the state, both alone and with her parents, and sharing photos from her travels on social media.[126] It soon became clear that Cheney's sights were set on 2014 and the Senate seat held by three-term Republican incumbent Mike Enzi, who had given no indications that he was considering retiring. Cheney's willingness to challenge an incumbent of her own party was not that surprising; 2010 and 2012 had seen high-profile primary challenges to multiple incumbent Senate Republicans, and several of these had succeeded. But Cheney chose poorly in her bid for elective office and was further doomed by running against the grain of a state political culture that prioritized personal ties and goodwill.

Mike Enzi and Wyoming Politics

There are United States Senators who seek and thrive in the spotlight, and then there are senators like Mike Enzi who avoid national publicity and focus on building and maintaining relationships in their home state while they work quietly in Washington. By 2014, Enzi had served three terms and was known for his "studious and low-key" style.[127] A former small-town mayor who had made the jump to federal office in 1996, Enzi had given Wyoming Republicans little reason to replace him with Cheney. While other Republicans who had lost primary challenges since 2010 had committed policy apostasies that alienated primary voters, cast too many votes favorable to Barack Obama, or been too moderate for their party's conservative base, Enzi was as close to a down-the-line conservative as one could find in the Senate.

Nor had Enzi neglected his home ties during the years he had served in Washington. As Cheney moved toward a candidacy, Enzi was not too humble to remind voters of his years of humble service to their state. His focus, he said, was not on the campaign but on doing "the job I was already elected to do" and "working behind the scenes."[128] He pointed to his duties in Washington and his full schedule of visits home for listening sessions and other meetings with constituents. He noted that fund-raising was at times "a problem" for him but that his priority would be representation: "My job is to be the U.S. Senator that I was elected to be . . . I do it pretty much full time, I'm in Wyoming every weekend, here during the time that we're voting out here." His plan, in response to Cheney's maneuvers, was to eschew campaigning in favor of continuing to do his job, "getting the opinions of the Wyoming people and traveling Wyoming and doing my job out here."[129] Enzi contrasted his experience representing the state to what he argued was Cheney's unfamiliarity with it: "She's never been to any of my listening sessions . . . I've done listening sessions in Wyoming where I actually listen to what the constituents have to say. I'm an old shoe salesman. I listen to the customer. I know who the customer is."[130]

Enzi's professed avoidance of campaigning was, of course, itself a form of campaigning; whenever he was asked about Cheney, Enzi emphasized the work he was doing on the behalf of Wyoming and his frequent travels to the state to hear from constituents. This was a sensible approach for a veteran legislator from a safe seat. In thoroughly Republican Wyoming, Enzi's only real electoral danger could ever come from a primary challenge. Making constituent relationships and interactions a central focus of his behavior in office was not just good representation, it was good politics, with the further benefit of not looking at all political, since it was simply part of the job. It just happened to be a part of the job with the power to help scare off potential challengers. Even as the campaign progressed and Cheney's criticisms became more aggressive, Enzi maintained his workhorse posture.

Also aiding Enzi was the political culture of Wyoming. Wyoming had not elected a Democrat to the Senate since Gale McGee was re-elected in 1972. Wyoming also has a long history of re-electing its members of Congress.[131] Enzi, as a conservative Republican, held views and cast votes in line with the views of his constituents. Cheney's challenge was out of sync with a state political culture in which incumbents tended to serve until they no longer want to serve. Previous candidates who tried to capitalize on a name shared with a past officeholder had met with little success in Wyoming.[132] But the most important cultural asset favoring Enzi was summed up in his comment on his relationship with Liz Cheney: "I thought we were friends."[133] This was not the plaintive cry of someone who feels wronged; this was Enzi reminding voters of the personal nature of politics in Wyoming.

As a largely rural state with no major metropolitan area and a population smaller than that of the District of Columbia dispersed across nearly ninety-eight thousand square miles, Wyoming's politics is lubricated, if not

entirely run, by interpersonal relationships. The reactions to Cheney from
influential actors in the state Republican Party make this clear. Alan Simpson, Enzi's predecessor in office, denounced a Cheney run not just because it
could hurt the state party, but because it created "a divisive, ugly situation."[134]
Later in the campaign, after a disagreement between Cheney and her sister
Mary over the issue of same-sex marriage went public and Mary announced
that she would not vote for her sister, Simpson complained that the Cheney
campaign was "destroying family relationships."[135] One Wyoming voter, after
describing her reservations about Cheney's campaign, then asked a reporter
not to use her name lest she "offend the Cheneys."[136]

Wyoming Republicans quickly lined up behind Enzi. The state's junior
senator, John Barrasso, described Enzi as a "tremendous senator," while its lone
House member, Cynthia Lummis, also endorsed Enzi, and further announced
that if Enzi chose not to run for another term, then she would become a
candidate for his seat.[137] Enzi also received support beyond Wyoming, from
fellow Republican senators, the National Republican Senatorial Committee, and
establishment figures like former White House press secretary Ari Fleischer.[138]
All of these supporters noted that they liked and respected Liz Cheney or
Dick Cheney or both Cheneys, but they argued that Enzi was doing a good
job, there was no need to replace him, and a bruising primary in Wyoming
endangered Republican efforts to win a majority in the Senate.

Enzi also used his position as the incumbent to frame both the primary
and Wyoming politics in ways that disadvantaged Cheney. When Cheney
announced her challenge in August of 2013, Enzi told reporters, "Nobody in
Wyoming likes a long campaign—anybody from Wyoming would know that,"
and he added that "you can't even file in Wyoming until May."[139] Representative Lummis struck a similar note, warning Cheney that she could "outraise
[Enzi] by factors of 10 or more and he will still win, because Wyoming is
grass-roots campaigning."[140] The message of Enzi and his supporters was
that the very fact of Cheney's campaign and the way she was conducting it
branded her as an outsider who did not understand the ways of Wyoming.

Carpetbagging in the Cowboy State

The logic behind Cheney's challenge was straightforward: Come back to Wyoming with outsized fundraising prowess and the Cheney name, scare Enzi
into retiring, and win first the primary and then the general election. If Enzi
declined to retire, Cheney would have to defeat him in the primary. Either
way, she would have to reestablish herself as a Wyomingite, not a transplanted

Virginian. This was a taller order than Cheney may have realized. Cheney had only lived in Wyoming full time for two years while she was growing up.[141] She had been born in Wisconsin, and went to high school in Virginia, college in Colorado, and law school in Illinois.[142] But she presented herself to voters as a local girl returned home. She described herself as a fourth-generation Wyomingite whose ancestors had helped establish Wyoming and her children as fifth-generation Wyomingites.[143] She emphasized national issues in her early campaign and argued that Enzi was insufficiently conservative, while she would apply "the cowboy code of the West" to know where to draw the line on compromises with Democrats and told voters her fourth-generation status meant she knew how to defend "Wyoming values and our freedom."[144] Her fundraising appeals warned that groups "from out of state" would be trying to "distract, mislead, and scare Wyoming voters."[145] But Cheney's careful self-presentation was undone by blunders that put her on the wrong side of the state's culture and traditions.

Perhaps the most significant of these was the revelation that Cheney had applied for and received the wrong kind of fishing license after her move back to Wyoming. Wyoming fishing licenses are less expensive for residents than they are for nonresidents, and residency requires 365 consecutive days living in the state. Cheney had not only received a resident license just 72 days after moving back to Wyoming, but her application listed her as a ten-year resident of the state.[146] Cheney argued that the clerk who had filled out her Game & Fish application must have made a mistake, but local Republicans told NBC News that the fishing store "would have spotted such an error."[147]

Worse than the specifics of the fishing license controversy was its larger symbolism. Fishing plays a central and complex role in Wyoming, just as it does in several other Mountain West states. One-third of citizens identify themselves as fishers, fishing plays a large role in the state's economy, and state and federal resource management of the state in large part focuses on protecting fishing; for many in Wyoming, fishing is an "invented tradition" linked to "notions of an authentic Western identity."[148] There is no small amount of tension at work here, however. On the one hand, fishing is part of the state's identity and attracts tourists and their disposable income to the state. But those tourists may not appreciate the state and its fishing traditions as Wyoming's residents do, and too many tourists and too much tourist fishing could damage the state's fisheries and fish populations. Many locals fear that, if left to their own devices, tourists would treat the state as a playground to exploit for their own benefit and gain, rather than a resource to be both enjoyed and managed thoughtfully. This tension can foster an insiders-versus-outsiders mindset among local residents.[149] One Wyoming fishing guide, attempting to navigate this dynamic, notes that it omits some fishing areas out of deference to local residents seeking to protect vulnerable fisheries from tourists.[150] By receiving a resident fishing license ahead of schedule, whether intentionally or accidentally, Cheney had, as one local newspaper column noted, "paid a fine for making the claim of residency before she was entitled to do so."[151] The column did not explicitly draw the parallel between the fishing license and Cheney's candidacy, but it was obvious to anyone reading it. In the eyes of the state Fish and Game Commission, Cheney, not yet a full resident of the state, had tried to pass herself off as one.

Cheney's response to the fishing license story drew her into conflict with another long-standing institution, the local newspapers of Wyoming. After she paid a $220 fine to resolve the matter,[152] Cheney attacked the *Jackson Hole News & Guide* and its editor for covering the story. She told an audience at a campaign event, "Newspapers are dying, and that's not a bad thing," and she suggested that her campaign supporters should go around established media to spread her message by word of mouth.[153] Wyoming's newspapers (like Mike Enzi, in Cheney's telling) needed to either step aside or be crushed by the future and its avatars. But local newspapers are an important part of day-to-day life in Wyoming. Just a few years before Cheney's campaign, a survey had found that 90 percent of adults in Wyoming read a newspaper each week and that newspapers were the chief means by which voters acquired information about politics.[154] In Wyoming's small cities and towns, as is the case in many other rural areas of the United States, local newspapers remain a vital, connective thread between neighbors and their communities.[155] In attacking her local paper, Cheney was demonstrating her lack of shared experience with the people of Wyoming.

While the fishing license controversy unspooled, it also turned out that Cheney's husband was registered to vote in both Virginia and Wyoming.[156] For anyone not married to a candidate for public office, this would be the sort of minor oversight that many people commit when they move from one state to another. But for the husband of someone facing accusations of being a carpetbagger, her husband's registration confusion was more fuel for the fire.

Enzi's long history in Wyoming and Cheney's lack of a compelling rationale for her primary challenge meant that she started the campaign at a disadvantage. Two July surveys found her badly trailing Enzi.[157] Half of the respondents in a Public Policy Polling survey did not think she was a Wyomingite and that she should have run in Virginia instead of Wyoming.[158] The same survey showed Cheney trailing Representative Cynthia Lummis in a hypothetical primary and Dave Freudenthal, a Democratic former governor, in a general election matchup. The fishing license fiasco and her attack on newspapers did nothing to improve primary voters' perceptions of her. Nor did the increasingly public dispute between Cheney and her sister Mary over the issue of same-sex marriage, which led to Mary Cheney telling her sister that her opposition to same-sex marriage put her "on the wrong side of history."[159] This family fight reinforced the concerns of Alan Simpson and others who complained that Cheney's run was divisive and harmful in a way that had no place in Wyoming politics.

On January 6, 2014, Cheney abruptly ended her campaign because of unspecified "serious health issues" in her family.[160] The same Wyoming GOP officials who had undercut her fishing license defense now applauded her decision and dubbed her "a rising star in Wyoming and national politics"[161] with a place waiting for her should she ever decide to return to the electoral arena—presumably, one suspects, as long as that did not involve a challenge to another incumbent Republican. Following Cheney's withdrawal, Senator Enzi was greeted by his fellow Republicans with high fives on the floor of the Senate.[162] But Cheney clearly had taken the words of encouragement from Wyoming Republicans to heart. Late in 2015, Cynthia Lummis announced she would not seek a fifth term representing Wyoming in the House of Representatives.[163] Cheney became one of nine candidates who sought the Republican nomination to succeed Lummis.[164] While the question of the strength of her ties to the state was an issue in the primary, just as it had been in 2014, the divided field and her fundraising prowess allowed her to win the primary with 40 percent of the vote.[165] She easily won the general election in her ruby red state and was sworn in on January 3, 2017.[166]

Discussion

All four of these candidates came to their races with the sorts of records and backgrounds that tend to make for credible candidacies. Former governors, members of Congress, presidential candidates, and national security officials who decide to run for office are normally taken seriously by their opponents, potential supporters, news outlets, and state political parties. Despite their credentials, neither Peabody, Keyes, Ford, nor Cheney was able to win election. Peabody and Keyes found themselves in the by-now-familiar situation of being given a party's nomination because that party had no better options and nothing to lose (though some Illinois Republicans might care to argue the latter case). And once the New Hampshire Democrats and Illinois Republicans had found a candidate to appear on the ballot, they treated those races—in terms of time, personnel, and other resources—like the impossible causes they were. They kept their distance and tried to limit the damage their losses would do to the rest of the party's candidates for other offices.

At least Peabody and Keyes were nominated by their parties. The cases of Ford and Cheney show that when state and national party leaders line up behind an incumbent (even an appointed one), it is virtually impossible for a carpetbagger to gain enough traction to become competitive. It may be tempting to look at these as cases no different than any other failed primary insurgency. But each offers important insights into the role the politics of place plays in American electoral politics. Ford's case demonstrates the limits of insider and media appeal. While Gillibrand's status as an appointee who had never won statewide made her a tempting target on paper, Ford eventually succumbed to the same logic that led Gillibrand's other potential challengers to decide against running. Her status as an appointed senator gave her a better platform and more opportunities to build support and engage in meaningful representational activity than Ford had as a carpetbagger. As for Cheney, once she failed to scare Enzi into retirement, her campaign was doomed. But a candidate with deeper ties to Wyoming might have realized just how difficult it would be to dislodge an unwilling Enzi and found a different avenue for her office-holding ambitions or not run in 2014 in the first place. But the fact that Cheney was able to rebound and win election to the House in 2016 has implications for carpetbagging and individual political careers and ambitions that will be discussed in the concluding chapter of this book.

The next chapter considers the most famous recent case of carpetbagging—former senator Scott Brown's 2014 attempt to win election in New Hampshire, just two years after his loss to Elizabeth Warren in Massachusetts. Like every other carpetbagger, he ran in part because both he and his new state's party lacked a better alternative. While he lost, however, his campaign enjoyed an unusual level of support from the national arms of the Republican Party. Closer examination will help determine whether Brown's campaign represents a new type of carpetbagger campaigning.

Chapter 7

Scott Brown

New Hampshire, 2014

Much of the story of Scott Brown's campaign will be familiar as it unfolds: the ambitious figure in want of a platform, the state party in need of a candidate, the charges of carpetbagging, and the carpetbagger's inability to put the issue to rest. But Brown's campaign is also distinct from those of the unsuccessful carpetbagger candidacies examined thus far. While Brown had served in another state before running in New Hampshire, he came closer to winning than any other unsuccessful carpetbagger examined in this book. Scott Brown's 2014 race raises the question of whether it represents a new type of carpetbagger campaign, and if so, what implications that development has for American politics.

Scott Brown in the Wilderness

Scott Brown's career is a classic example of progressive ambition. As a real estate lawyer in Wrentham, he worked his way up from local offices such as property assessor and town selectman to the Massachusetts state legislature.[1] He was elected to the lower house in 1998 and the state senate in 2004.[2] The state legislature's overwhelmingly Democratic composition meant that Republicans like Brown were a tiny minority with little actual power. But Brown did not plan to spend his career in the state legislature, and he made no secret of his interest in higher office. However, as a Republican in Democratic Massachusetts, there was a blue ceiling on his ambitions. Over time, the state had become less and less hospitable to Republicans: it had not elected a Republican to the United States Senate since Edward Brooke's re-election in 1972, and its House delegation became entirely Democratic while Brown was a state legislator. While the state had a tendency to elect moderate Republican governors like William Weld and Mitt Romney, it would be difficult for a little-known legislator like Brown to become competitive in a gubernatorial primary.[3]

However, Ted Kennedy's death in August of 2009 and the special election that followed in January presented Brown with an irresistible opportunity—a special election, when turnout was sure to be low, during the depths of an economic crisis under a Democratic administration. While better-known figures passed on the race, which they thought was unwinnable, Brown saw nothing to lose. The special election was the best chance he might ever have to move up from the state legislature, and even a losing campaign would make him better known beyond his state senate district and help him lay the groundwork for future runs for statewide office. Brown won, and much of the coverage of his victory focused on the style of his campaign: his everyman persona, his skill at retail politicking, his work shirts and jeans ensemble, and perhaps most of all, his red GMC pickup truck with over 200,000 miles on the odometer.[4] In 2012, however, when the economy was on the mend and turnout was higher, Brown lost his bid for a full term to Elizabeth Warren. Despite the loss and the often-negative tone of that campaign, he emerged from the race with many Massachusetts voters still thinking well of him. Six months after his loss, Brown's favorability rating in Massachusetts was 53 percent, and just 35 percent of those surveyed reported that they held an unfavorable view of Brown.[5] This was not that different from 2012 polling in which 57 percent of respondents—and 42 percent of Democrats—found Brown more likeable than Warren.[6] Brown's continued popularity led many to wonder what his next step would be. When President Barack Obama chose Senator John Kerry of Massachusetts to replace Hillary Clinton as secretary of state, many thought that Brown might run in the special election to fill the remainder of Kerry's term.[7] Early polling suggested that Brown would start such a race in a competitive position, or even with a lead.[8] By January of 2013 Brown appeared ready to run.[9] But in early February, Brown announced that he would not become a candidate.[10] One reason he offered was the grueling pace of campaigning: "I did a state senate run, then a special election and then a general election, and this special and general election would mean 5 elections in 5 years . . . It is too much right now after an intense election cycle."[11] There was also no guarantee that his lead over likely Democratic candidates would stick; one survey, conducted not long before Brown demurred on running, found that Brown had slipped to a statistical dead heat with Representative Ed Markey, who ultimately won the special election.[12] This poll suggested that Massachusetts' Democratic political gravity was too strong for Brown to get elected to the Senate a second time. A loss in the special election could turn him from a dragon slayer into an also ran and be fatal for his long-term political viability.

With his decision not to run in the special election, Brown was now in the political wilderness. He did the sorts of things former senators do: he took a job with Nixon Peabody, a law and lobbying firm, and signed on as a Fox News contributor.[13] But he did little to dissuade speculation about his political future. Might Brown run for governor of Massachusetts in 2014? A survey of Massachusetts voters conducted in May of 2013 found him with sizable leads over an array of potential Democratic opponents.[14] But, in August, Brown announced that he would not run for governor, in part because he was finding his new jobs "fulfilling and exhilarating."[15] One Republican strategist suggested that the state party's leaders saw Brown "more as a legislator than an executive," and others thought he may have been maintaining his visibility for a 2014 run for the Senate seat Ed Markey had won, or just enjoying the limelight without the pressures of an actual campaign.[16] The decision not to run also avoided a confrontation with Charlie Baker, the party's 2010 guber-natorial nominee, who was widely expected to, and did, run again in 2014.[17]

If Brown was not going to run for governor or in the special election, what was he going to do? He made several trips to Iowa, and hinted at possibly running for president in 2016; while many found this a dubious proposition, others noted that a campaign would put him back in the mix of the national political conversation and possibly on track to vice-presidential short lists or an executive branch appointment.[18] (With the benefit of hindsight, of course, we now know that Brown would have been far from the least experienced or most ludicrous candidate in the 2016 Republican field.) But Brown was even more noncommittal than the average potential presidential candidate and suggested that his trips to Iowa had no purpose besides visiting his in-laws.

Those who may or may not be running for president tend to visit New Hampshire, of course, as well as Iowa, and Brown began to appear in the Granite State at Republican fund-raisers and other party events. At these events, Brown started to drop hints about running in New Hampshire against the state's incumbent Democratic senator Jeanne Shaheen in 2014, when she would be up for election to a second term. As he told one reporter, "Noth-ing's off the table, but nothing's on the table, either."[19] Brown's own behavior suggested varying levels of interest at different times. Sometimes he engaged in traditional forms of not-quite-campaigning, as when he endorsed Republican mayoral candidates in several towns; at others, such as when he played guitar on stage with Cheap Trick while wearing an American flag shirt, he mainly seemed to be enjoying the spotlight.[20]

This "maybe, maybe not" approach did not impress many of the movers and shakers of the New Hampshire Republican Party. Tom Rath—the former state attorney general whom Endicott Peabody had once interrogated in the early 1980s—noted that for all the chatter about a Brown campaign, he didn't "know anyone who does campaigns in New Hampshire who has talked with him."[21] And campaign veteran Michael Dennehy said, "His comments make for fun talk around the water cooler but it is not realistic and not particularly respectful of the people of New Hampshire."[22] Another noted that Brown's carpetbagger status would be a tremendous drag on a candidacy.[23] But while Brown's haphazard potential candidacy was off-putting to many party actors, Jim Merrill, another veteran of many Republican campaigns, noted that for all of Brown's baggage, "there is a pent-up enthusiasm in favor of a strong challenge to Senator Shaheen."[24]

In other words, the elements of a by-now-familiar story were beginning to come together: Brown was an ambitious politician without a platform and no truly viable options in his home state of Massachusetts. Meanwhile, New Hampshire's Republican leaders were in sufficient need of a strong candidate in 2014 that they were willing to think about starting to talk themselves into getting behind a carpetbagger. To understand how they found themselves in that position, it is necessary to examine the career of Jeanne Shaheen and how the rise of the Democratic Party in New Hampshire left that state's Republicans with few viable, local options to run against her in 2014.

A Party without Options

In the aftermath of the 2012 election, Republicans across the country looked ahead to 2014. With many first-term Democratic senators seeking re-election in the second midterm election of President Obama's tenure, history suggested that Republicans were likely to do very well. In New Hampshire, however, one potential candidate after another declined to challenge Shaheen. Among those bowing out of a race were Jeb Bradley (state senate majority leader and former congressman) Charlie Bass (former representative), John Sununu (former senator), and Chris Sununu (executive councilor).[25] By September of 2013, only Jim Rubens, a former state senator, had officially entered the race.[26] But Rubens's candidacy was problematic. He favored abortion rights, same-sex marriage, and a carbon tax, putting him at odds with many Republicans, even in libertarian-minded New Hampshire, and he had not served in elected office since the late 1990s. He was soon joined by Karen Testerman, a conservative activist who had fared poorly in a 2010 run for governor.[27] Like Rubens, Testerman inspired little hope or excitement among Republicans who wanted to beat Senator Shaheen in 2014.

The lack of a viable, mainstream challenger provoked frustration among national and state Republicans. It also spoke to Shaheen's standing as a fixture of Granite State politics. Shaheen, who was born in Missouri, was a high school teacher in Mississippi when she married Bill Shaheen, a native of Dover attending law school at the University of Mississippi, and the Shaheens moved to New Hampshire after Bill finished law school.[28] The Shaheens' entry into politics came when they worked on Jimmy Carter's 1976 primary campaign, where they made such a mark that Jeanne would manage President Carter's campaign against Ted Kennedy's challenge in 1980 and the campaign that led to Gary Hart's surprise victory in the 1984 primary. In 1996, after three terms in the state senate, she was elected to the first of three, two-year terms as governor. She was the state's first elected woman governor.[29] She was also the first Democratic governor elected since 1980 and only the fourth Democrat elected governor in the twentieth century.[30]

Two factors help explain Shaheen's electoral successes in the 1990s. The first was the demographic shift taking place in the state, as an "in-migration of high-tech workers and professionals" from neighboring Massachusetts and other states proved more willing to vote Democratic than natives of the state had for many years.[31] The second was Shaheen's presentation of herself as a pragmatic, nonideological problem solver.[32] She was willing to take a pledge against any broad-based state tax that some past Democrats had eschewed and emphasized that she wanted to effect change without disrupting the state's "traditional values."[33] The image she crafted for herself helped her appeal to New Hampshire voters who would likely have rejected a Democrat running on a more liberal platform.

Shaheen's approach worked so well that both of the state's subsequent Democratic governors, John Lynch and Maggie Hassan, adapted it in their own campaigns, and it earned Shaheen a spot on Al Gore's short list of potential running mates in 2000.[34] Shaheen's success also led her, as the 2002 election neared, to launch a campaign for the US Senate seat then held by Republican Bob Smith. Smith was vulnerable. He had barely won re-election to a second term in 1996 and alienated many Republicans 1999 when he left the party, pursued a quixotic bid to become the candidate of the Taxpayers' Party, and then returned to the GOP in order to secure a committee chairmanship made available by the death of Rhode Island's John Chafee.[35] Smith's erratic behavior, Shaheen's standing in the state, and the fact that 2002 would be a midterm election during a Republican presidency would have made Shaheen a strong challenger to Smith.

However, the same logic that led Shaheen to run led many Republicans, including the George W. Bush White House, to support a primary challenge against Smith from Representative John H. Sununu. Sununu defeated Smith in the primary and Shaheen in the general election.[36] In 2008, Shaheen defeated Sununu in a rematch in part by tying him to the historically unpopular Bush administration.[37] As a senator, Shaheen generally supported the legislative agenda of Barack Obama, particularly during the president's first two years in office when Democrats had a large majority in the Senate. But she also attended to day-to-day priorities like federal transportation funding to widen Interstate 93, securing (with Republican Congressman Charlie Bass, in a mutually beneficial display of conspicuous bipartisanship) money to open the federal prison in Berlin, and protecting the Portsmouth Naval Yard from sequestration budget cuts (this time in tandem with another moderate Republican, Senator Susan Collins of Maine).[38] Shaheen's experience as governor and her loss in 2002 made her particularly aware of the need to both deliver for her swing state's voters and avoid perceptions that she was an ideologue or partisan.

Shaheen looked like a stronger favorite for re-election than many of the other freshman senators elected in 2008, and the perceptions of her strength increased as one potential opponent after another declined to run. Absent a strong challenger, Shaheen would win re-election easily; with such a challenger and a favorable political environment, however, there was at least a chance of defeating Shaheen. Her 2002 loss proved she was not invincible, and Republicans hoped 2014 would be at least as favorable an election year for them as 2002 had been. A strong challenger would also make it certain that Democrats would be forced to devote time, money, and resources to the race, rather than direct them toward first-term incumbents facing strong challengers in other states.

But the strongest potential candidates were uninterested in running. Contributing to this was the revival of the Democratic Party in New Hampshire in the preceding decades, thanks to the same demographic changes that gave Shaheen an opening in her campaigns for governor. In 1992, Bill Clinton became the first Democrat to carry the state in a presidential election since Lyndon Johnson; New Hampshire then supported Democrats in every subsequent presidential race but 2000, when it narrowly went for George W. Bush. In 2006, Democrats won both of the state's congressional seats and control of the state legislature; while Republicans came back in 2010, they again lost both House seats and the lower house of the state legislature in 2012. But for the single term of Republican Craig Benson, Democrats held the governorship from 1996 through the start of the 2014 election season. New Hampshire had quickly gone from a rock-ribbed Republican state to a genuinely competitive swing state,[39] with partisan advantage shifting so frequently from one party to the other that one longtime local analyst suggested that "observers could be forgiven for thinking that the sole swing state in New England had a malfunctioning pendulum."[40] The timing of Democrats' recent successes—holding the governorship and reclaiming both of the state's House seats in 2012—left the New Hampshire GOP with a dearth of successful potential candidates who might plausibly be looking to move up the political ladder. This led to the frustration Jim Merrill described: Shaheen, many Republican Party actors felt, was beatable; many of them had helped beat her in 2002. But there did not seem to be anyone in the state both capable of defeating her and willing to run against her. A Scott Brown candidacy held the potential to give the state's Republicans a path out of their conundrum. It would be good for the state's Republicans, who would see a Brown candidacy as a shot at defeating Shaheen, and for the national party, which would see Democrats put resources into New Hampshire that otherwise could have gone to more endangered Democrats.

But was Brown serious about a race? Throughout much of 2013, his haphazard barnstorming and unwillingness to declare a definitive interest in running led many Republican activists to dismiss Brown,[41] and an editorial in the conservative *Union Leader* in October of 2013 begged Brown to make up his mind, in part because the only real beneficiary of his flirtations with a run to that point had been the Shaheen campaign, which sent out a fundraising appeal every time Brown appeared in the state.[42]

Around the same time the *Union Leader* was chastising Brown, the political environment began to change in ways that nudged Brown closer to a candidacy and the state's Republicans closer to Brown. One event that changed the lay of the political landscape was the disastrous rollout of the Affordable Care Act. The botched launch of the health care exchanges appeared to live down to every Republican stereotype about both Obamacare and government. While the Obama administration eventually lurched the exchanges back into functionality, weeks of bad publicity hurt the president's approval ratings and made Republicans raise their already sky-high expectations for 2014. In New Hampshire, only one insurer took part in the state's health care exchange, and coverage purchased on the state's exchange did not extend to ten of the state's twenty-six hospitals.[43] For Brown, running in New Hampshire suddenly became a much more attractive prospect, and he took advantage of the opportunity with an email to the *Union Leader* in which he argued that Shaheen had not been honest with New Hampshire's voters in supporting Obamacare.[44] By mid-December, many of the same Republican leaders who had been rolling their eyes at Brown earlier in the year were speaking favorably of his potential candidacy, and Brown took the major step of moving full-time into his family's vacation home in Rye and transferring his official residency to New Hampshire.[45] On Twitter, he changed his handle from "ScottBrownMA" to the geographically nonspecific "ScottBrown."[46]

Another development further spurred Republicans' newfound willingness to embrace Brown. Bob Smith, the former senator ousted in the 2002 Republican primary, returned to New Hampshire and declared his candidacy for the Republican nomination. Smith had spent the years since his primary defeat as something of a political gadfly. He endorsed John Kerry for president in 2004,[47] and he flirted with the idea of running for the Senate in Florida, first in 2004 and again in 2010. [48] Much as New Hampshire's Democrats had been mortified in 1986 by the prospect of their nomination going to a LaRouchite, New Hampshire's Republicans panicked at the idea that Bob Smith could be their party's nominee in 2014.[49] In addition to the bad feelings and acrimony lingering from 2002, a Smith candidacy had the potential to turn a loss for the Senate seat—already a bad outcome—into a catastrophic defeat that would take down Republican candidates for other offices, too. Brown was no one's idea of a shoo-in to defeat Shaheen, but he was less likely than Smith to take the whole party down with him if he lost.

As 2014 neared, Brown demonstrated a new seriousness about becoming a candidate. He headlined the state party's holiday party and began to reach out to elected officials, making calls to Senator Kelly Ayotte, the state's last two Republican governors, Craig Benson and Steve Merrill, and party leaders in the state legislature and executive council.[50] Previously wary party figures started to offer their support; Charlie Bass, the former congressman, said Brown was the party's strongest opponent against Shaheen, and party chairwoman Jennifer Horn argued that Brown had the right message for New Hampshire.[51] The *Union Leader*, once critical of Brown's nascent candidacy, described him in a front page story about a polar bear swim to benefit the Special Olympics as "a longtime summer resident of Rye."[52] In March,

Brown began hiring staff and finally made his candidacy official at an event in Portsmouth on April 8, 2014, a year after he first suggested he might run in New Hampshire.[53]

The good news for Brown, compared to previous carpetbaggers, was that he had secured the support of his new state's elite party actors and that national Republicans were willing to commit resources to his campaign. In that respect, at least, his candidacy would not parallel that of his fellow Bay-Stater-turned-Grantie-Stater, Endicott Peabody. The bad news was that there was a long time between the day he made his candidacy official in April and the Republican primary in September and that he would face off against two idiosyncratic outsiders with little incentive not to attack him with any issue they thought might help their chances, up to and including his carpetbagger status.[54] On the far side of the primary waited Jeanne Shaheen, a veteran of state politics with a strong electoral track record. How did Brown seek to blunt the impact of the carpetbagger issue, and how did his opponents try to use it against him?

"Long and Strong Ties"

Brown faced the challenge every carpetbagger faces: convincing the residents of his new state that he was there to represent them and their interests; that he could do so better than an opponent who had been a fixture of state politics since the 1970s; and, finally, that his desire to win election from a new state less than two years after losing a race next door in Massachusetts, and actively flirting with campaigns for governor in Massachusetts and for president in 2016 was not motivated purely, or even primarily, by his ambition to hold elected office.

Brown took several approaches to explaining his candidacy to New Hampshire voters. The first of these was to emphasize his ties to New Hampshire. Previous chapters detailed how carpetbaggers have done this with varying degrees of credibility. On one end of the spectrum are carpetbaggers with fairly strong claims: Bill Brock's years living and paying taxes in Maryland, or James Buckley's longstanding family and business ties to Connecticut. On the other we have Bobby Kennedy's insistence that spending a few years of his childhood in Riverdale and Bronxville made him a New Yorker. In Scott Brown's case, he had several connections to his new state that he emphasized throughout his campaign. His family, he argued, had "nine generations of ties to New Hampshire."[55] Brown himself had been born at the Portsmouth Naval

Shipyard (though Democrats were quick to note that the shipyard is officially located in Maine, not New Hampshire).[56] Finally, Brown's mother, sister, and other family members lived in New Hampshire, and Brown had been paying New Hampshire taxes on his Rye vacation home for twenty years.[57] In Brown's view, as he told the Associated Press shortly before becoming a candidate, his ties to the state were "long and strong."[58]

Well-known state Republican figures supported Brown in this effort. Former governor John Sununu, speaking on Brown's behalf at his rally in Portsmouth, argued that Brown was born "virtually" in New Hampshire and had spent his "happiest days as a young man" in the state, while Shaheen had been born in Missouri and voted like she was "the third senator from Massachusetts."[59] While Sununu's enthusiasm was no doubt appreciated, his remarks illustrate the uphill climb facing Brown: his claims to being a New Hampshirite were somewhat slender, while trying to attack Shaheen as being less than fully a resident of the state only invited comparison between the length of the two candidates' residency in New Hampshire.

Brown therefore did not rest his appeal to voters solely on the strength of whatever ties to New Hampshire he could muster. He turned to retail, face-to-face politics, reasoning that making his case to voters in person would help minimize concerns about the recency of his residency. He was also aided by the fact that part of the legend that grew up around his 2010 upset victory involved his supposed preternatural skills as an in-person campaigner and the red pickup truck he used to get from one event to the next. This reputation was almost certainly overblown. Duquette argues convincingly that Brown's 2010 win was an anomaly caused by an unlikely confluence of unlikely events, rather than any campaigning superpowers Brown possessed.[60] However, playing up one of the best-known aspects of his political celebrity was smart politics, and Brown was willing to venture to small towns in the far north of the state that few candidates ever visited.[61] In addition to engaging in retail politics, Brown made a point of discussing how much retail politics he was doing and how much he enjoyed it. One early campaign commercial noted that Brown had been driving his pickup "all across New Hampshire, listening, learning—and what he's learned is pretty simple: People want an America that leads the world again, a health care system that works for New Hampshire and more good jobs."[62] This was not the formally structured listening tour that Hillary Clinton undertook, but its goal was the same: to introduce Brown to Granite State voters as a Granite Stater and convince them that he understood their concerns and could represent their interests. His personal campaigning was extensive; he visited "supermarkets, car shows, lobster shacks and a Harley

Davidson-themed cookout."[63] He campaigned during tailgating at a UNH football game not long before the election.[64] He also periodically stood in at bars throughout the state as a guest bartender, sometimes accompanied by supporters like John McCain and Kelly Ayotte.[65]

Brown also dealt with the carpetbagger issue by trying to nationalize the election and making it more about Barack Obama than Scott Brown. In this regard, Brown was little different from Republican Senate challengers across the country who focused on issues like immigration, the rise of ISIS, and public fears of an ebola outbreak while Democratic incumbents tried to focus on state and local matters. But, for Brown, focusing on these issues and on tying Shaheen to Obama, whose popularity in the New Hampshire had declined since 2012, could also help insulate him from the carpetbagger issue: If a voter wanted to express disapproval for the direction of the country, did it matter how recently Brown had moved to New Hampshire or had represented Massachusetts? By casting Shaheen's record of support for President Obama as fundamentally out of step with the interests of New Hampshire, Brown presented himself as the candidate better able to represent those interests.

In addition to endorsements from New Hampshire officials, like John Sununu, Brown offered testimonials from average citizens. One early Brown ad featured local veterans speaking highly of Brown's long record of National Guard service, and arguing that sending him to Washington would improve the quality of representation veterans received in Congress.[66] Other Brown supporters did not just talk up Brown, but tried to defuse the carpetbagger issue by talking about Hillary Clinton. Fergus Cullen, a former state GOP chair, wrote in the *Union Leader* that none of Brown's Democratic critics had criticized Clinton for running in New York in 2000.[67] By casting Democrats as selectively outraged over carpetbagging, such criticisms sought to defuse the issue by turning it into just another partisan attack.

Unlike Hillary Clinton, however, Brown did not have a cleared path to the Republican nomination; he would have to defeat Jim Rubens and Bob Smith before he would face off against Shaheen.

The Primary and General Elections

Rubens and Smith came to the primary with little to lose; neither had held office in years, and neither was particularly beloved by the state party's leaders. Brown spent the primary largely focusing on Jeanne Shaheen; the lateness of the September 9 primary meant that a bruising primary would leave Brown little time to pivot to his campaign against her, and his primary opponents were sufficiently obscure that sustained attention to them would have elevated their stature to voters. But their relative obscurity did not mean that they had no impact on the race. Both attacked Brown on areas where he was vulnerable, and while they did not prevent him from winning the nomination, they did well enough to make Brown's primary victory less than overwhelming.

Rubens was something of an idiosyncratic figure, thanks to positions on a host of social issues, as well as climate change and campaign finance reform, that put him well out of sync with most Republicans in 2014. In the primary, he emphasized his length of involvement in New Hampshire politics and cast himself as an antiestablishment Washington outsider, in contrast to Brown.[68] This approach won Rubens the support of some conservative groups, such as the Republican Liberty Caucus, and some prominent Republicans, including former US and state senator Gordon Humphrey and former executive council member Earl Rinker (who noted in his endorsement that Rubens was the only Republican candidate who had not moved to New Hampshire in order to run).[69] But for many Republicans, Rubens was reinventing himself one time too many with this campaign.[70] Rubens also enjoyed unexpected support from Mayday PAC, a group founded by Harvard Law School professor Lawrence Lessig to support candidates who favored campaign finance reform.[71] While this increased the visibility of Rubens's campaign, the issue of campaign finance reform is not exactly one that sets a Republican primary afire.

Former senator Bob Smith argued that Brown was too liberal for New Hampshire Republicans. Smith made much of the fact that he was the only one of the three Republican candidates to take a strong position against legalized abortion, for instance, and Smith particularly trained his fire on Brown on the issue of guns.[72] In this he was aided by Brown's own positions on the issue, which had zigzagged from supporting a federal ban on assault weapons after the Sandy Hook school massacre to proposing a ban on gun-free zones once he was running in New Hampshire.[73] In a debate just before the primary, Brown twice declined to say whether he still supported a federal ban on assault weapons. Smith used this nonanswer as an opportunity to doubly attack Brown: first as a Washington insider who could only offer New Hampshire Republicans "gobblydegook" rather than a clear position and then as someone who had voted with President Obama more than he supported Republican positions.[74] Where Rubens attacked Brown for his lack of true connections to New Hampshire, Smith accused him of being neither conservative enough nor Republican enough to represent the state's Republicans. Smith would likely have leveled this charge against any other Republican he faced in a primary election, but in this case it highlighted Brown's status as a newcomer with Massachusetts origins. Brown's initial support of a ban on assault weapons was a position he likely would not have taken to begin with had he imagined he'd ever be running in a Republican primary in New Hampshire.

Neither Rubens nor Smith made much headway against Brown; even after a final debate in which local television station WMUR's political analysts declared Smith the "clear winner" of the debate,[75] Brown won the primary. In terms of votes received, Brown won in a landslide. Neither Rubens nor Smith came within thirty thousand votes of Brown. But from another perspective, the result was not a terribly positive one for Brown. With the backing of the national Republican Party and many of the state party's most active and well-known figures, Brown received just 49.9 percent of the primary vote; the combined total for Smith and Rubens—45.6 percent—nearly matched Brown's vote.[76] In politics, a win is generally a win; however, this win suggested that Brown was entering the general election against Shaheen with a less than united party behind him.

Jeanne Shaheen did not attack Brown solely on the carpetbagger question; instead, she used it as a springboard from which to argue that he would not truly represent the interests of New Hampshire's citizens if he were to be elected. This approach allowed her to call attention to Brown's carpetbagger status without constantly using the word; in many ways it was reminiscent of her handling of gender in her earliest statewide runs for office. In those races, Shaheen had not defined herself as a female candidate but let the fact of her gender speak for itself and lend credibility to her positions on issues like education and health care.[77] Many of her attacks on Brown reminded voters that he had moved to the state in order to run there and then went a step further to call his motives and interests into question. Voters already knew Brown was a carpetbagger—a University of Massachusetts poll in October found that it was the most common one-word description of Brown offered by New Hampshire respondents[78]—and so charging Brown with being a carpetbagger would only remind voters of what they already knew about him. Shaheen instead used that knowledge as a starting point for arguments that questioned Brown's ability to represent New Hampshire and its citizens' interests.

Throughout the campaign, Shaheen argued time and time again that "New Hampshire is not a consolation prize."[79] This refrain did more than remind voters that Brown was new to the state. It also focused attention on the fact that Brown had spent much of 2013 weighing other campaigns and had finally settled on New Hampshire only after those other options proved unlikely to lead to a victory. This, the campaign argued in a memo to supporters, showed that "Scott Brown is out for himself, not New Hampshire."[80] This argument recurred throughout Shaheen's campaign, as she argued that "the question is not where he's from, the question is what he's for."[81]

Shaheen wove this theme into her discussions of issues throughout the campaign. In response to Brown's arguments about ISIS and other national security threats, she argued that she had been "asking questions about ISIS before my opponent ever moved to New Hampshire."[82] On economic issues, Shaheen argued that Brown's career showed a pattern of accepting support from corporate and oil interests and then acting on their behalf in office. Brown, Shaheen charged, "may have changed his address but he hasn't changed his stripes."[83] One Shaheen surrogate aptly summed up this line of attack against Brown when he declared, "I can get over that you are not from New Hampshire—but I cannot get over that you are not for New Hampshire!"[84] The point Shaheen argued was not that voters should vote against Brown because he was a carpetbagger, but that because he was a carpetbagger he would not represent the interests of the state if he won the election.

Shaheen further drove this argument home by deploying elected officials from Massachusetts as campaign surrogates. The fact of these surrogates' Massachusetts origins meant that news accounts of their events invariably discussed Brown's carpetbagger status, and some of them were willing to talk about the carpetbagger issue as itself disqualifying. Rob Dolan, the Democratic mayor of Melrose, Massachusetts, told a crowd that while he, like Brown, owned a summer home in New Hampshire, "I would feel I would have no right, although I've spent time in New Hampshire my whole life, to claim I'm from New Hampshire and certainly to reflect my views on the people or an opponent who's dedicated her life to improve this state."[85] Many of these surrogates were also chosen because they appealed to one or another of the constituencies Shaheen needed to mobilize—women, organized labor, progressives, and so on—to win the race.

Of these, the women's vote was perhaps the one to which Shaheen dedicated the most attention. She was aided in part by the fact that the Democratic candidates for other top offices in the state—governor and the state's two seats in the House of Representatives—were women, and the Republican candidates were all men. Even if Shaheen had never said a word about the gender dynamics of the race, the 2014 election in New Hampshire would still have notably been a battle of the sexes. But Shaheen made subtle and overt plays for the women's vote throughout the campaign. Some focused on policy, like her plan to make it easier for women to become business owners.[86] Some focused on criticisms of Brown's record on abortion as a state legislator in

Massachusetts.[87] Toward the end of the race, when polls started to tighten, Shaheen made this theme more explicit and told attendees at the state Democrats' Jefferson-Jackson dinner that they had the historic opportunity to make Brown "the only person to run for the Senate from two states to be defeated by two women."[88] Here, as in her other attacks on Brown, his carpetbagger status was the beginning, not the end, of her critique.

Unforced Errors

In his ideal campaign, Brown would have focused on more favorable issue territory than the carpetbagger question. But there were times throughout the campaign when Brown's words or actions reminded Granite Staters that Brown was a newcomer. Sometimes Brown was too glib about the carpetbagger question, as when, in response to a debate question about why he was running in New Hampshire, he responded by saying, "[B]ecause I live here."[89] While this was technically true, the answer ignored the fact that he had, just one year earlier, lived in Massachusetts or the representational concerns that this fact provoked. In some of his television advertising, Brown's campaign used green-screen technology to film him in a studio and insert a virtual setting behind him to make it appear that he was standing in an airport or on a farm owned by a former speaker of the New Hampshire state legislature.[90] While Brown was not the first candidate to use this technology, the symbolism of a carpetbagger using special effects to pretend to be somewhere he was not was painful.

Other verbal gaffes led Democrats to suggest that Brown could not keep track of which state he was in. Outside a fund-raiser in December 2013, for instance, Brown referenced "the issues that are affecting not only people here in Massachusetts—I mean New Hampshire—but also in Massachusetts obviously, and Maine."[91] In an interview with the *Boston Herald*'s radio station, Brown argued that his opposition to amnesty for undocumented immigrants and to the DREAM Act was "a big difference between Senator Shaheen and me and many other people in the Massachusetts delegation."[92] When President Obama visited Worcester, Massachusetts, in June, Brown asked why Shaheen wasn't appearing with him; while Brown's intention was to tie Shaheen to the unpopular president, he once again appeared to be confusing the state he had once represented and the one he was now running in.[93] The Brown campaign and New Hampshire Republicans argued that these and other, similar incidents were either slips of the tongue or misinterpretations of Brown's actual words.

But, unfortunately for Brown, whether these slips were innocent or Freudian, the coverage of each one reminded the state's voters once again that Brown was new to the state.

A final reminder of Brown's status as a carpetbagger came during the third and final debate of the campaign. Brown had given strong performances in the previous two debates, which made the stakes for this final confrontation high. Toward the close of the debate, James Pindell, the political director for Manchester's WMUR, asked Brown a question about the economy in Sullivan County, a county bordering Vermont. When Brown offered a response that focused on tourism and infrastructure and lacked any specific references to the economy of Sullivan County, Pindell interrupted Brown's answer, saying, "We're talking about Sullivan County and I think you're talking about the North Country."[94] From there, things devolved into a dispute over whether Sullivan County is located to the north or to the west of Concord; in fact, while Sullivan County is west of Concord, it is large enough that some parts of it are located to the north of the capitol city and some are to the south.[95] Pindell and WMUR were immediately and heavily criticized by the Brown campaign and the state Republican Party, and Pindell apologized for interrupting Brown on that night's 11:00 newscast.[96] Whoever was right or wrong was in many ways beside the point; Brown went into the closing days of the campaign in the wake of a very loud, very public debate over his knowledge of New Hampshire geography. Both candidates headed to Sullivan County that weekend. Shaheen was pouncing on an unexpected opportunity to highlight her message that Brown was neither from nor for New Hampshire. For Brown, who had been closing in on Shaheen in several predebate polls, it was damage control.

Results and Discussion

While Shaheen began the race well ahead of Brown, by the final days of the campaign, a Shaheen victory no longer seemed like a sure thing. The state Democratic Party abandoned all subtlety and peppered the state with signs that simply read "Massachusetts Carpetbagger" over a silhouette of the Bay State. But on election night, Shaheen won 51.6 percent of the vote to Brown's 48.4 percent. Shaheen had received exactly the same percentage of the vote in 2008. This suggests that Brown, whatever else, did not grossly underperform what was possible for a Republican candidate in this race. Unlike the losing carpetbagger candidates examined in earlier chapters, Brown turned what would likely have otherwise been a sleepy re-election campaign into a competitive race. In this respect, his candidacy fulfilled some of the hopes of the national Republicans who urged him to run and the state party actors who came to embrace his candidacy. But he also failed to prevent Shaheen from winning re-election. To what extent can this result be explained by Brown's carpetbagger status?

This is the sort of question that makes political scientists envy their friends in the physical sciences. While an experiment in physics or chemistry can be rerun as many times as needed to test the impact of changing aspects of the experiment, the same cannot be done in politics. We cannot run the 2014 New Hampshire US Senate election over again, but make Brown a New Hampshire native, or run a different Republican in his place, or keep Brown from being asked about Sullivan County. But we can turn to data about which New Hampshire voters chose Shaheen, which chose Brown, and whether the breakdown of support for each candidate suggests something about whether Brown's carpetbagger status factored into his loss. Exit polling conducted on Election Day sheds light on both of these questions.[97]

One question provides insight into the role Brown's Massachusetts origins may have played in the result of the election. Shaheen just barely defeated Brown among voters born in New Hampshire, winning their vote by just 50 percent to 49 percent, while Brown won among voters who had moved to New Hampshire from Massachusetts by a similar 51 to 48 percent. Among voters who (like Shaheen herself, as John Sununu once reminded voters) had moved to New Hampshire from a state other than Massachusetts, Shaheen beat Brown by 54 to 46 percent. This last category, composing 37 percent of the 2014 electorate, was actually larger than either the native-born segment (at 31 percent) or the Massachusetts expatriates (at 33 percent). As strong as New Hampshire's state image may be, native New Hampshirites were a small minority of voters in 2014 and split between the two candidates more or less equally. Women broke for Shaheen by a 59-40 percent margin, while men supported Brown by a margin of 55-44 percent. In other words, Shaheen did better among men than Brown did among women, and she further benefited from the fact that women made up 52 percent of the electorate, while men were only 48 percent of it. On the ideological front, self-identified liberals and moderates supported Shaheen by margins of 93 to 7 percent and 57 to 42 percent, respectively, while conservatives supported Brown over Shaheen by 89 to 11 percent. Shaheen won among Democrats, winning their support by 96 to 4 percent, and independents, winning by 51 to 49 percent, while Brown won the Republican vote by only 90 to 9 percent. On both the ideological and partisan fronts, Shaheen made small but meaningful inroads into segments of the electorate that one would have expected to support Brown, while Brown was unable to do the same in return. Brown's relative moderation may have harmed him here, especially given how nationalized the 2014 elections were. By emphasizing that his election would help put Republicans in control of the Senate, Brown neutralized whatever appeal he might have had to Democrats and liberals. On the other hand, Shaheen's decades-long presentation of herself as a pragmatic, nonideological problem solver focused on local concerns likely helped her with conservative- and Republican-identifying voters.

While Brown's emphasis on the issue shows that he hoped opposition to the Affordable Care Act, also known as Obamacare, would do for him in New Hampshire in 2014 what it had done for him in Massachusetts in 2010, more voters thought it should have done more or was about right (50 percent, combined) than went too far (46 percent), and only 25 percent of voters considered health care the most important issue in 2014. And even among voters who thought the law went too far, 18 percent more of them voted for Shaheen, who voted for and supported the law, than Brown, whose opposition to it was a central part of his campaign.

Brown also repeatedly tied Shaheen to President Obama. This was not a poor tactic in a state where the president's approval rating was underwater on election day, with 43 percent approving of his performance and 56 percent disapproving. But even here, Shaheen made inroads where Brown did not; 18 percent of those who disapproved of the president's job performance voted for her, rather than Brown.

To sum up, Shaheen managed to win some support among voters—Republicans, opponents of the Affordable Care Act, voters disapproving of President Obama's performance—whom we would not expect to vote for her. And Brown, despite his moderation relative to the national Republican Party, was unable to offset the votes he lost among members of these groups with support from equivalent voters such as Democrats, Obamacare supporters, or Obama supporters. Were Shaheen's unlikely levels of support from Republicans rooted in her long history in New Hampshire, her incumbency, or Brown's carpetbagger status?

One way to examine this question is to consider Shaheen's performance in the context of other Democratic senators first elected in 2008 and seeking re-election in 2014. Of the eight senators in that category, exit polling data is available for the campaigns of all but one of them, New Mexico's Tom Udall.

Table 7.1 shows each of the remaining seven incumbent Democratic freshman senators' support among voters who either approve or disapprove

Table 7.1. 2014 Senate Votes and Presidential Approval

Incumbent Democrat	Merkley (OR)	Franken (MN)	Shaheen (NH)	Hagan (NC)	Udall (CO)	Warner (VA)	Begich (AK)
Incumbent's vote share	55.8%	53.2%	51.6%	47.3%	46%	49.2%	45.6%
Challenger's vote share	37.3%	42.9%	48.4%	49%	48.5%	48.4%	48.8%
Obama approval	47%	47%	43%	43%	42%	40%	39%
% approve, voted D	89%	95%	94%	91%	88%	92%	81%
% approve, voted R	8%	4%	5%	8%	8%	7%	17%
Obama disapproval	51%	52%	56%	56%	56%	58%	59%
% disapprove, voted D	22%	20%	17%	13%	14%	15%	25%
% disapprove, voted R	66%	77%	81%	82%	78%	81%	68%

of President Obama's performance in office. Several points are worth not-ing here. First, Shaheen had the second-highest level of retention of voters approving of President Obama's performance in office, on par with what Al Franken received in Minnesota. While three other Democrats did better than Shaheen's performance among voters disapproving of the president's performance, two of them were Franken and Oregon's Jeff Merkley, both of whom faced underfunded political novices and were easily re-elected; the third was Alaska's Mark Begich, who, impressively for a Democrat, managed to win a quarter of the voters disapproving of the president while, impres-sively in a different way, losing 17 percent of those who did. Second, while voters in Minnesota and Oregon were more approving of the president than voters in most of the states where the Democratic class of 2008 was running for re-election, in New Hampshire the president's approval/disapproval was at 43 percent/56 percent—identical to what it was in North Carolina, where incumbent Kay Hagan lost a close race, in part because she retained only 91 percent of the voters approving the president and won only 13 percent of voters disapproving the president. It is therefore safe to say that Shaheen's performance was not the result of a state environment where the president was more popular than he was nationally. Instead, she managed to win—and Brown managed to lose—in a state where the president's standing helped a similar incumbent lose.

None of this definitively settles the question of whether Brown's car-petbagger status cost him a victory in New Hampshire in 2014. But these polling results do suggest that it dragged on his candidacy; as noted earlier, it was the first, and, as with past carpetbagger candidates, in many cases the only thing many voters knew about him. And in a close race, any drag can make the difference between victory and defeat. From a personal ambition perspective, the race was a failure for Scott Brown, and one that closed the door on any future opportunities to run for office in Massachusetts. From the perspective of state and national Republicans, however, his candidacy stopped that of Bob Smith, and as a result may have helped stave off a downballot disaster. From that perspective, the Brown campaign was at least a partial success. Brown also came far closer to winning than any of the other unsuc-cessful carpetbaggers examined in this book. The concluding chapter takes a step back to consider all of the candidates examined in this book as a whole and explores whether Scott Brown's candidacy represents a new, more viable model of carpetbagger and what that might mean for the prospects of car-petbagging in future elections.

Conclusion

After Robert Kennedy's victory in 1964, the *New York Times* editorial page declared that he had defeated not just his opponent, Senator Kenneth Keating, but also "the old tradition that a member of Congress should come from the state or district he represents."[1] The *Times* expressed the same concern that surfaces whenever carpetbaggers run for office—the fear that a lack of local ties between a carpetbagger and those he or she seeks to represent would prove costly to the interests of the represented and that any carpetbagger must seek office purely for the sake of unrestrained ambition, rather than to represent the state's interests.

This is, of course, a fear that any voter can fairly have regarding any political newcomer; in the absence of a record of representation in office, a voter has no guarantees that a given candidate is interested in anything more than winning office for its own sake. But most first-time candidates can usually point to local ties or nonpolitical reasons for having moved to a new place: education, family, career opportunities, and so on. A carpetbagger, however, lays bare ambition in a way that is impossible to ignore; the decision to run may even precede, rather than follow, a decision to move to a new place. This display of ambition made Robert Kennedy and Hillary Clinton fundamentally different, not just from Ken Keating and Rick Lazio but also from the thousands of people who move to New York in any given year in search of a fresh start, and conversely made Maggie Hassan different from Scott Brown even though both were originally from Massachusetts. Hassan had lived in New Hampshire for years before her first run for office, and she had been involved in public affairs before first seeking office. Brown, on the other hand, moved to the Granite State only so he could run for the Senate for a third time from a second state. Even candidates like Bill Brock and Endicott Peabody, who had lived for some time in their second states, found their past service in other states dragged their candidacies down, rather than helping them.

As the preceding chapters show, however, the fears of the *Times* editorial board have not quite come to pass. Runs by carpetbaggers have remained relatively rare since Kennedy's 1964 campaign in New York, and successful carpetbaggers rarer still; as of this writing, early in the spring of 2018, only Hillary Clinton, also in New York, won her election. Why has this been the case? Why has the tradition that the *Times* feared was imperiled remained so robust?

Part of the answer lies in the same ambition to hold office that leads carpetbaggers to run for office in new states. Every state in America has at least its fair share of ambitious, politically minded people who either hold office and would like to move up to higher office or would like to hold office in the first place. Each state also has its own political culture and partisan composition. This means that whenever an election for the Senate comes along, the best opportunities to run are likely to be seized by ambitious members of the state's existing body of potential candidates. If a popular incumbent is seeking another term and belongs to a party that dominates statewide politics (a Democrat in Hawaii, a Republican in Oklahoma), then few members of the opposing party are likely to seek their party's nomination in the expectation of having a real chance of winning. Such candidates might run for other reasons: the opportunity to discuss issues they feel passionately about, or winning the goodwill of party leaders and the exposure to voters to help a future run for another office. But these sorts of goals are unlikely to appeal to a would-be carpetbagger who has serious ambitions to win a seat in the US Senate: a loss might help a local candidate's long-term career goals, but a potential carpetbagger would likely find this an insufficiently appealing prospect to justify running.

On the other end of the spectrum are races where no incumbent is running, but one party is overwhelmingly likely to win the election, no matter who its candidate is. In these sorts of elections, competition among potential candidates for the dominant party's nomination is likely to be fierce because winning that nomination all but guarantees winning the general election. In such races a potential carpetbagger from the dominant party is likely to be confronted with a bevy of homegrown candidates who may have waited for many years for this seat to become available. As for the minority party, the same calculations described above come into play. The nomination is so unlikely to lead to a victory that carpetbagging is unappealing to those with a clear sense of how the election is likely to play out. For ambitious locals, on the other hand, this situation is still their best chance of winning the seat since there is no incumbent seeking re-election.

Then there are those elections in which both parties' nominations are likely to be valuable: those that take place in a state where both parties are roughly equal in strength and where no incumbent seeks re-election. Such races will not lack willing candidates because either party's nominee stands a good chance of winning the election. In these sorts of races, a potential carpetbagger in either party is, as in the previous types of elections, likely to encounter little interest or encouragement among party actors. The fact that American political parties, like American government, are federal in structure thus makes the likelihood of a carpetbagger having even a chance of being nominated very low—not because state parties are concerned with representation as an abstract matter, or even because they are concerned with winning, but because they are generally populated with ambitious men and women who want to hold elected office, and a nomination held by a carpetbagger is a nomination that is not held by a local figure. Therefore, in most elections in most states in most election years, there is little appetite or opportunity for a carpetbagger candidate.

"Most," however, is different from "all." As the previous chapters demonstrate, there are some elections in some states in some election years where a party finds itself in need of a candidate, no viable local options are available or willing to run, and therefore the idea of a carpetbagger candidate starts to become appealing. There are some features that crop up throughout these races. They tend to involve a party that is in the midst of or emerging from a period of decline, as was the case with New York's Democrats in 1964 and 2000, New Hampshire's Democrats in 1986 and Republicans in 2014, Illinois's Republicans in 2004, Connecticut's Republicans in 1980, and Maryland's Republicans in 1994. From a supply-and-demand perspective, this makes a certain amount of sense. When a party spends an extended period with little success in a state, it will have fewer quality candidates available to run for higher offices. In some cases, this may simply be a matter of unlucky timing; New Hampshire in the 2000s is a genuinely purple state, where each party has won statewide offices and control of the state legislature at various points and neither dominates the state's politics. But the bad year New Hampshire Republicans had in 2012 left them with few truly viable options heading into 2014 against incumbent Jeanne Shaheen. In other cases, a desperate party looks outside its state borders because it thinks a high-profile newcomer is preferable to an empty ballot line, as happened in 2004 in Illinois, or to prevent a truly disastrous outcome like having an extremist hijack a nomination, as in New Hampshire in 1986. Whatever the specific needs or motives of a particular party in a given year, the importance of state parties in recruiting or smoothing the path of a carpetbagger is a factor that the *Times* and other critics of carpetbagging often fail to consider. Of the candidates examined in the previous chapters, the two who fared so poorly that they ended their campaigns practically before they began were Harold Ford and Liz Cheney, who both tried to muscle aside incumbents without any sort of support for their challenges within their state parties.

This leads to another reason the *Times'* concerns following Robert Kennedy's election have not panned out. A carpetbagger candidacy requires a race that a state party thinks is winnable but lacks a viable candidate capable of winning or a party that thinks it needs a candidate from beyond the state's borders for other reasons. Such races are likely to be exceedingly rare. When a race looks winnable, local candidates are likely to come forward and run. Similarly rare are credible, ambitious candidates willing to undertake the difficult job of running as a newcomer to a state. Ambitious politicians tend to be strategic about whether and when to run for office and generally do so when they believe they are most likely to win their party's nomination and the general election. As the preceding chapters demonstrate, many of the people who become carpetbagger candidates do so not because they want to be carpetbaggers, but because becoming a carpetbagger is the best option available to them. But just because an option is the best one available relative to others, it does not necessary follow that that option is, in absolute terms, a terribly good one. Running as a carpetbagger means, at the very least, starting a campaign in a new state without the sorts of pre-existing ties to and knowledge of that state that a local candidate would possess. For candidates who had once held office in another state, the decision to run in a new state irrevocably breaks one's own ties to one's original state: Bill Brock, once he ran and lost in Maryland, could not turn around and run in Tennessee again, just as Scott Brown could not return to Massachusetts after his loss in New Hampshire.

These considerations mean that the supply of viable figures available who are free, willing, and need to run in a new state is always going to be profoundly limited. Robert Kennedy was a former cabinet secretary and the brother of a slain president. Hillary Clinton was a uniquely prominent first lady. Many people in these positions might decide to run for elective office at some point during their careers. But few would choose to do so in a new state, where they will be derided as carpetbaggers on top of every other attack they will face as a candidate, unless no better option were available to them.

Robert Kennedy would have had an easier time running in Massachusetts but could not do so without muscling his brother Ted out of the way—an option he apparently never considered and too ruthless for even the worst imaginable caricature of Kennedy. And running in New York was, to Kennedy, a preferable choice than running for governor in Massachusetts. Clinton, conversely, would have faced carpetbagger charges no matter where she ran. But it is hard not to think that if there had been an option available to her that did not raise those charges, she would have taken it. The fact that these are the only real success stories to be found in the annals of modern carpetbagging indicates yet another reason for the rarity of carpetbagger candidacies: no one with a better option becomes a carpetbagger, and most of those who are in a position to pull it off either don't want to or don't need to.

It is useful from this perspective to examine a recurring fantasy of political reporters during the Obama years: the prospect that First Lady Michelle Obama would run for the United States Senate from California, in something of a reenactment of Hillary Clinton's campaign in New York in 2000. Michelle Obama was a popular first lady and had become a top Democratic campaign surrogate over the course of her husband's presidency, particularly in 2014, when her approval ratings were much higher than his. Unlike Clinton, she had not had a controversial role in a high-profile policy failure, nor had her husband's administration been beset by the same sorts of scandals and scandalmongering that plagued Clinton's. No matter how often and how emphatically Michelle Obama herself said she had no interest in holding office, the prospect was an irresistible subject of speculation for many journalists. That speculation was fueled by the frequent outbreak of rumors that California Democrats were reaching out to Obama, much as New York's Democrats had done with Hillary Clinton in 1998 and 1999, to run if the state's longtime senator Dianne Feinstein retired in 2018.[2]

Culturally speaking, California makes sense as a state that could be receptive to a carpetbagger. Like New York, it is a state that has long been a place where Americans have ventured in search of a new start or a new chapter in life. Becoming a Californian is less culturally fraught process than becoming a Wyomingite, as Elizabeth Cheney found in 2013, because the state is so large and so diverse that there is no consensus idea of what a "Californian" is. As a state that has increasingly trended Democratic in recent decades, a nationally known and popular Democrat like Michelle Obama would be massively advantaged to win a Senate race, even in the event of a Democrat-versus-Democrat race like the one the state saw in 2016 thanks to its top-two primary system.

But these imaginings of a Michelle Obama campaign in California fail to consider a crucial part of the carpetbagger equation: a state party that needs the carpetbagger to become a candidate. California in the early twenty-first century does not lack ambitious Democrats interested in seeking statewide office. The state has so many well-known Democrats that two of them, Gavin Newsom and Kamala Harris, appear to have had an unofficial unspoken understanding not to run against one another for governor or senator and consulted with each other about their political futures when Barbara Boxer announced her retirement in 2015.[3] A state where Democrats are ascendant, several large cities routinely produce Democratic mayors, term limits cycle state legislators in and out of office on a steady basis, and that is home to any number of liberal, politically minded celebrities who might decide to follow in the footsteps of Ronald Reagan and Arnold Schwarzenegger, is unlikely to need to look beyond its borders to find viable potential Democratic candidates for a Senate seat in the near future. Any potential Michelle Obama campaign would know this; at best, Obama would come into such a race as one half of an intraparty conflict that could extend until the general election. It is difficult to see such a race being terribly appealing to her or to imagine many California Democrats reaching out to her when there are so many local options for Senate vacancies.

The *New York Times* in 1964 feared the death of what it called a "tradition" of candidates having strong ties to the places in which they ran for office. This book makes clear that that tradition is not supported solely by political norms, which have, in recent years, proven to be all too ephemeral. In fact, that tradition is not really a tradition at all. It is better understood as the manifestation of the interests and needs of both candidates and political parties. The best protection against widespread carpetbagging is not norms against it—as we have seen, it is occasionally successful and few carpetbaggers are laughed all the way off the ballot simply for being carpetbaggers—but the fact it is rarely in anyone's best interests to become a carpetbagger, or for a party to have a carpetbagger as its candidate. This truth is reflected by the poor electoral track record carpetbaggers have. Not only have few carpetbaggers won their elections, but most of those who run lose and lose badly.

However, some recent carpetbagger campaigns stand out as something of an exception, such as that of Scott Brown in 2014. While Brown did not defeat Jeanne Shaheen, he did perform respectably and turned what had looked like an easy re-election race for Shaheen into a competitive campaign decided by fewer than sixteen thousand votes out of nearly a half million cast. For Liz Cheney, her unsuccessful run in 2014 did not keep her from being either a viable candidate or a successful one in 2016. Do Brown and Cheney represent new models of carpetbagger? And does the state of American politics in the early decades of the twenty-first century have the potential to give carpetbaggers, when they decide to run, a better chance than they may have had in the past?

Whenever a carpetbagger runs for office, concerns arise about the importance of local ties for elected officials, and fears are expressed that this could be the beginning of an ominous trend. These fears should not be dismissed lightly, even though the record suggests they are overblown. While the motivations and incentives of multiple political actors and institutions collude to make carpetbagging a relatively rare phenomenon, it is also worth examining in the light of recent developments in American politics whether this is likely to remain the case. The United States in the second decade of the twenty-first century is a nation whose politics are defined in large part by weak parties and strong partisanship.[4] This has two practical effects on elections. The first is that parties often have limited influence over the outcomes of their nomination battles. The second is that once a candidate wins the nomination of a party, many partisans will vote for that candidate, no matter how flawed or out of the political mainstream that candidate may be. Also contributing to this state of affairs is a decades-long increase in what has been termed negative partisanship, in which voters' negative feelings toward the opposing party make them much less willing or likely to vote for candidates from the party to which they do not belong.[5]

This means that today's potential carpetbaggers might expect that voters will care less about a carpetbagger's newcomer status than might have been the case in an earlier era in American politics. In this view of things, a candidate like Elizabeth Cheney erred not in coming home to Wyoming after decades away to run for office, but in trying to muscle a well-liked incumbent into retirement. Cheney's success in her 2016 campaign for the House of Representatives suggests that the intraparty opposition to her 2014 candidacy was rooted less in a principled belief in the sanctity of the politics of place than it was in a desire to keep Mike Enzi in office. And this also suggests that local party leaders, in the absence of an incumbent with long ties to the party and state, may have less capacity today to prevent a carpetbagger's nomination than they once might have had. This would particularly be the case when a national party encourages a carpetbagger's candidacy over that of other candidates with stronger local ties, as in the case of Scott Brown's candidacy in New Hampshire in 2014. There is nothing new about national party leaders trying to influence who runs for office—Minnesotans with long political memories still remember the phone call from Dick Cheney that upended that state's races for governor and U.S. Senate in 2002—but when carpetbaggers are involved in a race issues of representation are implicated in a way that they are not in other, more conventional instances.[6] As partisans become increasingly unwilling to vote for candidates from the other party, representational concerns may come to carry less and less weight in general elections. Instead, it may be that nomination contests will provide the strongest opportunity to force carpetbaggers to attest to their ability to represent their state for its own sake. But in the event that party actors decide that a carpetbagger is the candidate they want, they are more likely to run interference for a carpetbagger rather than demand concrete demonstrations of a carpetbagger's local knowledge and capacity to represent the state's interests well.

Also potentially helping carpetbaggers in the future is the changed regulatory landscape of campaign finance and electioneering by independent organizations. While Endicott Peabody, for instance, came under fire when they turned out to have raised most of their campaign funds from out-of-state donors, in the modern era, donations directly to candidates routinely cross state borders. More potently, recent Supreme Court decisions have unleashed upon the political landscape SuperPACs and other independent organizations which can spend unlimited amounts of money on behalf of candidates. Among the effects of these developments is a diminished focus on candidates' specific fundraising sources and a flood of television, digital, and mail advertising in competitive races from many sources, little of which comes from sources known to voters. This may help lower the bar for becoming a carpetbagger. While past would-be carpetbaggers had to wonder not just whether they could raise enough money to compete, but whether they could do so in a manner that would not draw additional attention to their carpetbagger status, today a carpetbagger who secures a nomination can be confident that he or she will not be abandoned by his or her party's voters, and that if the race becomes competitive, campaign funding—either direct donations or independent dollars—will be made available.

This may make the case of Scott Brown a template for the sorts of carpetbagger campaigns we see in the future. Brown's candidacy began with his search for an opportunity to seek public office again after his 2012 loss and was eventually embraced by Republican Party actors who were perhaps less interested in winning an additional Senate seat than in forcing Democrats to expend resources defending a seat that every viable New Hampshire Republican had decided was out of reach. At worst, money spent re-electing Jeanne Shaheen would be money not available to other, more endangered

Democrats. At best, Scott Brown would surprise everyone again and add another member to the Republicans' senate caucus. In a year when the political tides are structurally likely to rise to the benefit of one party, it makes good political sense for that party to field plausible candidates in as many races as possible, even if some of those candidates are unlikely ones as well. When there are marginal races—races where lightning might strike, but more likely might not—and local candidates have passed on running, finding a willing carpetbagger might be a more attractive option than searching for a third- or fourth-tier local candidate. This would particularly be the case when the carpetbagger is well-known enough to attract more money and attention than an obscure in-state figure could.

Elizabeth Cheney's path in Wyoming may provide further encouragement for would-be carpetbaggers. While she failed to unseat Mike Enzi, two years later, she was able to muscle her way past a crowded primary field to win the Republican nomination for Wyoming's seat in the House of Representatives— largely thanks to the family name and fundraising prowess she'd hoped would scare Enzi into retirement in 2013. In this regard, Cheney was little different from any other candidate who runs for one office, loses, and wins a campaign for a second office a few years later. Her example suggests that a carpetbagger willing to play a long game might find that by a second campaign in a new state, the carpetbagger label will have faded from enough voters' memories to give the candidate a better shot at winning. Sticking around long enough to run in a subsequent election also demonstrates that the carpetbagger was willing to stay in the state for reasons beyond political ambition. Indeed, her case opens the door to the prospect that many carpetbaggers falter by seeking high-profile Senate seats. The comparatively lower profile of House seats, and the fact that few voters think of themselves in terms of congressional boundaries redrawn every ten years in the same way they think of themselves as residents of a particular state, might allow carpetbaggers a greater chance at victory were they to run. But that lower profile and that lower level of influence likely make House seats less appealing to would-be carpetbaggers. Running for a House seat in Massachusetts or even in New York does not appear to have been an option Bobby Kennedy even considered in 1964. But for carpetbaggers with more flexible ambitions, the prospect of running in a new state may be more attractive than it would be for those who cannot imagine settling for any title less impressive than "Senator."

This is not to say that carpetbaggers, in the future, are likely to become common; only a very small number of Senate campaigns in any given election year are likely to be ones where a state party's leaders would be open to a carpetbagger's candidacy, and in fewer still of those races is there likely to be someone who is both a credible potential candidate and willing to take the step of becoming a carpetbagger. But recent trends in American politics suggest that anyone who takes the step of becoming an actual carpetbagger may have a better shot of winning than past carpetbaggers have had.

As this book goes to press, yet another carpetbagger candidacy is underway. Mitt Romney, the former Massachusetts governor and 2012 Republican nominee, has announced that he is running for the Senate in Utah. In many ways, his candidacy similar to those of Robert Kennedy and Hillary Clinton. Romney is both personally ambitious and has been immersed in politics from a young age; both of his parents ran for office in Michigan, and Romney ran for the Senate in Massachusetts in 1994 before winning the governor's race in that state in 2002. Romney also ran for president in 2008 and lost the Republican nomination before winning it in 2012. Following his loss to Barack Obama, Romney found himself without a position in public life, and friends and advisors described him as being at loose ends.[7] He considered a third presidential bid in 2016 but decided against it; then, as Donald Trump made his way toward the Republican nomination, he spoke out forcefully against Trump in a speech at the University of Utah.[8] Following Trump's upset victory, Romney was publicly courted as a potential secretary of state but passed over. In this regard, Romney is reminiscent of other carpetbagger candidates who found themselves eager to remain in public life but lacked an obvious platform from which to do so.

Fortunately for Romney, Utah's longtime senator Orrin Hatch not only decided not to seek an eighth term in 2018, but began laying groundwork for Romney to succeed him in 2017.[9] This helped ease Romney's path into Utah politics, in notable contrast to the reception he received in 2002 when Romney put out trial balloons for restarting his political career in Utah after turning around the Salt Lake City Winter Olympics. Then, many Utah Republicans found Romney too moderate for their tastes. This chilly reception helped convince Romney to return to Massachusetts. Between 2002 and 2018, not only had Romney become a national political figure, but he had also become the most famous Mormon politician in American history, a fact that meant that many Utahns—the state is 55 percent Mormon[10]—have come to see him as "one of us" no matter where else he may have held office or owned homes beyond the one he built in Holladay, Utah, after his 2012 defeat.[11] That, combined with Utah's overwhelmingly Republican electorate, makes a Romney victory in 2018 extremely likely.

Advice to the Would-Be Carpetbagger

With all of this in mind, there are some recommendations that a would-be carpetbagger would be wise to bear in mind before running.

First, *get invited to run in your new state.* The more successful carpetbaggers do not show up in their new states, luggage in hand, and declare that they are running for office. Instead, they are asked to run by their party's state organization. If the party does not extend an invitation, ask them to ask you. The worst move you as a carpetbagger can make is to not only show up uninvited, but to try to muscle out an incumbent with no other justification than your desire for the office that incumbent is, inconveniently, holding. As a newcomer to a state, you will need known, local party leaders to attest to your fitness to serve, both in terms of your qualifications for office and your legitimacy as a resident of your new state. This will have the particular benefit of activating the partisan tendencies of voters who identify with your party and make them more likely to support your candidate. This takes you from being just a carpetbagger to being a Democratic carpetbagger or a Republican carpetbagger.

Next, *run in an uncontested primary or get nominated by a state party convention.* A contested primary campaign does two things, neither of them good for you. First, it opens you up to attacks on your carpetbagger status from within your own party. This hurts you in the long run by leading many members of your own party to oppose your candidacy and question your motives, and this will come back to haunt you in the general election. As a carpetbagger, you want attacks on your carpetbagger status to hold off until the general election, when they will be coming from your opponent and will therefore be seen by many voters as purely partisan attacks, and when your own party's voters will be inclined to set aside their misgivings about your state-hopping in favor of their partisan predispositions to support their own party and oppose the other party. A nominating convention could fit the bill as well, as long as any opponent who emerges to challenge you does not gain traction outside the convention, and your win there can be presented as one that is robustly supported by well-known figures in your state party.

If it is at all possible, you should already *be a nationally known political figure* before you become a carpetbagger. As the cases examined in this book demonstrate, carpetbaggers who have held office in another state have an extraordinarily difficult time overcoming the stigma of being a carpetbagger.

That fact, to residents of their new state, indelibly marks the carpetbagger's candidacy. Every reference to "Governor Peabody" or "Senator Brock" reminded voters in New Hampshire in 1986 and Maryland in 1994 that those candidates had not just held office in the past but that they had held it somewhere else. And, for many voters, this was the first—and possibly the only—thing that they learned about these candidates who were not, otherwise, terribly well known to the voters in their new states. Robert Kennedy and Hillary Clinton, in contrast, were already nationally known figures when they arrived in New York. While they had to work to convince voters of the credibility of their geographic bona fides, they did not have the baggage that came with having represented another state. Even Kennedy, whose Cape Cod tan and Harvard accent were seen by many as proof of his Massachusetts origins, could argue that he had spent most of his adult life working in and around Washington DC, rather than Boston. And neither Kennedy nor Clinton won a title by holding office someplace else.

Make sure you don't have a better option. If Bobby Kennedy had been able to run in Massachusetts in 1964, he would have done so and saved himself an awful lot of controversy and trouble. Bill Brock might have had more of a chance in 1994 as a prodigal son returned home to Tennessee than as a transplanted Marylander. Long absences are more forgivable and raise fewer questions than does a conveniently timed move to a new state—and this holds true even if, like Brock or Endicott Peabody, you've actually lived in your new state for some time before running there. So, before you announce your candidacy, sign a lease or rent a hotel suite, be absolutely sure there isn't a more geographically palatable choice you can make.

Run when the national political environment favors your party. In some election years, political and economic and other conditions combine to create a political landscape that dramatically favors one party or the other. It is not surprising, then, that many of the carpetbaggers studied in this book—even the very unsuccessful ones—chose to run in such years. Running in the year of a wave election benefits both carpetbaggers and, in many cases, the parties they belong to. For the carpetbagger, a favorable national tide could help their candidacy succeed by providing a final boost on Election Day; if the entire country is leaning toward your party, the impact of your newcomer status could be lessened. For state parties, a candidate from out of state is better than no candidate at all, especially when there are suggestions that this will be a big year for the party.

Be prepared. Even if you are the first lady, the fact that you are a carpetbagger will be the first thing anyone learns about your campaign. As a candidate, you must be ready to address this issue credibly. As we have seen, many carpetbaggers seem to have been caught unawares or expected voters to simply take the fact of their past service in another state as an impressive credential that helps justify their campaign. A smart carpetbagger must be ready to explain why he or she has come to a new state and is running for office, and take concrete steps to build a relationship with voters.

Your party is valuable and necessary. Every election cycle sees candidates win nominations without the backing of state and national party leaders. Perhaps they are activists or outsiders whom primary voters find more alluring than an establishment candidate. Perhaps they are political savants who recognize the chance for an upset when no one else does. Perhaps they are simply foolish but lucky. These candidates may give you the idea that you can get nominated without the support of the party in the state you are moving to in order to run. Anything is possible, but that is probably not going to happen. Those upstart candidates you are thinking of probably had the benefit of traditional ties to the state they ran in. As a newcomer to a state's political scene, you need local party leaders to vouch for you and reassure your new constituents that you are a solid candidate who has their best interests at heart. And you need that because, more than any other kind of candidate who runs for office, you've put your enormous ambitions on display for all to see. History suggests that you are almost certainly going to lose anyway—but without the support of state party figures, you might not even get nominated to run.

Be aware of the local political culture of your new state. Some states, like New York, have reputations as places where people move to begin a new chapter in their lives. Richard Nixon moved there twice in his career in search of a badly needed fresh start. Others, like Wyoming, are harder to crack. Within a state, as well, there are likely to be regional and other divisions that can be treacherous for a newcomer to navigate. Learn what your new state is like and seek out guidance from those who already know it well to avoid the sorts of geographical errors and other campaign flubs and snubs that can damage a candidacy and remind voters that you are not from around here. If your state is not a cosmopolitan state with a long history of welcoming newcomers, then you had better have some sort of tie to the culture and identity of your new state that you can draw upon.

Recommendations to a Party Considering Importing a Carpetbagger

Just as candidates considering hopping a state line in order to run for office need advice, so too are there questions state party leaders thinking about bringing in a carpetbagger to run must consider.

First, *are things really so bad that you need a carpetbagger?* The track record of candidates imported from out of state is not a stellar one. While nationally known candidates like Bobby Kennedy and Hillary Clinton won their races in New York and Scott Brown made his race in New Hampshire competitive, most carpetbaggers tend to lose badly. At best, they lose badly quietly, like Bill Brock in Maryland in 1994. At worst, they lose badly in dramatic and shambolic fashion, like Alan Keyes in Illinois in 2004. Your party must soberly assess whether the potential for a high-profile flameout is worth the risk of getting behind a carpetbagger. On the other hand, your party may have interests that take a higher priority than simply winning the general election; in both of New Hampshire's carpetbagger races, a state party turned to or embraced an outsider candidate in order to prevent a nomination from being hijacked by an extremist (in 1986) or won by a candidate who could cause an electoral wipeout (in 2014). If that is the case, however, be aware of that going in.

Next, *don't delude yourselves.* The fact that your party is thinking about bringing in a candidate from out of state is probably not a good sign. If the general election were that winnable, odds are that someone within your state would have stepped up to take a chance at running. When a potential candidate considers running as a carpetbagger, news coverage tends to mention three people: James Shields, who represented three states in the Senate, and the duo of Robert Kennedy and Hillary Clinton. This is because human beings tend to relate current events to similar events from the past, and memories of these successful candidates are far more accessible to us than the many unsuccessful candidacies of lesser-known carpetbaggers. But a hard-headed analysis should remind you that the fact that you have a carpetbagger race means the race is going to be uphill for you, no matter whom you recruit.

Finally, make sure *the party's leaders, factions, and important constituencies are all on board with this candidacy.* If you cannot guarantee your carpetbagger a glide path to the nomination, whether in a primary or a party convention or some other selection process, your carpetbagger will have to defend himself or herself from attacks by opponents for the nomination—and attacks from members of your party will stick with rank-and-file members of your party more than they will coming from the other party's candidate in a general election.

Finally, *is the carpetbagger a skilled candidate?* If part of the point of bringing in a carpetbagger is avoiding an electoral disaster, make sure the candidate brings something to the table. Scott Brown is a skilled retail campaigner. Kennedy and Clinton, while never naturals at campaigning, brought policy knowledge, name recognition, and ties to popular presidents to their races. Others, like James Buckley and Alan Keyes, did not have the gift for retail campaigning and lacked track records that would make anyone think otherwise. But in each of those latter two cases, parts of a state party swooned for the idea of their candidacies and never took a step back to consider that Buckley had won less than 40 percent of the vote in a multicandidate race in 1970 or that Keyes had never won an election.

While the recommendations for a carpetbagger candidate are specific to the circumstances of a carpetbagger, those to a party are not that different from the considerations sensible party leaders should make about any potential candidacy. There is one key difference, however; in the case of a carpetbagger's campaign, the support of a party's leaders can be critical to success. We see this most clearly in the abortive primary campaigns of Harold Ford and Elizabeth Cheney against incumbent senators. In both cases, key party leaders and constituencies positioned themselves behind the incumbents and gave the would-be challengers little opportunity to build their support. The final frontier in carpetbagging may be a carpetbagger who wins a nomination despite the open opposition of state party leaders. The political stars that would have to align for that to take place are many; however, American politics in recent years has taught us to never say never.

Life after Carpetbagging

While some of the candidates discussed in this book are well known to readers, others may be less familiar. Each carpetbagger's campaign was just one part of a long career in public service. As noted in chapter 6 and discussed earlier in this chapter, Elizabeth Cheney followed up her attempted run in 2014 with a successful campaign for Wyoming's seat in the House of Representatives in 2016. This book closes by taking note of what happened to the rest of these candidates following their campaigns.

Robert Kennedy was sworn in as New York's junior senator on January 3, 1965, alongside his brother Ted. However, Kennedy found life in the Senate, with its well-established seniority system and informal folkways, frustrating. Despite his political celebrity, he passed no major legislation of his own during his time in office.[12] Kennedy enjoyed something of a truce with President Lyndon Johnson early in his Senate tenure, but he soon began to break with Johnson on foreign policy and Johnson's conduct of the war in Vietnam.[13] In 1968, after Senator Eugene McCarthy of Minnesota embarrassed Johnson in the New Hampshire primary, Kennedy, too, became a candidate for president. His entry into the race helped convince Johnson not to seek another term. On June 4, 1968, Kennedy won the California presidential primary but was shot shortly after he addressed his supporters. He died two days later and is interred at Arlington National Cemetery alongside his brother John.

Hillary Clinton was easily re-elected in 2006 and ran for president in 2008, but she lost the Democratic nomination to Barack Obama. After winning the general election, President Obama appointed her as secretary of state, where she served until 2013. In 2016, she ran for president again and became the first woman to win a major party's nomination as well as the popular vote for president, but her narrow losses in Pennsylvania, Michigan, and Wisconsin enabled Republican Donald Trump to become the forty-fifth president. Clinton titled her memoir of the 2016 campaign *What Happened*.[14]

Shortly after Ronald Reagan was inaugurated in 1981, he appointed James Buckley as under secretary of state for coordination of security assistance programs.[15] From 1982 to 1985, he led Radio Free Europe.[16] In 1985, President Reagan nominated Buckley to sit on the Washington, DC, Circuit Court of Appeals. Controversy followed Buckley here as it had throughout his 1980 campaign. Reagan initially sought to name Buckley to the Second Circuit, but both of Connecticut's senators, Lowell Weicker and Christopher Dodd, objected. Buckley was ultimately confirmed by a vote of eighty-four to eleven.[17] These appointments make Buckley one of a very small number of people to have held high positions in all three branches of the federal government.

Like James Buckley, Bill Brock had served in appointed positions in the Reagan administration. But after his 1994 loss, without a Republican president in office to appoint him to a new position, Brock turned to the private sector, where he established a consulting firm and an education technology company.[18] He is also a counselor and trustee of the Center for Strategic and International Studies.[19] In recent years, Brock has advocated for improved science, technology, engineering, and mathematics (STEM) education, sometimes alongside former Democratic National Committee chairman Roy Romer.[20]

Endicott Peabody continued to run for office after his loss to Warren Rudman. In 1992, his name appeared on New Hampshire ballots no less than three times. He ran in both the Democratic and Republican vice-presidential primaries; while he received more votes than any other candidate on the Democratic ballot, he placed a distant fourth on the Republican side, with just 181 votes (Dan Quayle, the sitting vice president, came in second).[21] That fall, Peabody and his wife, Barbara, were the Democratic candidates for two seats in the state legislature representing Hillsborough; they came in third and fourth, respectively. Peabody died of leukemia in Hollis, New Hampshire, in 1997. One month before his death, he organized a New England town meeting at the John F. Kennedy Presidential Library to advocate for a ban on the use of land mines.[22]

Alan Keyes ran for president yet again in 2008 but received little attention among a large field that included John McCain, Rudy Giuliani, Fred Thompson, and Mitt Romney, and Keyes participated in just three primary debates.[23] Following his poor showing, Keyes left the GOP to seek the nomination of the Constitution Party but was unsuccessful.[24] He then appeared on the ballot in a handful of states as an independent.[25] Following the election of Barack Obama, Keyes made much of the fact that he had run against Obama in 2004. Keyes joined a lawsuit based on the groundless conspiracy theories about Obama's birth certificate, and declared himself "the only person ever to run against Barack Obama in a truly contested election—one featuring authentic moral conservatism vs. progressive liberalism."[26] He continues to speak and write at a number of venues, including his personal website, to which only paid subscribers receive unlimited access.

Harold Ford Jr. published a political memoir in 2010 and returned to the NBC fold as a contributor to the network's political coverage. In 2015, there was speculation that he might run for mayor of New York City in 2017, but Ford made no moves toward running.[27] Following the election of 2016, Ford's name surfaced as a potential nominee to lead the Department of Transportation, but no offer from the White House ever materialized.[28]

Scott Brown remained in New Hampshire after his loss to Jeanne Shaheen. He returned to his role as a Fox News contributor and spent a few days a week assembling bicycles at Gus' Bike Shop in North Hampton, New Hampshire.[29] During the 2016 presidential primary, Brown held a series of what he dubbed "No BS Backyard Barbecues" with candidates for the Republican nomination.[30] He surprised many when he endorsed Donald Trump just before the February 2016 primary, but the endorsement paid off.[31] While Brown was passed over as a running mate for Trump in the summer of 2016 and was not, despite some early speculation, named Secretary of Veterans Affairs, on April 25, 2017 Trump nominated Brown to become the United States' ambassador to New Zealand and Samoa.[32] His nomination received the immediate, and enthusiastic, endorsements of Senators Elizabeth Warren and Jeanne Shaheen.[33]

Notes

Chapter 1

1. "Raw Video: Scott Brown Delivers Concession Speech," *WMUR.com*. November 5, 2014, http://www.wmur.com/politics/raw-video-scott-brown-delivers-concession-speech/29541380.

2. Annie Linskey, "Brown's Move to New Hampshire Fuels Talk of Senate Race," *Bloomberg.com*, December 16, 2013, http://www.bloomberg.com/news/2013-12-16/brown-s-move-to-new-hampshire-fuels-talk-of-senate-race.html.

3. Jeanne Shaheen, "Shaheen at Fundrasier," *C-SPAN*, November 16, 2013, https://www.c-span.org/video/?c4488581/shaheen-fundrasier.

4. Casey Conley, "Shaheen and Brown Agree: No West Africa Travel Ban," *Fosters.com*, October 11, 2014, http://www.fosters.com/article/20141011/gjnews_01/141019883.

5. Molly Ball, "How She Does It," *The Atlantic*. April 11, 2014, http://www.theatlantic.com/politics/archive/2014/04/how-she-does-it/360471/.

6. Kyle Trygstad and Abby Livingston, "New Hampshire: Local Republicans Skeptical on Scott Brown," *Roll Call*, April 5, 2013, http://atr.rollcall.com/new-hampshire-local-republicans-skeptical-on-scott-brown/.

7. Rossiter Johnson and John Howard Brown, *The Twentieth Century Biographical Dictionary of Notable Americans*. Vol. 9, 10 vols. (Boston: Boston Biographical Society, 1904).

8. "The Hero's Luck: Shields Nominated for the Short Term," *St. Louis Globe-Democrat*, January 16, 1879, 1; "Senator Shields," *The Daily-Register Call*, January 22, 1879, 2.

9. "Lewis, James Hamilton (1863–1939)," *Biographical Directory of the United States Congress*, accessed February 13, 2015, http://bioguide.congress.gov/scripts/biodisplay.pl?index=L000284; William H. Condon, *Life of Major-General James Shields: Hero of Three Wars and Senator from Three States* (Chicago: Press of the Blakely Printing Company, 1900).

10. "Senator for Three States," *United States Senate: Senate History*, accessed January 30, 2015. https://www.senate.gov/artandhistory/history/minute/Senator_for_three_states.htm.

11. Steven Neal, *Happy Days Are Here Again: The 1932 Democratic Convention, the Emergence of FDR—and How America Was Changed Forever* (New York: William Morrow, 2004), 203; "Lewis, James Hamilton."

Chapter 2

1. "Free-Agent Clinton Signs Five-Year, $37 Million Deal with Argentina," *The Onion,* March 17, 1998, http://www.theonion.com/articles/freeagent-clinton-signs-fiveyear-37-million-deal-w,604/.

2. Richard N. Current, *Three Carpetbag Governors* (Baton Rouge: Louisiana State University, 1967).

3. Ted Tunnell, "Creating 'the Propaganda of History': Southern Editors and the Origins of Carpetbagger and Scalawag," *The Journal of Southern History* 72, no. 4 (November 2006): 789–822.

4. Ibid., 815.

5. Current, *Three Carpetbag Governors*, xi.

6. Richard N. Current, *Those Terrible Carpetbaggers* (Oxford: Oxford University Press, 1988).

7. "The Typical Carpet-bagger," *New York Times,* December 12, 1880, 4.

8. Meyer Berger, *The Story of the New York Times, 1851–1951* (New York: Simon and Schuster, 1951).

9. "The Typical Carpet-bagger," *New York Times,* December 12, 1880, 4.

10. Martin W. Sandler, *The Letters of John F. Kennedy* (New York: Bloomsbury, 2013), 40.

11. Michael O'Brien, *John F. Kennedy: A Biography* (New York: Thomas Dunne Books, 2005), 195–96.

12. Stephen Ansolabehere and Shanto Iyengar, *Going Negative: How Attack Ads Shrink and Polarize the Electorate* (New York: Free, 1995), 100.

13. Tom LoBianco, "Foes Allege Sen. Lugar Doesn't Really Live in Ind.," *Associated Press,* February 15, 2012, http://archive.boston.com/news/politics/articles/2012/02/15/foes_allege_sen_lugar_doesnt_really_live_in_ind/.

14. Dan Carden, "Lugar Appeals Ruling That He Is Not Indiana Resident," *NWI. com,* March 21, 2012, http://www.nwitimes.com/news/local/govt-and-politics/elections/lugar-appeals-ruling-that-he-is-not-indiana-resident/article_dcd1ede5-cf1c-596a-b4e1-691b76698d68.html; Rebecca Stewart, "Lugar Beats Back Residency Challenge," *CNN Politics,* February 24, 2012, http://politicalticker.blogs.cnn.com/2012/02/24/lugar-beats-back-residency-challenge/.

15. Jonathan Martin, "Lacking a House, a Senator Is Renewing His Ties in Kansas," *New York Times,* February 7, 2014, https://www.nytimes.com/2014/02/08/us/senator-races-to-show-ties-including-an-address-in-kansas.html.

16. Joseph A. Schumpeter, *Capitalism, Socialism and Democracy* (New York: Harper Perennial Modern Classics, 2008).

17. Hanna Fenichel Pitkin, *The Concept of Representation* (Berkeley and Los Angeles, California: University of California Press, 1967).

18. Jane Mansbridge, "Should Blacks Represent Blacks and Women Represent Women? A Contingent 'Yes,'" *Journal of Politics* 61, no. 3 (August 1999): 628–57.

19. Cindy Simon Rosenthal, *Women Transforming Congress* (Norman: University of Oklahoma Press, 2003).

20. Andrew Rehfield, *The Concept of Constituency: Political Representation, Democratic Legitimacy, and Institutional Design* (New York: Cambridge University Press, 2005), 8.

21. Richard F. Fenno Jr., *Home Style: House Members in Their Districts* (Boston: Little, Brown, 1978); Morris P. Fiorina and David W. Rohde, "Richard Fenno's Research Agenda and the Study of Congress," in *Home Style and Washington Work: Studies of Congressional Politics*, ed. Morris P. Fiorina and David W. Rohde (Ann Arbor: University of Michigan Press, 1989), 1–16.

22. Fenno Jr., *Home Style*, 59.

23. Rob Gandy, "An Investigation of Politician Mobility in the United Kingdom," *British Politics* 9, no. 2 (June 2014): 182–209.

24. Sarah Childs and Philip Cowley, "The Politics of Local Presence: Is There a Case for Descriptive Representation?" *Political Studies* 59, no. 1 (March 2011): 1–19.

25. Philip Cowley, "Why Not Ask the Audience? Understanding the Public's Representational Priorities," *British Politics* 8, no. 2 (June 2013): 138–63.

26. Alexander Hamilton, James Madison, and John Jay, *The Federalist (with Letters of "Brutus")*, edited by Terence Ball (Cambridge: Cambridge University Press, 2003).

27. Joseph A. Schlesinger, *Ambition and Politics: Political Careers in the United States* (Chicago: Rand McNally, 1966).

28. David Maraniss, "Before Race Began, Clinton Resolved Pledge Not to Run," *Washington Post*, July 15, 1992, https://www.washingtonpost.com/archive/politics/1992/07/15/before-race-began-clinton-resolved-pledge-not-to-run/696cb650-3dab-4fcc-97dd-8bdcbb4b50f5/?utm_term=.2efd204bcb69.

29. Gerald Gardner, *Robert Kennedy in New York* (New York: Random House, 1965), 154.

30. Sheryl Gay Stolberg," Testing Presidential Waters as Race at Home Heats Up," *New York Times*, March 26, 2006, A26; Edward A. Lynch, *Starting Over: A Political Biography of George Allen* (Lanham, Maryland: Hamilton Books, 2011), 223.

31. Daniel J. Elazar, *American Federalism: A View from the States* (2nd) (New York: Thomas Y. Crowell, 1972).

32. Jody L. Fitzpatrick and Rodney E. Hero, "Political Culture and Political Characteristics of the American States: A Consideration of Some Old and New Questions," *Western Political Quarterly* 41, no. 1 (March 1988): 145–53.

33. Richard F. Fenno Jr., *The United States Senate: A Bicameral Perspective* (Washington, DC: American Enterprise Institute Press, 1982).

34. John Hibbing and Sara L. Brandes, "State Population and the Electoral Success of U.S. Senators," *American Journal of Political Science* 27, no. 4 (November 1983): 808–19.

35. Fenno referred to the members he wrote about in *Home Style* only by letters; later books used his subjects' actual names.

36. Fenno Jr., *Home Style*, 73.

37. Gary C. Jacobson, *The Politics of Congressional Elections* (6th) (New York: Pearson Longman, 2004).

38. Jeffrey S. Banks and D. Roderick Kiewiet, "Explaining Patterns of Competition in Congressional Elections," *American Journal of Political Science* 33, no. 4 (November 1989): 997–1015.

39. Richard F. Fenno Jr., *Senators on the Campaign Trail* (Norman and London: University of Oklahoma Press, 1996).

Chapter 3

1. "Bobby Kennedy: Is He the 'Assistant President'?" 1962.

2. Robert A. Caro, *The Years of Lyndon Johnson: The Passage of Power* (New York: Alfred A. Knopf, 2012), 61–63.

3. Ibid., 129–34.

4. Jeff Shesol, *Mutual Contempt: Lyndon Johnson, Robert Kennedy, and the Feud that Defined a Decade* (New York: W. W. Norton, 1997), 99; Caro, *The Years of Lyndon Johnson*, 243, 104.

5. Shesol, *Mutual Contempt*, 151–55.

6. Ibid., 157.

7. Ibid., 178.

8. W. Marvin Watson and Sherwin Markman, *Chief of Staff: Lyndon Johnson and His Presidency* (New York: Thomas Dunne Books-St. Martin's, 2004), 61.

9. Shesol, *Mutual Contempt*, 198.

10. Ibid., 179–81.

11. Karen Markoe, "A Short History of New York's Two Major Parties," in *New York State Today: Politics, Government, Public Policy*, 2nd ed., ed. Peter W. Colby and John Kenneth White (Albany: State University of New York Press. 1989), 69.

12. Thomas Oliphant and Curtis Wilkie, *The Road to Camelot: Inside JFK's Five-Year Campaign* (New York: Simon & Schuster, 2017).

13. R. W. Apple Jr., "Stratton Assails Race by Kennedy: Says It Shows Bankruptcy of Party Leadership," *New York Times*, August 26, 1964, 25.

14. Edward J. Silberfarb, "Kennedy No Peril to Me—Wagner," *New York Herald Tribune*, August 29, 1964.

15. Arthur M. Schlesinger Jr., *Robert Kennedy and His Times*, vol. 2 (Boston: Houghton Mifflin, 1978), 699.

16. Statement, George Backer and others to Robert F. Kennedy, August 16, 1964, box 27, folder "Correspondence," Robert F. Kennedy Senate Papers 1964–1968, John F. Kennedy Library, National Archives and Records Administration, Boston, MA.

17. Memorandum, "Kennedy and Reform," no date, box 30, folder "Keating, Kenneth," Robert F. Kennedy Senate Papers 1964–1968, John F. Kennedy Library, National Archives and Records Administration, Boston, MA.

18. Schlesinger Jr., *Robert Kennedy and His Times*, 698.

19. Memorandum, "Mr. Kennedy's Childhood," no date, box 26, folder "Kennedy, Robert F.," Robert F. Kennedy Senate Papers 1964–1968, John F. Kennedy Library, National Archives and Records Administration, Boston, MA; Manuscript by Robert F. Kennedy, "Why I Would Like to Be Senator from New York," October 7, 1964, box 20, folder "10/7/64, 'Why I Would Like to Be Senator from New York,'" *Journal-American*, Robert F. Kennedy Senate Papers 1964–1968, John F. Kennedy Library, National Archives and Records Administration, Boston, MA.

20. Memorandum, Milton Gwirtzman to Robert F. Kennedy, no date, box 37, folder "Memoranda," Robert F. Kennedy Senate Papers 1964–1968, John F. Kennedy Library, National Archives and Records Administration, Boston, MA.

21. Speech, "RFK TV Speech—Why I Am Running for Senate," no date, box 30, folder "Kennedy, Robert F.," Robert F. Kennedy Senate Papers 1964–1968, John F. Kennedy Library, National Archives and Records Administration, Boston, MA.

22. Memorandum, "Carpetbagger," no date, box 25, folder " 'Carpetbag' Issue," Robert F. Kennedy Senate Papers 1964–1968, John F. Kennedy Library, National Archives and Records Administration, Boston, MA.

23. As We See It, "Will Kennedy Claim New York Citizenship?" *Albany Times-Union*, 1964.

24. Report, "Kennedy-Johnson Accomplishments for New York," no date, box 25, folder "Kennedy-Johnson Accomplishments for New York," Robert F. Kennedy Senate Papers 1964–1968, John F. Kennedy Library, National Archives and Records Administration, Boston, MA.

25. Statement, George Backer and others to Robert F. Kennedy, August 16, 1964.

26. Fenno Jr., *Senators on the Campaign Trail*.

27. Speech, Robert F. Kennedy to New York State Democratic Convention, September 1, 1964, box 20, folder "9/1/64. Acceptance Speech for Democratic Nomination," Robert F. Kennedy Senate Papers 1964–1968, John F. Kennedy Library, National Archives and Records Administration, Boston, MA.

28. Report, "Residence in State (for H of R), Wed., Aug. 8, 1787," no date, box 25, folder " 'Carpetbag' issue," Robert F. Kennedy Senate Papers 1964–1968, John F. Kennedy Library, National Archives and Records Administration, Boston, MA.

29. Report, "Senators Born in Other States," no date, box 25, folder " 'Carpetbag' issue," Robert F. Kennedy Senate Papers 1964–1968, John F. Kennedy Library, National Archives and Records Administration, Boston, MA.

30. Speech, Robert F. Kennedy to New York State Democratic Convention.

31. Kennedy, "Why I Would Like to Be Senator from New York."

32. Ibid.

33. Gardner, *Robert Kennedy in New York*, 112.

34. Speech, Robert F. Kennedy at Madison Square Garden, October 31, 1964, box 21, folder "10/31/64, Democratic Rally Madison Square Garden," Robert F. Kennedy Senate Papers 1964–1968, John F. Kennedy Library, National Archives and Records Administration, Boston, MA.

35. Max Lerner, "N.Y. Senate Race," *New York Post*, September 27, 1964, 41.

36. Kennedy, "Why I Would Like to Be Senator from New York."

37. Speech, Robert F. Kennedy to New York State Democratic Convention.

38. Ibid.

39. Statement, George Backer and others to Robert F. Kennedy, August 16, 1964.

40. Gardner, *Robert Kennedy in New York*, 78.

41. R.W. Apple, Jr., "Kennedy Edge 6-5: Keating's Defeat Is Termed a 'Tragedy' by Rockefeller," *New York Times*, November 4, 1964, 1.

42. Speech, Thomas E. Dewey Address for Senator Keating, October 7, 1964, box 20, folder "10/7/64, Thomas E. Dewey Address for Senator Keating," Robert F. Kennedy Senate Papers 1964–1968, John F. Kennedy Library, National Archives and Records Administration, Boston, MA.

43. Transcript, WCBS-TV Interview with Senator Keating, October 27, 1964, box 21, folder "10/27/64, WCBS-T.7 Interview with Senator Keating: Transcript," Robert F. Kennedy Senate Papers 1964–1968, John F. Kennedy Library, National Archives and Records Administration, Boston, MA.

44. Transcript, WCBS-TV Interview with Senator Keating.

45. Flyer, Democrats for Keating, Johnson, & Humphrey regarding Negro vote, no date, box 30, folder "Keating's Unprincipled Bid for Ethnic Votes," Robert F. Kennedy Senate Papers 1964–1968, John F. Kennedy Library, National Archives and Records Administration, Boston, MA.

46. Flyer, N.Y. State Democratic Committee regarding myth of Keating's liberalism, no date, box 30, folder "Keating, Kenneth," Robert F. Kennedy Senate Papers 1964–1968, John F. Kennedy Library, National Archives and Records Administration, Boston, MA.

47. Speech, Thomas E. Dewey Address for Senator Keating.

48. Kennedy, "Why I Would Like to Be Senator from New York." 7.

49. "1964 Senatorial General Election Results—New York," *Dave Leip's Atlas of U.S. Presidential Elections,* accessed August 2, 2017, http://uselectionatlas.org/RESULTS/state.php?year=1964&off=3&elect=0&fips=36&f=01964 Senatorial General Election Results-New York 2014.

50. David Halberstam, "The Morning After in Keating's Suite: Dawn of Reflection," *New York Times*, November 5, 1964, 30; Warren J. Weaver, Jr., "Keating Assays Defeats in State: Says He Would Have Won if Goldwater Had Not Run," *New York Times*, November 25, 1964, 22.

Chapter 4

1. John R. Zaller, "Monica Lewinsky's Contribution to Political Science," *PS: Political Science and Politics* 31, no. 2 (June 1998): 182–89.

2. Barry C. Burden and Anthony Mughan, "Public Opinion and Hillary Rodham Clinton," *Public Opinion Quarterly* 63, no. 2 (Summer 1999): 237–50.

3. Janell Ross, "Hillary Clinton Will No Longer Be Called 'Rodham.' Here's Her Complicated History with Her Maiden Name," *Washington Post*, November 30, 2015, https://www.washingtonpost.com/news/the-fix/wp/2015/11/19/the-fascinating-history-of-when-hillary-clinton-has-chosen-to-use-her-maiden-name/; Lauren Easton, "Updating AP style on Hillary Clinton," Associated Press—Announcements, November 30, 2015, https://blog.ap.org/announcements/updating-ap-style-on-hillary-clinton.

4. Michael Tomasky, *Hillary's Turn: Inside Her Improbable, Victorious Senate Campaign* (New York: Free, 2001), 37.

5. Judith S. Trent and Cady Short-Thompson, "From First Lady to United States Senator: The Role and Power of Image in the Transmorgifying of Hillary Rodham Clinton," in *Images, Scandal, and Communication Strategies of the Clinton Presidency* (Praeger Series in Presidential Studies), ed. Robert E. Jr. Denton and Rachel L. Holloway (Westport, CT: Praeger Publishers, 2003), 113.

6. Ibid., 117.

7. "Millennium Council—Save America's Treasures 2000," Clinton White House Website Archives, accessed September 4, 2015, https://clintonwhitehouse4.archives.gov/WH/EOP/First_Lady/html/treasures/index2.html.

8. Jeffrey C. Kraus, "Case: Showdown in the Empire State—Clinton versus Lazio," in *Campaigns and Elections: Issues, Concepts, Cases*, ed. Robert P. Watson and Colton C. Campbell (Boulder, Colorado: Lynne Rienner, 2003), 229; Tomasky, *Hillary's Turn*, 33–34.

9. David Kaufer, Shawn J. Parry-Giles, and Beata Beigman Klebanov, "The "image bite," political language, and the public/private divide," *Journal of Language and Politics* 11, no. 3 (November 2012): 336–356.

10. David Axelrod, *Believer: My Forty Years in Politics* (New York City: Penguin Press, 2015), 115.

11. Tomasky, *Hillary's Turn*, 49.

12. Ibid., 290.

13. Ibid., 35–36.

14. Geraldine Baum, "Hillary Clinton's Campaign Off to Pastoral Start," *Los Angeles Times*, July 8, 1999, 12.

15. Jayson Blair, "Senator Moynihan Objects to Being Spliced in Step with Lazio," *New York Times*, July 26, 2000, B5.

16. David L. Brown and Stefan Rayer, "The Volume and Composition of Internal Migration to and from New York," in *New York State in the 21st Century*, ed. Thomas A. Hirschl and Tim B. Heaton (Santa Barbara, CA: Praeger), 230.

17. Jeffrey M. Stonecash, "Political Parties and Partisan Conflict," in *Governing New York State*, ed. Jeffrey M. Stonecash, John Kenneth White, and Peter W. Colby (Albany: State University of New York Press, 1994), 84.

18. Paul Riede, "Ed Koch and 'Gingham Dresses': Upstate Never Forgets," *Syracuse Post-Standard*, February 1, 2013.

19. Teri Weaver, "Syracuse, New York Leaders React to Death of NYC Mayor Ed Koch," *Syracuse Post-Standard*, February 1, 2013.

20. Derek Rose, "Irish Eyes Will Be Smiling On . . . ," *New York Daily News*, March 10, 2001, 10.

21. Thomas J. Lueck, "Mrs. Clinton Explains Kiss in Middle East," *New York Times*, July 14, 2000, B4.

22. "Does Hillary Agree with Suha?" *New York Post*, November 23, 1999, 28.

23. Tomasky, *Hillary's Turn*, 123.

24. Damian Whitworth, "Hillary Clinton Losing Support among Women: The Decline in the Polls Could Lead to Her Defeat in the N.Y. Senate Race," *Vancouver Sun*, February 24, 2000, A16; Lenore Skenazy, "Hil Has Woman Troubles, Too," *New York Daily News*, April 5, 2000, 35.

25. Tomasky, *Hillary's Turn*, 39.

26. Andrew D. Wolvin, "Listening Leadership: Hillary Clinton's Listening Tour," *International Journal of Listening* 19, no. 1 (2005): 34.

27. Ibid., 35.

28. Anne Gearan, "Mrs. Clinton may find tough crowd in upstate New York," *The Argus-Press*, July 8, 1999, 15.

29. Andrew D. Wolvin, "Listening Leadership: Hillary Clinton's Listening Tour," *International Journal of Listening* 19, no. 1 (2005): 34.

30. Tomasky, *Hillary's Turn*, 179.

31. Karrin Vasby Anderson, "From Spouses to Candidates: Hillary Rodham Clinton, Elizabeth Dole, and the Gendered Office of U.S. President," *Rhetoric & Public Affairs* 5, no. 1 (Spring 2002): 105–32.

32. Erica Scharrer, "An 'Improbable Leap': A Content Analysis of Newspaper Coverage of Hillary Clinton's Transition from First Lady to Senate Candidate," *Journalism Studies* 3, no. 3 (2002): 398.

33. Katherine Q. Seelye, "Mrs. Clinton May Steal Mayor's Yankee Fan Base," *New York Times*, June 11, 1999, B1.

34. Joe Mahoney, "Rick Takes Homegrown Approach to Lure Women," *New York Daily News*, October 21, 2000, 6.

35. There were many polls on this issue, but the Marist data has the twin virtues of covering the entirety of the campaign and using the same question wording in each survey.

36. Trent and Short-Thompson, 128.

37. Grant C. Cos and Brian J. Snee, "New York, New York: Being and Creating Identity in the 2000 New York State Senate Race," *American Behavioral Scientist* 44, no. 12 (August 2001): 2018.

38. Ibid., 2026.

39. Steve Kornacki, "The Clintons Take New York," *Politico New York*, December 11, 2013, https://www.politico.com/states/new-york/albany/story/2013/12/the-clintons-take-new-york-067223.

40. "New York," 2000 U.S. Senate Results, Federal Election Commission, https://transition.fec.gov/pubrec/fe2000/2000senate.htm#NY.

41. "Hillary Clinton Elected to Senate From New York," *New York Times*, November 8, 2000, http://www.nytimes.com/2000/11/08/politics/hillary-clinton-elected-to-senate-from-new-york.html.

42. "2000 Presidential General Election Results—New York," *Dave Leip's Atlas of U.S. Presidential Elections*, accessed August 14, 2017, http://uselectionatlas.org/RESULTS/state.php?fips=36&year=2000.

43. Kraus, "Case: Showdown in the Empire State—Clinton versus Lazio," 236.

Chapter 5

1. Special to the *New York Times*, "Buckley Waging First Campaign in State Where He Was Raised," *New York Times*, September 10, 1980, B6.

2. Gerald Sirkin and Natalie Sirkin, "The Unplanned Admirable Life of James Buckley," *Connecticut Commentary: Red Notes from a Blue State,* February 26, 2007, http://donpesci.blogspot.com/2007/02/.

3. Timothy J. Sullivan, *New York State and the Rise of Modern Conservatism: Redrawing Party Lines* (Albany: State University of New York Press, 2009).

4. Leslie Bennetts, "Buckley Stressing 'Emotional Roots' in Connecticut Campaign for Senate," *New York Times*, June 14, 1980, 25.

5. Rachelle Patterson, "GOP: Senate Can Be Ours," *Boston Globe*, October 25, 1979, 6.

6. Richard L. Madden, "A Senator and His Party Boss at Loggerheads in Connecticut," *New York Times*, February 18, 1979, E6.

7. Robert G. Kaiser, "Sen. Ribicoff Announces Retirement," *Washington Post*, May 4, 1979, A3.

8. Ibid.; Madden, "A Senator and His Party Boss at Loggerheads in Connecticut," E6.

9. Diane Henry, "Kissinger Holds Hartford Parley on Senate Race: Discusses Joining Contest for G.O.P. Nomination," *New York Times*, February 7, 1979, B2.

10. Richard Madden, "POLITICS: A Hungry G.O.P. Eyes the Senate Race," *New York Times*, June 24, 1979, CN16.

11. Steven Slosberg, "Buckley Assesses Chances in State," *The Day*, January 3, 1980, 1; Clyde Haberman and Albin Krebs, "Notes on People: James Buckley Shifts Registration to Connecticut," *New York Times*, August 24, 1979, B5.

12. Madden, "POLITICS: A Hungry G.O.P. Eyes the Senate Race," CN16.

13. Richard L. Madden, "Buckley Confronts 'Carpetbagger' Issue," *New York Times*, December 16, 1979, CN26.

14. Matthew L. Wald, "James Buckley Weighs Senate Bid," *New York Times*, November 2, 1979, B4.

15. Richard L. Madden, "Buckley and the '80 Senate Race," *New York Times*, September 2, 1979: CN20.

16. Ibid.; "Buckley To Attend Fund-Raiser," *The Hartford Courant*, September 6, 1979, 217. Wald, "James Buckley Weighs Senate Bid," B4.

18. Associated Press, "Connecticut Legislator Opens G.O.P. Contest fora U.S. Senate Seat: Ribicoff Stepping Down," *New York Times*, December 2, 1979: 55.

19. Richard L. Madden and Matthew L. Wald, "Talking Politics: James L. Buckley," *New York Times*, June 22, 1980, CN1.

20. "AROUND THE WORLD: Republican Eyes Senate Anew," *The Globe and Mail*, December 12, 1979, 20.

21. Richard L. Madden, "James Buckley Says He Will Run for Ribicoff's Seat in U.S. Senate," *New York Times*, December 12, 1979, A1.

22. Richard L. Madden, "Buckley Confronts 'Carpetbagger' Issue," *New York Times*, December 16, 1979, CN26.

23. Diane Henry, "Kissinger Holds Hartford Parley on Senate Race: Discusses Joining Contest for G.O.P. Nomination," *New York Times*, February 7, 1979, B2.

24. Edward C. Burks, "Weicker, Still an Unrepentant Maverick: Weicker Weathers 'Winds of Sentiment,'" *New York Times*, August 12, 1979, CN1.

25. Steven Slosberg, "Buckley Assesses Chances in State," *The Day*, January 3, 1980, 1.

26. Weicker was always willing to speak his mind, but his exceptional candor in this case may have stemmed from his feud with William F. Buckley Jr., which dated back to their undergraduate days as members of the Yale Political Union. Weicker's ongoing opposition to James Buckley's campaign only exacerbated the feud and contributed to the Buckleys' formation of a political action committee to back Democrat Joe Lieberman over Weicker in 1988 (May 1988). Weicker's loss did not put the feud to rest; in 2007, William F. Buckley Jr. speculated that his brother might be drafted to run for the Connecticut Senate seat that would open in 2012 if Chris Dodd's presidential campaign went poorly enough to end Dodd's Senate career (Buckley 2007). Buckley was prescient about the end of Dodd's Senate career, but the prophesied draft movement never emerged.

27. Richard L. Madden, "G.O.P. Senate Race Closer Than Expected: Both Contestants Have Delegates to Force Primary Bozzuto and Buckley In Tight G.O.P. Race," *New York Times*, June 15, 1980, CN1.

28. Richard L. Madden, "Buckley Confronts 'Carpetbagger' Issue," *New York Times*, December 16, 1979, CN26.

29. Madden, "G.O.P. Senate Race Closer Than Expected," CN1.

30. Matthew L. Wald, "A Foe of Buckley Is Confident: Buckley's Foe in G.O.P. Says He Expects to Win," *New York Times*, July 22, 1980, B1.

31. Barrett, "It's Conservative vs. Conservative in Connecticut."

32. Wald, "A Foe of Buckley Is Confident," B1.

33. Associated Press, "Connecticut Legislator Opens G.O.P. Contest for a U.S. Senate Seat: Ribicoff Stepping Down," *New York Times*, December 2, 1979, 55.

34. Madden, "G.O.P. Senate Race Closer Than Expected," CN1.

35. Wald, "A Foe of Buckley Is Confident," B1.

36. Associated Press, "Connecticut Legislator Opens G.O.P. Contest," 55.

37. Matthew L. Wald, "Talking Politics: Richard C. Bozzuto: The Candidates on the Issues," *New York Times*, June 15, 1980, CN1.

38. Madden, "G.O.P. Senate Race Closer Than Expected," CN1.

39. Madden and Wald, "Talking Politics," CN1.

40. Wald, "Talking Politics," CN1.

41. Leslie Bennetts, "Buckley Stressing 'Emotional Roots' in Connecticut Campaign for Senate," *New York Times*, June 14, 1980, 25.

42. Madden and Wald, "Talking Politics," CN1; Richard L. Madden, "McKinney Tells Why He Is Backing Buckley for Senate," *New York Times*, May 25, 1980, CN20.

43. Nancy M. Tracy, "Senate Race Down to the Wire: James Buckley," *Fairpress*, October 29, 1980, A1, A6.

44. Matthew L. Wald, "Bozzuto vs. Buckley: Issues and Nonissues," *New York Times*, August 10, 1980, CN24.

45. Jacqueline Huard, "Weicker Reaffirms His Support of Bozzuto," *The Hour*, August 5, 1980, 3.

46. Ibid.

47. Richard L. Madden, "Factors Behind Buckley Victory: G.O.P. Convention: A Primary Warmup," *New York Times*, August 3, 1980, CN1.

48. "Buckley wins Conn. GOP vote," *Boston Globe,* July 27, 1980, 29.

49. Huard, "Weicker Reaffirms His Support of Bozzuto," 3.

50. Chris Black, "In US Senate Race in Ct., Ethnic Vote Is Crucial," *Boston Globe*, September 1, 1980, 25.

51. Tracy, "Senate Race Down to the Wire," A1, A6; David Lieberman, "Connecticut: Buckley Woos the Blues," *The New Republic*, October 10, 1980.

52. Black, "In US Senate race in Ct., Ethnic Vote Is Crucial," 25.

53. Tracy, "Senate Race Down to the Wire, A1, A6.

54. Lieberman, "Connecticut," 13.

55. Wald, "Dodd Makes Bid forNomination to Ribicoff Post: Kennedy Backer Modifies Opposition to Carter," *New York Times*, January 10: B2.

56. Lieberman, "Connecticut," 13.

57. Black, "In US Senate Race in Ct., Ethnic Vote Is Crucial," 25; Richard L. Madden, "Buckley Pleads for G.O.P. Unity in Contest against Dodd," *New York Times*, September 11, 1980, B4.

58. Black, "Buckley Fights to Close Gap with Dodd," *Boston Globe*, October 22, 1980 24.

59. Matthew L. Wald, "Buckley and Dodd Take Up Positions," *New York Times*, September 21, 1980, CN1.

60. Black, "In US Senate Race in Ct., Ethnic Vote Is Crucial," 25.

61. George B. Merry, "Classic Connecticut Battle: Buckley vs. Dodd," *Christian Science Monitor*, October 28, 1980, http://www.csmonitor.com/1980/1028/102837.html.

62. Richard L. Madden, "Buckley and Dodd Sharpen Senate Campaign Barbs," *New York Times*, October 17, 1980, B2.

63. Madden, "Buckley Confronts 'Carpetbagger' Issue," CN26.

64. Madden, "Buckley Pleads for G.O.P. Unity in Contest against Dodd," B4.

65. Richard L. Madden, "A Buckley-Dodd Debate Emphasizes Differences," *New York Times*, September 16, 1980, B1.

66. "1980 Senatorial General Election Results—Connecticut," *Dave Leip's Atlas of U.S. Presidential Elections,* accessed May 23, 2017, https://uselectionatlas.org/RESULTS/state.php?fips=9&year=1980&f=0&off=3&elect=0.

67. Stan DeCoster, "Buckley Was Gracious to the End," *The Day*, November 5, 1980, 5.

68. Jeffrey William Burris, "The Senatorial Election of 1970: Brock vs. Gore" (Honors thesis, University of Tennessee Knoxville, 1994).

69. Gerald R. Ford, *A Time to Heal: The Autobiography of Gerald R. Ford* (New York: Harper & Row, 1979), 143.

70. David M. Brodsky and and Robert H. Swansbrough, "Tennessee: A House Divided," in *The 1988 Presidential Election in the South: Continuity Amidst Change in Southern Party Politics*, ed. Laurence W. Moreland, Robert P. Steed, and Tod A. Baker (New York: Praeger, 1991), 204.

71. Charles Babington, "Brock, Sarbanes Launch All-Out Attacks; Tense Moments, Accusations Define Maryland Candidates' First Debate," *Washington Post*, October 20, 1994, C1.

72. "Governor Bill Brock?" *Baltimore Sun*, February 1, 1993, http://articles.baltimoresun.com/1993-02-01/news/1993032037_1_republican-candidates-maryland-gop-bill-brock.

73. C. Fraser Smith, "Maryland GOP May End Up Doing the Tennessee Waltz," *Baltimore Sun*, February 3, 1993, http://articles.baltimoresun.com/1993-02-03/news/1993034135_1_maryland-gop-maryland-republican-party-bill-brock.

74. "Governor Bill Brock?" *Baltimore Sun*, February 1, 1993, http://articles.baltimoresun.com/1993-02-01/news/1993032037_1_republican-candidates-maryland-gop-bill-brock.

75. Frank Langfitt, "GOP Candidates Narrow Sarbanes' Lead for Senate," *Baltimore Sun*, July 21, 1994, http://articles.baltimoresun.com/1994-07-21/news/1994202016_1_yesterday-poll-sarbanes-republican-candidates.

76. "GOP: Grand Old Pot-shotters," *Baltimore Sun*, September 2, 1994, http://articles.baltimoresun.com/1994-09-02/news/1994245178_1_bill-brock-pierpont-franks.

77. Charles Babington, "Montgomery Lawyer Joins Senate Race," *Washington Post*, April 6, 1994, B7.

78. Charles Babington, "GOP Senate Candidate in Maryland Attacks Brock, Sarbanes in Ad Debut," *Washington Post*, April 16, 1994, B5.

79. Babington, "Montgomery Lawyer Joins Senate Race," B7.

80. Frank Langfitt, "After Taking Many Blows, Brock Strikes Back at Aron," *Baltimore Sun*, September 9, 1994, http://articles.baltimoresun.com/1994-09-08/news/1994251044_1_bill-brock-aron-term-limits.

81. "Aron's Failed Lawsuit 1994 Senate Primary: Unsuccessful Candidate Sought Limits on What Opponents Can Say," *Baltimore Sun*, March 15, 1996, http://articles.baltimoresun.com/1996-03-15/news/1996075083_1_aron-brock-ruthann.

82. Frank Langfitt, "Brock Leads Senate Race, Polls Show," *Baltimore Sun*, September 10, 1994, http://articles.baltimoresun.com/1994-09-10/news/1994253040_1_bill-brock-aron-unfavorable-rating.

83. Charles Babington, "Sarbanes Account Full; Brock's Cash Dwindles; Challenger Spends on Staff, Volunteer Organizing," *Washington Post*, July 16, 1994, D4.

84. Charles Babington, "Senate Race Lacks Issue to Rouse Voters; While Sarbanes Lies Low, Brock Leaves Some Confused about His Message," *Washington Post*, October 15, 1994, B1.

85. Charles Babington, "Sarbanes Disputes the Theory of Relative Senate Success," *Washington Post*, October 24, 1994, D1.

86. Michael Olesker, "Brock's Record Mostly a Secret to Marylanders," *Baltimore Sun*, October 2, 1994, http://articles.baltimoresun.com/1994-10-02/news/1994275068_1_make-brock-bill-brock-new-brock.

87. Frank Langfitt, "Brock Trails Sarbanes, Despite Heavy Spending," *Baltimore Sun*, November 5, 1994, http://articles.baltimoresun.com/1994-11-05/news/1994309044_1_bill-brock-sarbanes-brock-looked.

88. Charles Babington, "Brock, Sarbanes Launch All-Out Attacks; Tense Moments, Accusations Define Maryland Candidates' First Debate," *Washington Post*, October 20, 1994, C1.

89. Charles Babington, "U.S. SENATE; Political Veterans Differ on Views," *Washington Post*, November 3, 1994, M1.

90. Babington, "Brock, Sarbanes Launch All-Out Attacks," C1.

91. Babington, "Senate Race Lacks Issue to Rouse Voters," B1.

92. Frank Langfitt, "Sarbanes Sweeps to 4th Term; Brock Says He Has No Regrets," *Baltimore Sun*, November 9, 1994, http://articles.baltimoresun.com/1994-11-09/news/1994313162_1_sarbanes-maryland-republicans-brock.

93. Babington, "Brock, Sarbanes Launch All-Out Attacks," C1.

94. Ibid.

95. "Sauerbrey Close Brock Not," *Baltimore Sun*, September 29, 1994, http://articles.baltimoresun.com/1994-09-29/news/1994272094_1_sauerbrey-glendening-brock.

96. Babington, "Senate Race Lacks Issue to Rouse Voters," B1.

97. Ibid.; Frank Langfitt, "Brock Television Ads Call Sarbanes Soft on Crime," *Baltimore Sun*, October 13, 1994, http://articles.baltimoresun.com/1994-10-13/news/1994286043_1_senator-sarbanes-bill-brock-soft-on-crime.

98. Babington, "Brock, Sarbanes Launch All-Out Attacks," C1.

99. Langfitt, "Brock Trails Sarbanes, Despite Heavy Spending."

100. "Sauerbrey Close Brock Not."

101. John T. Willis and Herbert C. Smith, *Maryland Politics and Government: Democratic Dominance* (Lincoln: University of Nebraska Press, 2012).

Chapter 6

1. Dennis King, *Lyndon LaRouche and the New American Fascism* (New York: Doubleday, 1989), 102–103.

2. This is, perhaps, why Peabody was not much of a factor in Milton Gwirtzman's evaluation of the 1964 governor's race as an option for Robert Kennedy's political future.

3. "Endicott Peabody: Endicott 'Chub' Peabody, a Quixote of Politics, Died on December 2nd, Aged 77," *The Economist*, December 11, 1997, https://www.economist.com/node/109195.

4. Charles Brereton, "A Look at Endicott Peabody," *Nashua Telegraph*, April 22, 1986, 22.

5. Jane F. Taylor, "Mrs. Endicott Peabody Explains Why Her Husband Seeks Vice Presidency," *Nashua Telegraph*, February 29, 1972, 20.

6. Peabody's vote in the vice presidential primary exceeded the 33,007 votes won by second-place finisher and eventual nominee George McGovern in the presidential primary (New Hampshire Public Radio n.d.).

7. Brereton, "A Look at Endicott Peabody," 22.

8. Rod Paul, "Should Attorney General Be Elected?" *Nashua Telegraph*, May 22, 1984, 28.

9. "N.H. Democrats Seek Dignity," *Nashua Telegraph*, April 13, 1986, A10.

10. Steve Sakson, "Mayor Has 'No Intention' Of Running This Year," *Nashua Telegraph*, April 10, 1986, 64.

11. Michael Mokrzycki, "Bruno Challenges Rudman To Limit Campaign Spending," *Nashua Telegraph*, April 12, 1986, 1.

12. Rod Paul, "Endicott Peabody 'Never Considered the Possibility of Being out of Politics,'" *Nashua Telegraph*, June 4, 1986, 34.

13. "Robert L. Dupay," NHPR State of Democracy, accessed March 16, 2016, http://nh.electionstats.com/candidates/view/Robert-L-Dupay.

14. Steve Sakson, "Peabody Asked to Run against Sen. Rudman," *Nashua Telegraph*, April 4, 1986, 12.

15. Steve Sakson, "Rudman Campaign Chest 6 Times Opponents' Combined," *Nashua Telegraph*, August 28, 1986, 16.

16. Joann Goslin, "Candidate Dupay Says Nuclear Issue Top Priority," *Nashua Telegraph*, July 20, 1986, 36.

17. "Tucker to Seek Re-Election," United Press International, June 4, 1986, https://www.upi.com/Archives/1986/06/04/Tucker-to-seek-re-election/1505518241600/.

18. Sakson, "Peabody Asked to Run against Sen. Rudman," 12.

19. Ibid.

20. Richard March, "Democrats Warn against LaRouche 'Nazi' Movement," United Press International, August 29, 1986, https://www.upi.com/Archives/1986/08/28/Democrats-warn-against-LaRouche-Nazi-movement/9845525585600/.

21. "1986 U.S. Senate Democratic Primary," NHPR State of Democracy, accessed May 23, 2016, http://nh.electionstats.com/elections/view/60451/.

22. Warren B. Rudman, *Combat: Twelve Years in the U.S. Senate* (New York: Random House, 1996), 65.

23. Steve Sakson, "Rudman Campaign Chest 6 Times Opponents' Combined," 16.

24. Ibid.

25. Paul, "Endicott Peabody 'Never Considered the Possibility of Being out of Politics,'" 34.

26. Claude R. Marx, "Gloves Come Off in State Campaigns: Gramm Visits Nashua with Rudman to Aid Campaign," *Nashua Telegraph*, October 16, 1986, 12.

27. Clay F. Richards, "Negative Ads a Big Factor in '86 Campaigns," United Press International, October 31, 1986, https://www.upi.com/Archives/1986/10/31/Negative-ads-a-big-factor-in-86-campaigns/8936531118800/.

28. Steve Gerstel, "Sleepers Could Pull Some Senate Surprises," United Press International, October 30, 1986, https://www.upi.com/Archives/1986/10/30/Sleepers-could-pull-some-Senate-surprises/3943531032400/.

29. "1986 U.S. Senate General Election," NHPR State of Democracy, accessed May 23, 2016, http://nh.electionstats.com/elections/view/60604/.

30. Bernard Schoenburg, "Rauschenberger Won't Run; Drafting Ditka for Senate Race Excites Some in GOP," *The State Journal-Register*, July 9, 2004, 1; Kevin McDermott, "Ryan Fiasco Adds to Burden of Struggling Illinois GOP," *St. Louis Post-Dispatch*, June 27, 2004.

31. Liam Ford and Rudolf Bush, "Ryan Quits Race: State GOP Scrambles to Find Replacement to Face Obama; Republican Senate Nominee Cites Fixation on Divorce Files," *Chicago Tribune*, June 26, 2004, http://www.chicagotribune.com/chi-0406260116jun26-story.html.

32. Brendan Koerner, "Why Unseal Ryan's Divorce Papers?" *Slate*, June 23, 2004, http://www.slate.com/articles/news_and_politics/explainer/2004/06/why_unseal_ryans_divorce_papers.html.

33. Monica Davey, "The 2004 Campaign: The Illinois Primary; From Crowded Field, Democrats Choose State Legislator to Seek Senate Seat," *New York Times*, March

17, 2004, http://www.nytimes.com/2004/03/17/us/2004-campaign-illinois-primary-crowded-field-democrats-choose-state-legislator.html.

34. Eric Krol, "Ryan Denies Sex Club Claim Senate Hopeful Insists He Won't Quit over Ex-Wife's Allegations," *Chicago Daily Herald*, June 22, 2004, 1.

35. Ibid.

36. Eric Krol, "Ryan Event Canceled When Hastert Bails Out; Spokesman Says Candidacy Not in Trouble," *Chicago Daily Herald*, June 24, 2004, 1.

37. Hastert was later revealed to be a serial child molester; the reader is invited to reflect on the irony of Hastert playing a role in forcing Jack Ryan out of the race over a sex scandal in which no one actually had any sex.

38. Eric Krol, "Facing 'Brutal' Campaign, Ryan Quits GOP Leaders Breathe Sigh of Relief, Begin Search for Replacement," *Chicago Daily Herald*, June 26, 2004 1.

39. Ford and Bush, "Ryan Quits Race."

40. Eric Krol and John Patterson, "Top Prospects Won't Take Ryan's Place," *Chicago Daily Herald*, June 26, 2004, 5.

41. Stephen Kinzer, "Candidate, under Pressure, Quits Senate Race in Illinois," *New York Times*, June 26, 2004, Late Edition, A8.

42. Schoenburg, "Rauschenberger Won't Run," 1.

43. Eric Krol, "Gidwitz Bows Out, But GOP May Have Another Senate Option," *Chicago Daily Herald*, July 2, 2004, 13.

44. Eric Krol, "Salvi Says No To Senate Race Unless Bush Calls," *Chicago Daily Herald*, July 22, 2004, 1.

45. Eric Krol and John Patterson, "Political Glare Too Harsh for Ditka," *Chicago Daily Herald*, July 15, 2004, 1.

46. Eric Krol, "A Political Campaign Would Put a Halt to Mike Ditka's Lucrative Endorsements and ESPN Gig, Making a Run for the Senate . . . a Costly Venture," *Chicago Daily Herald*, July 14, 2004, 1.

47. Bernard Schoenburg, "Ryan out of the Running; GOP Works on Recovering from Scandal," *The State Journal-Register*, June 24, 2004, 1.

48. Monica Davey, "In a Star's Shadow, Republicans Strain to Find Opponent," *New York Times*, July 29, 2004, P6.

49. Stephen Kinzer, "Ex-Coach Won't Run for Senate, and G.O.P. Woes Grow in Illinois," *New York Times*, July 15, 2004, A14.

50. "A Bear Market for Republicans," *The State Journal-Register*, July 14, 2004, 6.

51. Jo Napolitano, "Illinois G.O.P. Finally Picks a Candidate," *New York Times*, August 5, 2004, A17.

52. Eric Krol, "GOP List Down to a Surprising Pair: Former Bush Anti-Drug Official and Radio Talk Show Host from Maryland Up for Senate Candidacy," *Chicago Daily Herald*, August 4, 2004, 1.

53. Kevin McDermott, "Keyes May Expose GOP Rift: 'If Jim Edgar or Jim Thompson Don't Like the Choice, They Should Have Stepped Forward and Given Us

a (Expletive) Candidate!,'" *St. Louis Post-Dispatch*, August 8, 2004, Sunday Five Star Late Lift Edition ed, B06.

54. Eric Krol, "Keyes Makes GOP Wait; Maryland Conservative Gets the Offer, but He Delays Commitment," *Chicago Daily Herald*, August 5, 2004, 1.

55. Rick Pearson and John Chase, "How Illinois Gop Imploded," *Chicago Tribune*, January 16, 2005, 1.

56. Colin Devenish, *Rage against the Machine* (New York: St. Martin's Griffin, 2001), 128.

57. Ron Strom, "MSNBC Pulling Plug on Keyes," *WorldNetDaily*, June 19, 2002, http://www.wnd.com/2002/06/14279/.

58. Krol, "Keyes makes GOP wait," 1.

59. Kevin McDermott, "Illinois GOP Narrows Senate List to Two," *St. Louis Post-Dispatch*, August 4, 2004, Five Star Edition, A01.

60. Kevin McDermott, "Illinois Republicans Pick Keyes as Senate Candidate," *St. Louis Post-Dispatch*, August 5, 2004, Five Star Late Lift Edition, B02.

61. Juliet Eilperin, "Keyes to Face Obama In U.S. Senate Race; Ill. Election to Ensure Nation's 5th Black Senator," *Washington Post*, August 9, 2004, A08.

62. Kevin McDermott, "Keyes Enters Senate Contest," *St. Louis Post-Dispatch*, August 9, 2004, Five Star Lift Edition, A01.

63. Krol, "Keyes Makes GOP Wait," 1.

64. Patrick Waldron, "Hastert Says He'll Back Keyes' Senate Campaign," *Chicago Daily Herald*, August 7, 2004, 3.

65. "Nothing against Keyes, but How about an Illinoisan?" *Chicago Daily Herald*, August 5, 2004, 14.

66. "Plan B for Illinois," *New York Times*, August 10, 2004, 20.

67. "The GOP's Rent-A-Senator," *Chicago Tribune*, August 6, 2004, http://articles.chicagotribune.com/2004-08-06/news/0408060313_1_mr-keyes-judy-baar-topinka-alan-keyes.

68. Jennifer Skalka and Ofelia Casillas, "Keyes Takes Jabs at His Own Party," *Chicago Tribune*, September 1, 2004, http://articles.chicagotribune.com/2004-09-01/news/0409010139_1_mr-keyes-selfish-hedonist-keyes-comments.

69. "Keyes Left off Illinois GOP Flier," *Chicago Tribune*, October 21, 2004, 33.

70. Rick Pearson, "Keyes, State GOP Gearing Up Blame Campaign," *Chicago Tribune*, September 5, 2004, 6.

71. John Kass, "Keyes' Antics Just What GOP Old Guard Wants," *Chicago Tribune*, September 5, 2004, A1–A2.

72. Liam Ford and David Mendell, "Keyes Sets Up House in Cal City," *Chicago Tribune*, August 13, 2004, http://articles.chicagotribune.com/2004-08-13/news/0408130201_1_senate-candidate-alan-keyes-obama-senate-sen-peter-fitzgerald.

73. Kevin McDermott, "Keyes Enters Senate Contest," *St. Louis Post-Dispatch*, August 9, 2004, Five Star Lift Edition, A01.

74. John Chase and Liam Ford, "Senate Debate Turns Personal," *Chicago Tribune*, October 22, 2004, 1.

75. "Keyes Vows More Provocative Campaigning," United Press International, September 14, 2004, http://www.upi.com/Top_News/2004/09/14/Keyes-vows-more-provocative-campaigning/77071095186946/.

76. John S. Jackson, "The Making of a Senator: Barack Obama and the 2004 Illinois Senate Race" (Southern Illinois University Carbondale, the Simon Review: Occasional Papers of the Paul Simon Public Policy Institute, 2006).

77. "CNN.com Election Results: U.S. Senate Illinois Exit Polls 2004," CNN.com, accessed August 16, 2016, http://www.cnn.com/ELECTION/2004/pages/results/states/IL/S/01/epolls.0.html.

78. Jackson, "The Making of a Senator: Barack Obama and the 2004 Illinois Senate Race."

79. "2006 Senatorial General Election Results—Tennessee," *Dave Leip's Atlas of U.S. Presidential Elections*, accessed August 16, 2017, http://uselectionatlas.org/RESULTS/state.php?fips=47&year=2006&f=0&off=3&elect=0&class=1.

80. Bill Dries, "Ford on Governor's Race: 'Not the Right Time,'" *The Daily News*, April 15, 2009, https://www.memphisdailynews.com/news/2009/apr/15/ford-on-governors-race-not-the-right-time.

81. Michael M. Grynbaum, "Spitzer Resigns, Citing Personal Failings," *New York Times*, March 12, 2008, http://www.nytimes.com/2008/03/12/nyregion/12cnd-resign.html.

82. Peter Baker and Helene Cooper, "Clinton Set for State Dept., Fed Official for Treasury: Ex-Rivals Uniting," *New York Times*, November 22, 2008, A1.

83. Nicholas Confessore and Danny Hakim, "Kennedy Drops Bid for Senate Seat, Citing Personal Reasons," *New York Times*, January 21, 2009, http://www.nytimes.com/2009/01/22/nyregion/22caroline.html.

84. Danny Hakim and Nicholas Confessore, "Paterson Picks Gillibrand for Senate Seat," *New York Times*, January 24, 2009, http://www.nytimes.com/2009/01/24/nyregion/24senator.html.

85. Ibid.

86. Mike Madden, "Blanche Lincoln Stuns Bill Halter," *Salon*, June 9, 2010, http://www.salon.com/2010/06/09/bill_halter_blanche_lincoln_runoff/.

87. Jackson Baker, "Harold Ford's Imperfect Storm," *Memphis Flyer*, November 8, 2006, http://www.memphisflyer.com/memphis/harold-fords-imperfect-storm/Content?oid=1131123.

88. Melissa Russo, "NRA Shoots Down Gillibrand's 'Grade,'" *NBC New York*, September 29, 2010, http://www.nbcnewyork.com/news/local/NRA-Shoots-Down-Kirsten-Gillibrands-Rating—104050029.html.

89. Eve Fairbanks, "150 Minutes with Carolyn McCarthy," *New York*, February 15, 2009, http://nymag.com/news/intelligencer/encounter/54343/.

90. Michelle Norris, "Democratic Rep. McCarthy Blasts Gillibrand Pick," National Public Radio, January 23, 2009, http://www.npr.org/templates/story/story.php?storyId=99816999.

91. "Congressman Israel Will Not Run for Senate," *Plainview Old Bethpage Herald*, May 21, 2009, http://plainviewoldbethpageherald.com/2009/05/21/congressman-israel-will-not-run-for-senate/; Aaron Blake, "Serrano, McCarthy Say No to Gillibrand Challenge," *The Hill*, August 10, 2009, http://thehill.com/homenews/campaign/54223-serrano-mccarthy-say-no-to-gillibrand-challenge; Reid Pillifant, "The Last Gillibrand Fighter," *Observer*, November 9, 2009, http://observer.com/2009/11/the-last-gillibrand-fighter/.

92. Associated Press, "Rural Senator-to-Be Visits Harlem," *Denver Post*, January 24, 2009, http://www.denverpost.com/2009/01/24/rural-senator-to-be-visits-harlem/.

93. Ben Terris, "Kirsten Gillibrand's Improbable Path to Liberal Stardom," *The Atlantic*, October 26, 2013, http://www.theatlantic.com/politics/archive/2013/10/kirsten-gillibrands-improbable-path-to-liberal-stardom/280872/.

94. Eric Kleefeld, "Gillibrand Inches Leftward, Now Supports Gay Marriage," *Talking Points Memo*, January 23, 2009, http://talkingpointsmemo.com/dc/gillibrand-inches-leftward-now-supports-gay-marriage.

95. Tom Wroblewski, "Gillibrand Boosts Stimulus, Obama Economic Team," *Staten Island Live*, April 15, 2009, http://blog.silive.com/politics/2009/04/gillibrand_boosts_stimulus_oba.html.

96. Aaron Blake and and Roxana Tiron, "Gillibrand Mulls Move Left on Gays in Military," *The Hill*, July 13, 2009, https://www.thehill.com/homenews/senate/50115-gillibrand-mulls-move-left-on-gays-in-military.

97. Dan Margolis, "N.Y. Progressives Begin to Line Up behind Gillibrand," *People's World*, February 18, 2010, http://www.peoplesworld.org/article/n-y-progressives-begin-to-line-up-behind-gillibrand/.

98. Jonathan Van Meter, "In Hillary's Footsteps: Kirsten Gillibrand," *Vogue*, October 19, 2010, http://www.vogue.com/865477/in-hillarys-footsteps-kirsten-gillibrand/.

99. Macon Phillips, "President Obama on the Selection of Kirsten Gillibrand," *Obama White House*. January 23, 2009, https://obamawhitehouse.archives.gov/blog/2009/01/23/president-obama-selection-kirsten-gillibrand; Dan Amira, "Rahm Emanuel Gave Gillibrand Opponent an Offer He Couldn't Refuse," *New York*, May 22, 2009, http://nymag.com/daily/intelligencer/2009/05/rahm_emanuel_gave_gillibrand_o.html.

100. Raymond Hernandez, "N.Y.'s Junior Senator Gains a Defender: The Senior Senator," *New York Times*, May 8, 2009, A1.

101. Josh Kraushaar, "Big Endorsement for Gillibrand," *Politico*, January 28, 2009, http://www.politico.com/blogs/scorecard/0109/Big_endorsement_for_Gillibrand.html?showall; Zachary Abrahamson, "Gillibrand Gets NARAL Endorsement," *Politico*, June 30, 2009, http://www.politico.com/story/2009/06/gillibrand-gets-naral-endorsement-024355.

102. Irene Jay Liu, "Gillibrand Gets CSEA Endorsement," *Times Union*, July 31, 2009, http://www.timesunion.com/local/article/Gillibrand-gets-CSEA-endorsement-553224.php.

103. Margolis, "N.Y. Progressives Begin to Line Up behind Gillibrand."

104. Irene Jay Liu, "Gillibrand Snags Endorsement over Sausage," *Times Union*, September 1, 2009, http://blog.timesunion.com/capitol/archives/17818/gillibrand-snags-endorsement-over-sausage/; Kyle Trygstad, "Gillibrand Racking Up Endorsements," *RealClearPolitics*, May 18, 2009, http://www.realclearpolitics.com/politics_nation/2009/05/gillibrand_racking_up_endorsem.html.

105. Glenn Thrush, "King Iffy on NY Senate after Intel Appointment," *Politico*, June 29, 2009, http://www.politico.com/blogs/on-congress/2009/06/king-iffy-on-ny-senate-after-intel-appointment-019473; Danny Hakim, "For Nixon In-Law, G.O.P. Post and a Giuliani Clash," *New York Times*, September 29, 2009, A30; "3/29: Gillibrand and Pataki in Virtual Dead Heat," Marist Poll, March 29, 2009, http://maristpoll.marist.edu/329-gillibrand-and-pataki-in-virtual-dead-heat/.

106. Ben Smith and Jonathan Martin, "Harold Ford's Gilded New York," *Politico*, January 13, 2010, http://www.politico.com/story/2010/01/harold-fords-gilded-new-york-031455.

107. Michael Barbaro, "Senate Hopeful in New State Airs Evolving Views," *New York Times*, January 12, 2010, A1.

108. Peter Beinart, "Harold Ford Implodes," *Daily Beast*, January 13, 2010, http://www.thedailybeast.com/articles/2010/01/14/harold-ford-implodes.html.

109. Robin Toner, "Ad Seen as Playing to Racial Fears," *New York Times*, October 26, 2006, A1.

110. Beinart, "Harold Ford Implodes."

111. Tom Humphrey, "Harold Ford Jr. to Lose TN Voter Registration," *KnoxBlogs.com*, August 31, 2010, http://knoxblogs.com/humphreyhill/2010/08/31/harold_ford_jr_to_lose_tn_vote/; Hilary Elkins, "Harold Ford Jr. Gets Stonewalled," *GQ*, February 25, 2010, http://www.gq.com/story/harold-ford-jr-gets-stonewalled.

112. John Cook, "Harold Ford Tries, Fails to Give a Straight Answer on Whether He's Paid New York Taxes," *Gawker*, February 15, 2010, http://gawker.com/5472029/harold-ford-tries-fails-to-give-a-straight-answer-on-whether-hes-paid-new-york-taxes; John Cook, "Harold Ford's Tennessee Tax Dodge," *Gawker*, February 12, 2010, http://gawker.com/5470445/harold-fords-tennessee-tax-dodge.

113. Raymond Hernandez, "N.Y.'s Junior Senator Gains a Defender: The Senior Senator," *New York Times*, May 8, 2009, A1.

114. Kevin Robillard, "Harold Ford's Comments on Abortion Prompt Charges of Flip-Flopping," *Politifact*, January 19, 2010, http://www.politifact.com/truth-o-meter/statements/2010/jan/19/harold-ford-jr/harold-ford-flip-flopped-abortion/.

115. Michael Barbaro, "Senate Hopeful in New State Airs Evolving Views," A1.

116. Michael Barbaro, "Gillibrand Responds to Ford's Challenge, Calling Him out of Touch with New York," *New York Times*, January 13, 2010, A30.

117. Barbaro, "Senate Hopeful in New State Airs Evolving Views," A1.

118. Michael Barbaro, "Ford Decides Not to Run for Senate Seat," *New York Times*, March 2, 2010, A18.

119. Beinart, "Harold Ford Implodes."

120. Michael Barbaro, "Harold Ford Jr. Weighs a Challenge to Gillibrand," *New York Times*, January 5, 2010, A16; "A Proxy Battle, Senate-style," *Crain's New York Business*, January 19, 2010, http://www.crainsnewyork.com/article/20100119/INS/1001 19881.

121. Sewell Chan, "Bloomberg Leaving Republican Party," *New York Times*, June 19, 2007, https://cityroom.blogs.nytimes.com/2007/06/19/bloomberg-leaving-republican-party/.

122. Michael Crowley, "Ford Theater: The Crazy Logic of an Outsider/ Insider Carpetbagger Candidacy," *New York*, March 5, 2010, http://nymag.com/news/intelligencer/64602/.

123. Harold Ford, Jr., "Why I'm Not Running for the Senate," *New York Times*, March 2, 2010, A23.

124. Frances Martel, "Harold Ford, Jr. Goes on Morning Joe and Finally Sounds like a Senator," *Mediaite*, March 2, 2010, http://www.mediaite.com/print/harold-ford-jr-goes-on-morning-joe-and-finally-sounds-like-a-senator/.

125. Ben Smith, "Liz Cheney Takes On 'Radical' W.H.," *Politico*, October 13, 2009, http://www.politico.com/story/2009/10/liz-cheney-takes-on-radical-wh-028212.

126. Jonathan Martin, "In Wyoming, a Cheney Run Worries G.O.P.," *New York Times*, July 6, 2013, A1.

127. Ibid.

128. Trevor Brown, "Liz Cheney to Challenge Enzi for Senate Seat," *Wyoming Tribune Eagle-Wyoming News,* July 17, 2013, http://www.wyomingnews.com/news/liz-cheney-to-challenge-enzi-for-senate-seat/article_fafa7562-6620-57ff-94ed-616a8a4e1d76.html#.VOuHSXzF9Ao.

129. Sean Sullivan and Ed O'Keefe, "Liz Cheney Will Challenge Sen. Mike Enzi," *Washington Post*, July 16, 2013, 6.

130. John McCormick, "Cheney Bid Divides Wyoming Republicans Puzzled by Timing," *Bloomberg*, July 17, 2013, http://www.bloomberg.com/news/articles/2013-07-18/cheney-bid-divides-wyoming-republicans-puzzled-by-timing.

131. Cal Clark and Janet Clark, "Wyoming Political Surprises in the Late 1980s: Deviating Elections in a Conservative Republican State," *Great Plains Quarterly* 11, no. 3 (Summer 1991) 181–97.

132. Jonathan Martin, "For Cheney, Realities of a Race Outweighed Family Edge," *New York Times*, January 7, 2014, A9.

133. Sean Sullivan and Ed O'Keefe, "Liz Cheney Will Challenge Sen. Mike Enzi," 6.

134. Jonathan Martin, "In Wyoming, a Cheney Run Worries G.O.P.," *New York Times*, July 6, 2013, A1.

135. Daniel Strauss, "Alan Simpson: Liz Cheney 'Destroying Family Relationships' Because of Senate Race," *TPM*, November 19, 2013, http://talkingpointsmemo. com/livewire/alan-simpson-liz-cheney-destroying-family-relationships-because-of-senate-race.

136. Martin, "In Wyoming, a Cheney Run Worries G.O.P.," A1.

137. Sean Sullivan and Ed O'Keefe, "Liz Cheney Will Challenge Sen. Mike Enzi," *Washington Post*, July 16, 2013, 6; Jonathan Martin, "In Wyoming, a Cheney Run Worries G.O.P.," *New York Times*, July 6, 2013, A1.

138. Burgess Everett, "GOP senators to Cheney: We Like Mike," *Politico*, July 28, 2013, http://www.politico.com/story/2013/07/mike-enzi-liz-cheney-wyoming-senate-race-94846.html#ixzz2aRGFjP4Q; Perry Stein, "Rand Paul Voices Support for Sen. Enzi as Liz Cheney Considers WY Challenge," *TPM*, July 11, 2013, http:// talkingpointsmemo.com/livewire/rand-paul-voices-support-for-sen-enzi-as-liz-cheney-considers-wy-challenge; Perry Stein, "NRSC: 'Our Mission Is to Reelect Our Incumbents,' " *TPM*, July 16, 2013, http://talkingpointsmemo.com/livewire/nrsc-our-mission-is-to-reelect-our-incumbents; Ari Fleischer (@AriFleischer), "I'm a big fan of Liz Cheney. But not in this race," Tweet, July 16, 2013, https://twitter.com/AriFleischer/status/357249872174395393?ref_src=twsrc%5Etfw.

139. Sullivan and O'Keefe, "Liz Cheney Will Challenge Sen. Mike Enzi," 6.

140. McCormick, "Cheney Bid Divides Wyoming Republicans Puzzled by Timing."

141. Kyle Roerink, "Liz Cheney Features Daughters in Campaign Ad Touting Family's Wyoming History," *Casper Star-Tribune*, November 25, 2013, http://trib.com/ news/state-and-regional/govt-and-politics/liz-cheney-features-daughters-in-campaign-ad-touting-family-s/article_81862c67-91ca-50cb-b65c-4ea861356105.html.

142. McCormick, "Cheney Bid Divides Wyoming Republicans Puzzled by Timing."

143. Trevor Brown, "Liz Cheney Promises Stiff Opposition to President Obama," *Wyoming Tribune Eagle-WyomingNews.com*, July 18, 2013, http://www. wyomingnews.com/news/liz-cheney-promises-stiff-opposition-to-president-obama/article_cc6e8ea1-df2a-583b-92be-17089b6ca7fa.html#.VOuHS3zF9Ao; Daniel Strauss, "Liz Cheney's First Campaign Ad Touts Family's Ties to Wyoming," *TPM*, November 14, 2013, http://talkingpointsmemo.com/livewire/liz-cheney-releases-first-campaign-ad-focusing-on-family-s-ties-to-wyoming.

144. Trevor Brown, "Liz Cheney Promises Stiff Opposition to President Obama"; Roerink, "Liz Cheney Features Daughters in Campaign Ad Touting Family's Wyoming History."

145. Trevor Brown, "Senate Race Money Is Pouring In," *Wyoming Tribune Eagle-WyomingNews.com*, October 16, 2013, http://www.wyomingnews.com/news/senate-race-money-is-pouring-in/article_fa52ea6f-d8af-5b50-b9e2-fa4d095ce75d.html#.VOuJBXzF9Ao.

146. Kyle Roerink, "Liz Cheney Listed As 10-Year Wyomingite, Gets Resident Fishing License Early," *Casper Star Tribune*, August 5, 2013, http://trib.com/news/state-

and-regional/govt-and-politics/liz-cheney-listed-as—year-wyomingite-gets-resident-fishing/article_d764ebbc-7d00-5358-88f2-8029198beff7.html.

147. Jessica Taylor, "Cheney Family Dispute Inflames Tensions in Wyoming Race," *MSNBC.com*, November 19, 2013, http://www.msnbc.com/the-daily-rundown/cheney-family-dispute-inflames-tensions.

148. Adrian A. Bantjes, "Introduction: Bourdieu on the Bighorn? Or, Towards a Cultural History of Fly-Fishing in Wyoming and the Rocky Mountain West," *Annals of Wyoming: The Wyoming History Journal* 76, no. 2 (Spring 2004): 2–5.

149. Paul Schullery, *Cowboy Trout: Western Fly Fishing as If It Matters* (Helena, MT: Montana Historical Society Press, 1993); Jen Corrine Brown, *Trout Culture: How Fly Fishing Forever Changed the Rocky Mountain West* (Seattle, Washington: University of Washington Press, 2015).

150. Kenneth L. Graham, *Fishing Wyoming: An Angler's Guide to More than 200 Sites* (Helena, MT: Falcon, 1998).

151. Bob Bonnar, "Newspapers Alive and Well," *Wyoming Tribune Eagle-Wyoming News.com*, October 13, 2013, http://www.wyomingnews.com/opinion/newspapers-alive-and-well/article_471f9b1b-528b-5ba7-9d8a-4e1e3efa80cd.html#.VOuJBXzF9Ao.

152. Angus M. Thuermer Jr., "Breaking News: Cheney Pays $220 for Fishing License Ticket," *Jackson Hole News & Guide*, August 21, 2013, http://www.jhnewsandguide.com/news/top_stories/breaking-news-cheney-pays-for-fishing-license-ticket/article_89978870-ee8f-533d-a0b0-648d9a2c34df.html.

153. Michael Polhamus, "Cheney Knocks Obama, Papers," *Jackson Hole News & Guide*, September 4, 2013, http://www.jhnewsandguide.com/news/top_stories/cheney-knocks-obama-papers/article_a4adf4d5-7977-546a-838b-6f66edc5f518.html.

154. Bonnar, "Newspapers Alive and Well."

155. Geoff McGhee, "Rural Newspapers Doing Better Than Their City Counterparts," Rural West Initiative, July 14, 2011, http://web.stanford.edu/group/ruralwest/cgi-bin/drupal/content/rural-newspapers.

156. Kyle Roerink, "Wyoming U.S. Senate Candidate Liz Cheney's Husband Caught in Voter Registration Snafu," *Casper Star-Tribune*, December 19, 2013, http://trib.com/news/state-and-regional/govt-and-politics/wyoming-u-s-senate-candidate-liz-cheney-s-husband-caught/article_f7fe8c69-4d5d-581f-920c-2326e9d66096.html.

157. Trevor Brown, "Enzi Leads in Early Poll," *Wyoming Tribune Eagle-Wyoming-News.com*, July 20, 2013, http://www.wyomingnews.com/news/enzi-leads-in-early-poll/article_f83e42ac-dde0-53ae-bf72-1ed349122733.html#.VOuHY3zF9Ao; Tom Jensen, "Uphill Battle for Cheney in Wyoming," PublicPolicyPolling.com, July 22, 2013, http://www.publicpolicypolling.com/pdf/2011/PPP_Release_WY_723.pdf.

158. Ibid.

159. Jonathan Martin, "Dispute over Gay Marriage Erupts in Cheney Family," *New York Times*, November 17, 2013, A1.

160. James Hohmann, Tal Kopan, and Alexander Burns, "Cheney: 'I Have Decided to Discontinue My Campaign,'" *Politico*, January 6, 2014, http://www.politico.com/story/2014/01/liz-cheney-wyoming-senate-race-101767.

161. John King and Peter Hamby, "Liz Cheney Abandons Senate Bid," *CNN*, January 6, 2014, http://www.cnn.com/2014/01/05/politics/liz-cheney-senate-race/.

162. Caitlin Macneal, "Enzi Greeted with High Fives on Senate Floor Following Cheney News (VIDEO)," *TPM*, January 4, 2014, http://talkingpointsmemo.com/livewire/enzi-greeted-with-high-fives-on-senate-floor-following-cheney-news.

163. Eli Yokley, "Cynthia Lummis Will Not Seek Fifth Term in House," *The Hill*, November 12, 2015, http://www.rollcall.com/news/home/cynthia-lummis-will-not-seek-fifth-term-house.

164. Emmarie Huetteman, "Liz Cheney to Run for Wyoming's Only House Seat," *New York Times*, January 30, 2016, https://www.nytimes.com/2016/01/31/us/politics/liz-cheney-to-run-for-wyomings-only-house-seat.html.

165. Laura Hancock, "Liz Cheney Wins Republican Primary for U.S. House," *Casper Star-Tribune*, August 16, 2016, http://trib.com/news/state-and-regional/govt-and-politics/liz-cheney-wins-republican-primary-for-u-s-house/article_e3b38943-8bba-5c87-8a02-7f87d9c53841.html.

166. Rema Rahman, "Liz Cheney Wins Wyoming House Seat," *Roll Call*, November 8, 2016, http://www.rollcall.com/news/politics/liz-cheney-wins-wyoming-house-seat.

Chapter 7

1. J. K. Trotter, "Why Scott Brown Might Run for Governor Instead of John Kerry's Senate Seat," *The Atlantic*, January 14, 2013, https://www.theatlantic.com/politics/archive/2013/01/why-scott-brown-might-run-governor-instead-john-kerrys-senate-seat/319502/.

2. "Massachusetts Vote: Scott Brown Profile," *The Telegraph*, January 19, 2010, http://www.telegraph.co.uk/news/worldnews/northamerica/usa/7023400/Massachusetts-vote-Scott-Brown-profile.html.

3. Frank Bruni, "Where Scott Brown Is Coming From," *New York Times Magazine*, February 22, 2010, MM24.

4. Chris Woodyard, "Scott Brown Drives His GMC Pickup to U.S. Senate Victory," *USA Today*, January 20, 2010, http://content.usatoday.com/communities/driveon/post/2010/01/scott-brown-drives-his-gmc-pickup-truck-to-us-senate-victory/1#.WZrkqD6GPcc;Sarah Laskow, "The Truck behind the Man," *Newsweek*, October 29, 2010, http://www.newsweek.com/truck-behind-man-74091.

5. Tom Jensen, "Dems Favored for MA-Gov.—Unless Brown Runs," Public Policy Polling, May 7, 2013, http://www.publicpolicypolling.com/main/2013/05/dems-favored-for-ma-govunless-brown-runs.html.

6. Aaron Blake, "Scott Brown, Elizabeth Warren and the 'Have a Beer' Factor," *Washington Post*, April 2, 2012, https://www.washingtonpost.com/blogs/the-fix/post/scott-brown-elizabeth-warren-and-the-have-a-beer-factor/2012/04/02/gIQAQGIxqS_blog.html?utm_term=.cfee8b479f45.

7. Harry J. Enten, "If John Kerry Makes Secretary of State, Can Scott Brown Win His Senate Seat?" *The Guardian*, December 14, 2012, https://www.theguardian.com/commentisfree/2012/dec/14/john-kerry-secretary-state-scott-brown-senate; Aaron Blake, "Another Massachusetts Special Election?" *Washington Post*, November 13, 2012, https://www.washingtonpost.com/news/the-fix/wp/2012/11/13/another-massachusetts-special-election/?utm_term=.08cf7375db5a.

8. Richard Rizzuto, "Poll: Scott Brown Holding Slight Lead over Ed Markey in Massachusetts Senate Race," *MassLive*, January 30, 2013, http://www.masslive.com/politics/index.ssf/2013/01/poll_scott_brown_holding_sligh.html; Richard Rizzuto, "Scott Brown Carries Double Digit Lead over Ed Markey in Massachusetts Special Election," *MassLive*, January 25, 2013, http://www.masslive.com/politics/index.ssf/2013/01/scott_brown_carries_double_dig.html.

9. Shira Schoenberg, "Scott Brown 'Leaning Strongly' toward Another Massachusetts U.S. Senate Run, AP Reports," *MassLive*, January 30, 2013, http://www.masslive.com/politics/index.ssf/2013/01/scott_brown_leaning_strongly_t.html.

10. "Scott Brown Will Not Run in the Special Election for U.S. Senator," *Western Mass News*, February 1, 2013, http://www.westernmassnews.com/story/20935790/scott-brown-will-not-run-in-the-special-election-for-us-senator.

11. "Scott Brown Not Running for Open Senate Seat," CBS Boston, February 1, 2013, http://boston.cbslocal.com/2013/02/01/ap-scott-brown-not-running-for-open-senate-seat/.

12. Martin Finucane, "Markey, Brown in Statistical Dead Heat, Poll Shows," *Boston Globe*, January 30, 2013, https://www.bostonglobe.com/metro/2013/01/30/new-poll-finds-markey-brown-statistical-dead-heat-hypothetical-senate-race/0jcrsghKfpTx5fbzVbaHXO/story.html.

13. Kevin Bogardus, "Scott Brown Joins Law and Lobby Firm," *The Hill*, March 11, 2013, http://thehill.com/business-a-lobbying/287329-scott-brown-joins-law-and-lobby-firm; Irena Briganti, "Fox News Channel Signs Former Sen. Scott Brown to Contributor Role," FOXNews.com, February 2013, http://press.foxnews.com/2013/02/fox-news-channel-signs-former-sen-scott-brown-to-contributor-role/.

14. Richard Rizzuto, "Despite Absence from Politics Poll Shows Republican Scott Brown Is Favorite for Governor of Massachusetts in 2014 Race," *MassLive*, May 8, 2014, http://www.masslive.com/politics/index.ssf/2013/05/despite_absence_from_politics.html.

15. Sean Sullivan, "Scott Brown Won't Run for Governor of Massachusetts," *Washington Post*, August 21, 2013, https://www.washingtonpost.com/news/post-politics/wp/2013/08/21/scott-brown-wont-run-for-governor-of-massachusetts/?utm_term=.a58195a69b67.

16. Jim O'Sullivan, "Scott Brown Will Not Run for Governor in 2014," *Boston Globe*, August 21, 2013, A1.

17. James Hohmann, "Why Scott Brown Might Run for Governor, Not Senate," *Politico*, January 13, 2013, http://www.politico.com/story/2013/01/why-scott-brown-might-run-for-governor-not-senate-86102_Page3.html.

18. Peter Hamby, "Scott Brown in 2016: Why Not?" CNN, August 19, 2013, http://www.cnn.com/2013/08/19/politics/scott-brown-2016.

19. Gregory Wallace, "Brown Stirs Speculation with Another New Hampshire Visit," CNN, April 13, 2013, http://politicalticker.blogs.cnn.com/2013/04/13/brown-stirs-speculation-with-another-new-hampshire-visit/.

20. Noah Bierman, "Scott Brown Gets a Plea to Run in N.H.," *Boston Globe*, November 8, 2013, A1.

21. Karen Tumulty, "Scott Brown: Will He Or Won't He Run for Senate from New Hampshire?" *Washington Post*, February 9, 2014, https://www.washingtonpost.com/politics/scott-brown-will-he-or-wont-he-run-for-senate-from-new-hampshire/2014/02/09/1b4fdce0-8ffe-11e3-84e1-27626c5ef5fb_story.html?utm_term=.05cf2ccdbfe6.

22. Sean Sullivan and Aaron Blake, "The Fix's Top 10 Senate Races of 2014," *Washington Post*, April 5, 2014, https://www.washingtonpost.com/news/the-fix/wp/2013/04/05/the-fixs-top-10-senate-races-of-2014-2/?utm_term=.6bf2a5f4b2e8.

23. Kyle Trygstad, "New Hampshire: Local Republicans Skeptical on Scott Brown," *Roll Call*, April 5, 2013, http://www.rollcall.com/politics/new-hampshire-local-republicans-skeptical-on-scott-brown/.

24. Noah Bierman, "Scott Brown Gets a Plea to Run in N.H.," *Boston Globe*, November 8, 2013, A1.

25. Ben Leubsdorf, "N.H. Senate Leader Jeb Bradley Won't Run for U.S. Senate in 2014," *Concord Monitor*, September 4, 2013, http://www.concordmonitor.com/Archive/2013/09/JebBradley-CM-090413; Ben Leubsdorf, "Charlie Bass Passes on 2014 Senate Run against Incumbent Democrat Jeanne Shaheen," *Concord Monitor*, October 5, 2013, http://www.concordmonitor.com/Archive/2013/11/CharlieBass-CM-110513; John DiStaso, "Former Sen. John E. Sununu Won't Run for Office in 2014," *New Hampshire Union Leader*, April 12, 2013, http://www.unionleader.com/article/20130412/NEWS0 6/130419623&template=mobileart; John Celock, "Chris Sununu Says He Won't Run for New Hampshire Governor in 2014," *Huffington Post*, July 18, 2013, http://www.huffingtonpost.com/2013/07/18/chris-sununu-governor_n_3617739.html.

26. Kevin Landrigan, "Jim Rubens Becomes First GOPer to Officially Oppose NH's Shaheen," *Nashua Telegraph*, September 19, 2013.

27. Ben Leubsdorf, "NH Republican Activist Karen Testerman to Run for US Senate," *Concord Monitor*, October 14, 2013, http://www.concordmonitor.com/Archive/2013/10/TestermanSenate-CM-101513.

28. Dante Scala, *Stormy Weather: The New Hampshire Primary and Presidential Politics* (New York: Palgrave Macmillan, 2003), 88; Doris Weatherford, *Women in American Politics: History and Milestones* (Thousand Oaks, CA: CQ, 2012), 236.

29. Vesta M. Roy, president of the New Hampshire state senate, acted as governor for seven days following the death of Governor Hugh Gallen in 1982, just before his term ended (Associated Press 2002).

30. "New Hampshire: Past Governors Bios," *National Governors Association*, accessed August 17, 2017, https://www.nga.org/cms/home/governors/past-governors-bios/page_new_hampshire.html.

31. Linda L. Fowler, "New Hampshire Senate: Down to the Wire in New Hampshire," in *Midterm Madness: The Elections of 2002*, ed. Larry Sabato (Lanham, MA: Rowman & Littlefield, 2003) 125–35.

32. Christopher J. Galdieri, "50 Takes on Trump: New Hampshire," Utica College Center of Public Affairs and Election Research. May 10, 2017, https://www.ucpublic affairs.com/home/2017/5/10/50-takes-on-trump-new-hampshire-by-christopher-galdieri.

33. Robin Toner, "Political Briefs," *New York Times*, May 2, 1996, http://www.nytimes.com/1996/05/02/us/political-briefs.html.

34. Christopher J. Devine and Kyle C. Kopko, *The VP Advantage: How Running Mates Influence Home State Voting in Presidential Elections* (Manchester: Manchester University Press, 2016), 147.

35. Fowler, "New Hampshire Senate," 125–35.

36. Ibid.

37. Jesse Richman, "Congress on the Line: The 2008 Congressional Election and the Obama Presidency," *White House Studies* 9, no. 1 (2009): 21–34.

38. Jim Haddadin, "Shaheen Prods U.S. House on Transportation Funding Bill," *Fosters Daily Democrat*, March 28, 2012, http://www.fosters.com/article/20120328/GJNEWS_01/703289957. 2012; Edith Tucker, "Congress Passes Funds to Open Berlin Prison," *Salmon Press*, November 22, 2011, http://www.newhampshirelakesand mountains.com/Articles-Berlin-Reporter-c-2011-11-21-155084.113119-Congress-passes-funds-to-open-Berlin-Prison.html; "Shaheen, Collins Call for Action to Avoid Potential Cuts to Portsmouth Naval Shipyard," *New Hampshire Union Leader*, February 4, 2013, http://www.unionleader.com/article/20130204/NEWS06/130209643/1013/NEWS11.

39. Dante J. Scala, "New Hampshire: The Swing State Swings Right," in *Pendulum Swing*, ed. Larry Sabato (Hoboken: Pearson Longman: 2011), 329–34.

40. Dante J. Scala, "Politics in New Hampshire," *New England Journal of Political Science* 7, no. 1 (Spring 2013): 142–48.

41. Noah Bierman, "Scott Brown Gets a Plea to Run in N.H.," *Boston Globe*, November 8, 2013, A1.

42. "Hey, Scott Brown Stop Flirting with NH," *New Hampshire Union Leader*, September 30, 2013, http://www.unionleader.com/article/20131001/OPINION01/13100 9992/-1/opinion01.

43. Thomas B. Edsall, "The Obamacare Crisis," *New York Times*, November 19, 2013, http://www.nytimes.com/2013/11/20/opinion/edsall-the-obamacare-crisis.html; Jonathan Weisman, "In Fracas on Health Coverage, Some Democrats Feel Exposed," *New York Times*, November 16: A1.

44. Bierman, "Scott Brown Gets a Plea to Run in N.H.," A1.

45. Alex Roarty, "Republicans to Scott Brown: Oh, You're Serious?" *National Journal*, December 10, 2013; Hilary Chabot, "As N.H. Pols Buzz, Scott Brown Moves In," *Boston Herald*, December 19, 2013, http://www.bostonherald.com/news_opinion/us_politics/2013/12/as_nh_pols_buzz_scott_brown_moves_in.

46. James Pindell, "What's in a Twitter Name? Scott Brown Drops 'MA' from His Handle," WMUR.com, November 27, 2013, http://www.wmur.com/article/what-s-in-a-twitter-name-scott-brown-drops-ma-from-his-handle/5186378.

47. John Nichols, "Even Republicans Fear Bush," *The Nation*, October 31, 2004, https://www.thenation.com/article/even-republicans-fear-bush/.

48. Andrew Glass, "Sen. Bob Smith Switches Back to GOP, Nov. 1, 1999," *Politico*, October 31, 2015, http://www.politico.com/story/2015/10/sen-bob-smith-switches-back-to-the-gop-nov-1-1999-215242 2015.

49. Roarty, "Republicans to Scott Brown: Oh, You're Serious?"

50. Paul Steinhauser, "Brown Stokes More Speculation about Senate Run in NH," CNN.com, December 3, 2013, http://politicalticker.blogs.cnn.com/2013/12/03/brown-stokes-more-speculation-about-senate-run-in-nh/; John DiStaso, "Is He In? Scott Brown Making Private Calls to Prominent NH Republicans," *New Hampshire Union Leader*, February 21, 2014, http://www.unionleader.com/article/20140221/NEWS0602/140219339.

51. Bierman, "Scott Brown Gets a Plea to Run in N.H."; Joe Battenfeld, "GOP Chief Sees N.H. 'Opportunity' for Scott Brown," *Boston Herald*, December 11, 2013, http://www.bostonherald.com/news_opinion/columnists/joe_battenfeld/2013/12/battenfeld_gop_chief_sees_nh_opportunity_for_scott.

52. Gretyl Macalester, "Penguin Plunge Raises $600,000 over Weekend," *New Hampshire Union Leader*, February 2, 2014, 1.

53. James Pindell, "Scott Brown to Formally Enter Senate Contest Thursday," WMUR.com, April 7, 2014, http://www.wmur.com/article/scott-brown-to-formally-enter-senate-contest-thursday/5189402.

54. Karen Testerman ended her campaign by the summer of 2014 in a bid to avoid diluting the conservative vote (see Bookman).

55. Gregory Wallace, "Brown Stirs Speculation with Another New Hampshire Visit," CNN, April 13, 2013, http://politicalticker.blogs.cnn.com/2013/04/13/brown-stirs-speculation-with-another-new-hampshire-visit/.

56. Warren Richey, "Resolved: Where Maine Begins and N.H. Ends," *Christian Science Monitor*, May 31, 2001, https://www.csmonitor.com/2001/0531/p2s2.html.

57. Rachel Weiner, "Scott Brown Not Ruling Out New Hampshire Bid," *Washington Post*, April 4, 2013, https://www.washingtonpost.com/news/post-politics/wp/2013/04/04/scott-brown-not-ruling-out-new-hampshire-bid/?utm_term=.ec7d22c77710.

58. Paige Lavender, "Gov Brags That Scott Brown, Who Was Born in Maine, Was 'Born Virtually' in New Hampshire," *Huffington Post*, April 14, 2014, http://www.huffingtonpost.com/2014/04/14/scott-brown-new-hampshire_n_5145796.html.

59. Chris Moody, "The Second Coming of Scott Brown," Yahoo News, April 14, 2014, https://www.yahoo.com/news/scott-brown-new-hampshire-2014-015538246.html.

60. Jerold J. Duquette, "The 'Scott Brown Era' in Massachusetts Politics," *New England Journal of Political Science* 7, no. 1 (Spring 2013): 120–41.

61. Drew Cline, "Scott Brown Plans to Win Over NH One Handshake at a Time," *New Hampshire Union Leader*, July 10, 2014, 7.

62. Paul Steinhuaser, "Brown Stokes More Speculation about Senate Run in NH," CNN.com, December 3, 2014, http://politicalticker.blogs.cnn.com/2013/12/03/brown-stokes-more-speculation-about-senate-run-in-nh/.

63. Paul Lewis, "Scott Brown: Fallout from Hobby Lobby Decision Puts Senate Bid in Tight Spot," *The Guardian*, July 16, 2014, https://www.theguardian.com/world/2014/jul/16/scott-brown-republican-senate-campaign-hobby-lobby-women.

64. Benny Johnson, "Bartender Scott Brown," *National Review*, November 3, 2014, http://www.nationalreview.com/article/391703/bartender-scott-brown-benny-johnson.

65. Ibid.

66. Scott Brown, "Scott Brown: Proud to Serve," YouTube.com, May 12, 2014, https://www.youtube.com/watch?v=PEQ15NIE6_0&feature=youtu.be.

67. Fergus Cullen, "Welcome to New Hampshire, Scott Brown," *New Hampshire Union Leader*, January 3, 2014, 18.

68. Ella Nilsen, "Jim Rubens Tries to Win Over Votes as 'Reform' Candidate," *SentinelSource.com*, August 13, 2014, http://www.sentinelsource.com/news/local/jim-rubens-tries-to-win-over-votes-as-reform-candidate/article_ca0c1176-afc7-5886-a2ee-2089ff876d9a.html.

69. "Conservative New Hampshire Group Endorses Brown Rival for Senate," *Chicago Tribune*, May 29, 2014, http://articles.chicagotribune.com/2014-05-29/news/sns-rt-us-usa-new-hampshire-senate-20140529_1_new-hampshire-republican-scott-brown-karen-testerman; Tony Schinella, "Humphrey Backs Rubens in Race against Shaheen," *Patch.com*, January 10, 2014, https://patch.com/new-hampshire/concord-nh/humphey-backs-rubens-in-race-against-shaheen; Earl A. Rinker III, "Earl Rinker Endorses Jim Rubens for US Senate," *NH Insider*, August 23, 2014, http://www.nhinsider.com/letters-to-the-editor/2014/8/23/earl-rinker-endorses-jim-rubens-for-us-senate.html.

70. Grant Bosse, "Jim Rubens Goes from Centrist to Anti-Republican," *New Hampshire Union Leader*, March 7, 2016, 6.

71. Timothy B. Lee, "Larry Lessig Backs a Long-Shot Republican in His Campaign to Clean Up Money in Politics," *Vox*, July 29, 2014, https://www.vox.com/2014/7/29/5947835/larry-lessig-backs-a-long-shot-republican-in-his-campaign-to-clean-up.

72. Kathleen Ronayne, "Smith, Rubens Go after Brown in GOP U.S. Senate Debate," *Concord Monitor*, September 4, 2014, http://web.archive.org/web/20140908005802/http://www.concordmonitor.com/news/campaignmonitor/13424061-95/smith-rubens-go-after-brown-in-gop-us-senate-debate. See Wayback Machine at www.archive.org.

73. Richard Rizzuto, "Sen. Scott Brown Says He Now Supports a Federal Ban on Assault Weapons," *MassLive*, December 19, 2012, http://www.masslive.com/politics/index.ssf/2012/12/sen_scott_brown_says_he_now_su.html; Greg Sargent, "Scott Brown Lurches to the Right on Guns," *Washington Post*, May 27, 2014, https://www.washingtonpost.com/blogs/plum-line/wp/2014/05/27/scott-brown-lurches-to-the-right-on-guns/?utm_term=.734605de3d4f.

74. Ronayne, "Smith, Rubens Go after Brown in GOP U.S. Senate Debate."

75. Dave Martinez, "Smith 'Clear Winner' in Debate, Anti-Brown Candidate," *Girard at Large*, September 5, 2014, http://www.girardatlarge.com/2014/09/smith-clear-

winner-in-debate-anti-brown-candidate/; Smith for U.S. Senate, "WMUR TV: Bob Smith Wins US Senate Debate," *NH Insider*, September 6, 2014, http://www.nhinsider.com/press-releases/2014/9/6/smith-for-us-senate-wmur-tv-bob-smith-wins-us-senate-debate.html.

76. "2014 U.S. Senate Republican Primary," NHPR State of Democracy, accessed August 17, 2017, http://nh.electionstats.com/elections/view/49560/.

77. Brenda DeVore Marshall and Molly A. Mayhead, "The Changing Face of the Governorship," in *Navigating Boundaries: The Rhetoric of Women Governors*, ed. Brenda DeVore Marshall and Molly A. Mayhead (Westport, CT: Praeger, 2000): 1–14.

78. "Analysis of Respondents Mentioning 'Carpetbagger,'" UMass Poll, October 20, 2014, http://www.umass.edu/poll/pdfs/20141020_carpetbagger.pdf.

79. Alex Rogers, "Jeanne Shaheen Admits to Headwinds in New Hampshire Debate," *Time*, October 21, 2014, http://time.com/3530397/jeanne-shaheen-scott-brown-new-hampshire-debate/.

80. Shira Schoenberg, "Jeanne Shaheen Uses Massachusetts Politicians to Attack Scott Brown in NH Senate Race," MassLive, October 21, 2014, http://www.masslive.com/politics/index.ssf/2014/10/jeanne_shaheen_uses_massachuse.html.

81. Erin Dooley, "New Hampshire Senate Debate Live Updates," ABCNews.com, October 30, 2014, http://liveblog.abcnews.go.com/Event/New_Hampshire_Senate_Debate_Live_Updates.

82. Katherine Q. Seelye, "New Hampshire's Tight Senate Race Keeps Focus on Baggage," *New York Times*, October 26, 2014, A16.

83. "Excerpts: Shaheen to Address Supporters in Manchester on Primary Night," JeanneShaheen.org, September 9, 2014, http://jeanneshaheen.org/news/excerpts-shaheen-address-supporters-manchester-primary-night/.

84. "Massachusetts governor helps rally Carroll County Democrats at annual Grover Cleveland Dinner," *Conway Daily Sun*, September 15, 2014, https://www.con-waydailysun.com/news/massachusetts-governor-helps-rally-carroll-county-democrats-at-annual-grover/article_6e5ddfea-c427-5cdd-86e1-cf17c9b92c8e.html.

85. Schoenberg, "Jeanne Shaheen Uses Massachusetts Politicians to Attack Scott Brown in NH Senate Race."

86. James Hohmann, "How Shaheen Plans to Defeat Brown," *Politico*, March 30, 2014, http://www.politico.com/story/2014/03/new-hampshire-senate-race-2014-jeanne-shaheen-scott-brown-105149?o=1.

87. Schoenberg, "Jeanne Shaheen Uses Massachusetts Politicians to Attack Scott Brown in NH Senate Race."

88. Maggie Haberman, "Brown Gains on Shaheen in N.H.," *Politico*, October 21, 2014, http://www.politico.com/story/2014/10/scott-brown-jeanne-shaheen-senate-new-hampshire-elections-112086.

89. Kaitlin Flanigan and Josh Brogadir, "Shaheen, Brown Clash in New Hampshire Senate Debate," NECN.com, October 21, 2014, http://www.necn.com/news/new-england/Jeanne-Shaheen-Scott-Brown-Set-To-Debate-in-New-Hampshire-Senate-Race-279946572.html.

90. Dorsey Shaw, "Scott Brown's Campaign Ads Feature Green Screened Stock Footage," *Buzzfeed*, July 29, 2014, https://www.buzzfeed.com/dorsey/scott-browns-campaign-ads-feature-green-screened-stock-foota?utm_term=.jl3zP46wM#.hjleD 09Rx.

91. Alexandra Jaffe, "Scott Brown Forgets He's in New Hampshire," *The Hill*, December 6, 2013, http://thehill.com/blogs/ballot-box/senate-races/192295-scott-brown-forgets-what-state-hes-visiting.

92. "Brown Forgets Where He's Running," NHDP Video, YouTube.com, July 15, 2014, https://www.youtube.com/watch?v=gPkVn6VduQE.

93. Colby Itkowitz, "Which Town Is Brown's Town?" *Washington Post*, June 11, 2014, https://www.washingtonpost.com/blogs/in-the-loop/wp/2014/06/11/which-town-is-browns-town/?utm_term=.ff3a9b25c598.

94. "New Hampshire Senate Debate," C-SPAN, October 30, 2014, 2017, https://www.c-span.org/video/?322395-1/new-hampshire-senate-debate#.

95. Josh Rogers, *Shaheen, Brown Press Their Cases In Final Debate*, New Hampshire Public Radio, October 31, 2014, http://nhpr.org/post/shaheen-brown-press-their-cases-final-debate#stream/0.

96. Jeremy Diamond, *Apology, Geography Lesson Follow New Hampshire Debate*, CNN.com, October 31, 2014, http://www.cnn.com/2014/10/31/politics/scott-brown-geography-fact-check/index.html.

97. This discussion uses the data released by NBC News available at http://www.nbcnews.com/politics/elections/2014/us/exit-polls.

Conclusion

1. "The Kennedy Victory," *New York Times*, November 4, 1964, 38.

2. Husna Haq, "Senator Michelle Obama? Is the First Lady Eyeing a Senate Seat?" *Christian Science Monitor*, October 27, 2014, http://www.csmonitor.com/USA/Politics/Decoder/2014/1027/Senator-Michelle-Obama-Is-the-first-lady-eyeing-a-Senate-seat; Chris Sheridan, "Michelle Obama for President?" Al Jazeera—*Reporter's Notebook*, October 28, 2016, http://www.aljazeera.com/blogs/americas/2016/10/michelle-obama-president-161028033947102.html.

3. Alex Isenstadt and Tarini Parti, "Newsom Won't Run for Calif. Senate Seat; All Eyes on Harris," *Politico*, January 12, 2015, http://www.politico.com/story/2015/01/gavin-newsom-not-running-barabara-boxer-seat-114178; Philip Matier, Andrew Ross, and Carolyn Lochhead, "Race for U.S. Senate: Gavin Newsom out, Kamala Harris in," SFGate.com, January 13, 2015, http://www.sfgate.com/bayarea/article/Gavin-Newsom-won-t-run-for-Barbara-boxer-s-6009753.php.

4. Julia Azari, "Weak Parties and Strong Partisanship Are a Bad Combination," *Vox*, November 3, 2016, http://www.vox.com/mischiefs-of-faction/2016/11/3/13512362/weak-parties-strong-partisanship-bad-combination.

5. Alan I. Abramowitz and Steven Webster, "The Rise of Negative Partisanship and the Nationalization of U.S. Elections in the 21st Century," *Electoral Studies* 41 (March 2016): 12–22.

6. Michael Khoo, "White House Call Reshapes Senate Race," Minnesota Public Radio, April 18, 2001, http://news.minnesota.publicradio.org/features/200104/18_khoom_pawlenty/.

7. Philip Rucker, "A Detached Romney Tends Wounds in Seclusion after Failed White House Bid," *Washington Post*, December 1, 2012, https://www.washingtonpost.com/politics/a-detached-romney-tends-wounds-in-seclusion-after-failed-white-house-bid/2012/12/01/4305079a-38a9-11e2-8a97-363b0f9a0ab3_story.html?utm_term=.805df2c4d864.

8. "Full transcript: Mitt Romney's Remarks on Donald Trump and the 2016 Race," *Politico*, March 3, 2016, https://www.politico.com/story/2016/03/full-transcript-mitt-romneys-remarks-on-donald-trump-and-the-2016-race-220176.

9. Matt Viser, "Romney Was Recruited to Run for Senate in Utah by Hatch," *Boston Globe*, February 6, 2018, https://www.bostonglobe.com/news/politics/2018/02/05/the-seeds-mitt-romney-senate-bid-were-planted-marriott-meeting-with-orrin-hatch/YfY1zZxVK49WBrZiaz6LSK/story.html.

10. "Religious Landscape Study," Pew Research Center, accessed March 30, 2018, http://www.pewforum.org/religious-landscape-study/state/utah/.

11. Catalina Camia, "Mitt Romney Building House in Utah," *USA Today*, May 15, 2013, https://www.usatoday.com/story/onpolitics/2013/05/15/mitt-romney-house-utah/2162533/.

12. Evan Thomas, *Robert Kennedy: His Life* (New York: Simon and Schuster, 2013).

13. Joseph A. Palermo, *In His Own Right: The Political Odyssey of Senator Robert F. Kennedy* (New York: Columbia University Press, 2002).

14. Hillary Clinton, *What Happened* (New York: Simon and Schuster, 2017).

15. "Nomination of James L. Buckley to Be an Under Secretary of State," Nominations, January 29, 1981, https://www.reaganlibrary.archives.gov/archives/speeches/1981/12981a.htm.

16. Gerald Russello, "Mr. Buckley Goes to Washington," *The American Conservative*, April 14, 2011, http://www.theamericanconservative.com/articles/mr-buckley-goes-to-washington.

17. Mitch Sollenberger, Jack Rossotti, and Mark J. Rozell, "Reagan and the Courts," In *The Reagan Presidency: Assessing the Man and His Legacy*, ed. Paul Kengor and Peter Schweitzer (Lanham, MD: Rowman & Littlefield, 2005), 93–114.

18. "William Brock," Bloomberg, accessed August 18, 2017, https://www.bloomberg.com/profiles/people/1503150-william-e-brock.

19. "William E. Brock, CSIS Counselor and Trustee," Center for Strategic and International Studies, accessed August 18, 2017, https://www.csis.org/people/william-e-brock.

20. "Sen. Brock on education," *Times Free Press*, March 30, 2010, http://www.timesfreepress.com/news/opinion/freepress/story/2010/mar/30/fp2-sen-brock-on-education/11254/; Earl Lane, " 'Letter on STEM Education' Urges Parents to Demand Better Science Classes," American Association for the Advancement of Science, December 13, 2012, https://www.aaas.org/news/letter-stem-education-urges-parents-demand-better-science-classes.

21. "1992 Vice President Democratic Primary," NHPR State of Democracy, http://nh.electionstats.com/elections/view/58606/; "1992 Vice President Republican Primary," NHPR State of Democracy, http://nh.electionstats.com/elections/view/58605/.

22. Irvin Molotsky, "Endicott Peabody, 77, Dies; Governor of Massachusetts in 60's," *New York Times*, December 4, 1997, B13.

23. Mike Dec, "Alan Keyes Announces for President!" 4president.org, September 16, 2007, http://blog.4president.org/2008/2007/09/alan-keyes-anno.html.

24. Matt Lewis, "Alan Keyes Loses Constitution Party Bid," *TownHall.com*, April 28, 2008, https://townhall.com/tipsheet/mattlewis/2008/04/29/alan-keyes-loses-constitution-party-bid-n689396.

25. Jack Kenny, "Alan Keyes Still Running for President," *New American*, October 1, 2008, https://www.thenewamerican.com/usnews/politics/item/2433-alan-keyes-still-running-for-president.

26. Andrew Malcolm, "Alan Keyes Stokes Obama Birth Certificate Controversy," *Top of the Ticket: Political Commentary from* The LA Times, February 21, 2009, http://latimesblogs.latimes.com/washington/2009/02/obama-birth-cer.html; Alan Keyes, "Alan Keyes Column," *Renew America*, http://www.renewamerica.com/columns/keyes.

27. Jackson Baker, "Harold Ford Jr. for Mayor?" *Memphis Flyer*, June 1, 2015, https://www.memphisflyer.com/JacksonBaker/archives/2015/06/01/harold-ford-jr-for-mayor.

28. Marcy Kreiter, "Who Is Harold Ford Jr.? Former Tennessee Rep. May Be Transportation Secretary in Trump Cabinet," *International Business Times*, November 22, 2016, http://www.ibtimes.com/who-harold-ford-jr-former-tennessee-rep-may-be-transportation-secretary-trump-cabinet-2450078.

29. Casey Conley, "Scott Brown Goes from Senate to Cycle Assembly," *Fosters Daily Democrat*, June 14, 2015, http://www.seacoastonline.com/article/20150614/NEWS/150619571.

30. Marc Fortier, "Scott Brown to Host Donald Trump at N.H. Barbecue Event," NECN.com, January 12, 2016, http://www.necn.com/news/politics/Scott-Brown-to-Host-Donald-Trump-at-NH-Barbecue-Event-365010401.html.

31. James Pindell, "Scott Brown Endorses Donald Trump," *Boston Globe*, February 2, 2016, https://www.bostonglobe.com/news/politics/2016/02/02/scott-brown-endorse-trump/Iz7bBu2IJoq4EDTFEIK3mM/story.html.

32. Allie Morris, "Capital Beat: VP Chatter Includes Scott Brown," *Concord Monitor*, July 10, 2016, http://www.concordmonitor.com/Scott-Brown-Donald-Trump-

Vice-President-Consideration-3286848; Jim O'Sullivan and Travis Andersen, "Scott Brown Being Considered for Trump Cabinet position," *Boston Globe*, November 18, 2016, https://www.bostonglobe.com/news/politics/2016/11/18/scott-brown-being-considered-for-trump-cabinet-position/1FQmz71id2nTVO80gqGsgN/story.html?s_campaign=bdc:article:stub; Jim O'Sullivan, "Scott Brown Nominated as Ambassador to New Zealand, Samoa," *Boston Globe*, April 25, 2017, https://www.bostonglobe.com/metro/2017/04/25/scott-brown-nominated-ambassador-new-zealand-samoa/tJeG43FR-W4oevyqccYZXdP/story.html.

33. Rebecca Savransky, "Warren Congratulates Scott Brown on Ambassador Nomination," *The Hill*, April 20, 2017, http://thehill.com/homenews/senate/329732-warren-congratulates-scott-brown-on-ambassador-nomination; Tony Schinella, "Jeanne Shaheen to Support Scott Brown Ambassador Nomination," Patch.com, May 16, 2017, https://patch.com/new-hampshire/portsmouth-nh/jeanne-shaheen-support-scott-brown-ambassador-nomination.

Bibliography

Abrahamson, Zachary. "Gillibrand Gets NARAL Endorsement." *Politico*, June 30, 2009. http://www.politico.com/story/2009/06/gillibrand-gets-naral-endorsement-024355.

Abramowitz, Alan I., and Steven Webster. "The Rise of Negative Partisanship and the Nationalization of U.S. Elections in the 21st Century." *Electoral Studies* 41 (2016): 12–22.

Amira, Dan. "Analysis of Respondents Mentioning 'Carpetbagger.'" *UMass Poll*. October 20, 2014. http://www.umass.edu/poll/pdfs/20141020_carpetbagger.pdf.

———. "Rahm Emanuel Gave Gillibrand Opponent an Offer He Couldn't Refuse." *New York*, May 22, 2009. http://nymag.com/daily/intelligencer/2009/05/rahm_emanuel_gave_gillibrand_o.html.

Anderson, Karrin Vasby. "From Spouses to Candidates: Hillary Rodham Clinton, Elizabeth Dole, and the Gendered Office of U.S. President." *Rhetoric & Public Affairs* 5 (1) (2002): 105–32.

Ansolabehere, Stephen, and Shanto Iyengar. *Going Negative: How Attack Ads Shrink and Polarize the Electorate*. New York: The Free Press, 1995.

Apple, R.W., Jr. "Kennedy Edge 6–5: Keating's Defeat Is Termed a 'Tragedy' by Rockefeller." *New York Times*, November 4, 1964: 1.

———. "Stratton Assails Race by Kennedy: Says It Shows Bankruptcy of Party Leadership." *New York Times*, August 26, 1964: 25. http://0-search.proquest.com.library.anselm.edu/docview/115614100?accountid=13640.

"AROUND THE WORLD Republican Eyes Senate Anew." *The Globe and Mail*. December 12, 1979: 20.

Associated Press. "Buckley Running for Senate." *Sarasota Herald-Tribune*, December 12, 1979: 9-A. https://news.google.com/newspapers?nid=1755&dat=19791212&id=gDweAAAAIBAJ&sjid=Ir8EAAAAIBAJ&pg=5327,6522683&hl=en.

———. "Connecticut Legislator Opens G.O.P. Contest for a U.S. Senate Seat: Ribicoff Stepping Down." *New York Times*, December 2, 1979: 55.

———. "Rural Senator-to-Be Visits Harlem." *Denver Post*, January 24, 2009. http://www.denverpost.com/2009/01/24/rural-senator-to-be-visits-harlem/.

————. "Vesta Roy, 76, New Hampshire Ex-Governor." *New York Times*, February 22, 2002: B9.

As We See It. "Will Kennedy Claim New York Citizenship?" *Albany Times-Union*, 1964.

Axelrod, David. *Believer: My Forty Years in Politics*. New York City: Penguin, 2015.

Azari, Julia. "Weak Parties and Strong Partisanship Are a Bad Combination." *Vox*, November 3, 2016. http://www.vox.com/mischiefs-of-faction/2016/11/3/13512362/weak-parties-strong-partisanship-bad-combination.

Babington, Charles. "Brock, Sarbanes Launch All-Out Attacks; Tense Moments, Accusations Define Maryland Candidates' First Debate." *Washington Post*, October 20, 1994: C1.

————. "GOP Senate Candidate in Maryland Attacks Brock, Sarbanes in Ad Debut." *Washington Post*, April 16, 1994: B5.

————. "Montgomery Lawyer Joins Senate Race." *Washington Post*, April 6, 1994: B7.

————. "Sarbanes Account Full; Brock's Cash Dwindles; Challenger Spends on Staff, Volunteer Organizing." *Washington Post*, July 16, 1994: D4.

————. "Sarbanes Disputes the Theory of Relative Senate Success." *Washington Post*, October 24, 1994: D1.

————. "Senate Race Lacks Issue to Rouse Voters: While Sarbanes Lies Low, Brock Leaves Some Confused about His Message." *Washington Post*, October 15, 1994: B1.

————. "U.S. SENATE; Political Veterans Differ on Views." *Washington Post*, November 3, 1994: M1.

Backer, George, et al. "Statement Urging RFK to Run." August 16, 1964.

Baker, Jackson. "Harold Ford's Imperfect Storm." *Memphis Flyer*, November 8, 2006. http://www.memphisflyer.com/memphis/harold-fords-imperfect-storm/Content?oid=1131123.

————. "Harold Ford Jr. for Mayor?" *Memphis Flyer*, June 1, 2015. https://www.memphisflyer.com/JacksonBaker/archives/2015/06/01/harold-ford-jr-for-mayor.

Baker, Peter, and Helene Cooper. "Clinton Set for State Dept., Fed Official for Treasury: Ex-Rivals Uniting." *New York Times*, November 22, 2008: A1. http://www.nytimes.com/2008/11/22/us/politics/22obama.html.

Ball, Molly. "How She Does It." *The Atlantic,* April 11, 2014. http://www.theatlantic.com/politics/archive/2014/04/how-she-does-it/360471/.

Banks, Jeffrey S., and Kiewiet, D. Roderick. "Explaining Patterns of Competition in Congressional Elections." *American Journal of Political Science* 33 (1989): 997–1015.

Bantjes, Adrian A. "Introduction: Bourdieu on the Bighorn? Or, Towards a Cultural History of Fly-Fishing in Wyoming and the Rocky Mountain West." *Annals of Wyoming: The Wyoming History Journal* 76 (2) (2004): 2–5.

Barbaro, Michael. "Ford Decides Not to Run for Senate Seat." *New York Times*, March 2, 2010: A18. http://www.nytimes.com/2010/03/02/nyregion/02ford.html?_r=0.

————. "Gillibrand Responds to Ford's Challenge, Calling Him Out of Touch with New York." *New York Times*, January 13, 2010: A30. http://www.nytimes.com/2010/01/14/nyregion/14ford.html.

————. "Harold Ford Jr. Weighs a Challenge to Gillibrand." *New York Times*, January 5, 2010: A16. http://www.nytimes.com/2010/01/06/nyregion/06ford.html.

————. "Senate Hopeful in New State Airs Evolving Views." *New York Times*, January 12, 2010: A1. http://www.nytimes.com/2010/01/13/nyregion/13ford. html?ref=nyregion.

Barrett, David S. "It's Conservative vs. Conservative in Connecticut." *Washington Post*, September 6, 1980. https://www.washingtonpost.com/archive/politics/1980/09/06/its-conservative-vs-conservative-in-connecticut/e6e5434f-ae04-4108-9f64-d2196c2c2431/?utm_term=.7359cf275b9e.

Battenfeld, Joe. "GOP Chief Sees N.H. 'Opportunity' for Scott Brown." *Boston Herald*, December 11, 2013. http://www.bostonherald.com/news_opinion/columnists/joe_battenfeld/2013/12/battenfeld_gop_chief_sees_nh_opportunity_for_scott.

Baum, Geraldine. "Hillary Clinton's Campaign Off to Pastoral Start." *Los Angeles Times*, July 8, 1999: 12.

Beinart, Peter. "Harold Ford Implodes." *Daily Beast*, January 13, 2010. http://www.thedailybeast.com/articles/2010/01/14/harold-ford-implodes.html.

Bennetts, Leslie. "Buckley Stressing 'Emotional Roots' in Connecticut Campaign for Senate." *New York Times*, June 14, 1980: 25.

Berger, Meyer. *The Story of the New York Times, 1851–1951*. New York: Simon and Schuster, 1951.

Bierman, Noah. "Scott Brown Gets a Plea to Run in N.H." *Boston Globe*, November 8, 2013: A1. http://www.bostonglobe.com/news/politics/2013/11/08/national-republicans-drafting-scott-brown-for-senate-new-hampshire-granite-staters-grow-impatient/A4Me0f4Q25O3FAHMK4JY2J/story.html.

Black, Chris. "Buckley Fights to Close Gap with Dodd." *Boston Globe*, October 22, 1980: 24.

————. "In US Senate Race in Ct., Ethnic Vote Is Crucial." *Boston Globe*, September 1, 1980: 25.

Blair, Jayson. "Senator Moynihan Objects to Being Spliced in Step with Lazio." *New York Times*, July 26, 2000: B5.

Blake, Aaron. "Another Massachusetts Special Election?" *Washington Post*, November 13 2012. https://www.washingtonpost.com/news/the-fix/wp/2012/11/13/another-massachusetts-special-election/?utm_term=.08cf7375db5a.

————. "Scott Brown, Elizabeth Warren and the 'Have a Beer' Factor." *Washington Post*, April 2, 2012. https://www.washingtonpost.com/blogs/the-fix/post/scott-brown-elizabeth-warren-and-the-have-a-beer-factor/2012/04/02/gIQAQGIxqS_blog. html?utm_term=.cfee8b479f45.

————. "Serrano, McCarthy Say No to Gillibrand Challenge." *The Hill*, August 10, 2009. http://thehill.com/homenews/campaign/54223-serrano-mccarthy-say-no-to-gillibrand-challenge.

Blake, Aaron, and Roxana Tiron. "Gillibrand Mulls Move Left on Gays in Military." *The Hill*, July 13, 2009. https://www.thehill.com/homenews/senate/50115-gillibrand-mulls-move-left-on-gays-in-military.

Bogardus, Kevin. "Scott Brown Joins Law and Lobby Firm." *The Hill*, March 11, 2013. http://thehill.com/business-a-lobbying/287329-scott-brown-joins-law-and-lobby-firm.

Bonnar, Bob. "Newspapers Alive and Well." *Wyoming Tribune Eagle—WyomingNews. com*. October 13, 2013. http://www.wyomingnews.com/opinion/newspapers-alive-and-well/article_471f9b1b-528b-5ba7-9d8a-4e1e3efa80cd.html#.VOuJBXzF9Ao.

Bookman, Todd. "Testerman Out, Backs Bob Smith in U.S. Senate Race." *New Hampshire Public Radio*, June 13, 2014. http://nhpr.org/post/testerman-out-backs-bob-smith-us-senate-race#stream/0.

Bosse, Grant. "Jim Rubens Goes from Centrist to Anti-Republican." *New Hampshire Union Leader*, March 7, 2016: 6. http://www.unionleader.com/Grant-Bosse-Jim-Rubens-goes-from-centrist-to-anti-Republican.

Boston Globe. "Buckley Wins Conn. GOP vote." July 27, 1980: 29.

Brereton, Charles. "A look at Endicott Peabody." *Nashua Telegraph*, April 22, 1986: 22. https://news.google.com/newspapers?nid=2209&dat=19860425&id=xZ4rAAAA IBAJ&sjid=NfwFAAAAIBAJ&pg=4967,7245605&hl=en.

Briganti, Irena. "Fox News Channel Signs Former Sen. Scott Brown to Contributor Role." *FOXNews.com*. February 2013. http://press.foxnews.com/2013/02/fox-news-channel-signs-former-sen-scott-brown-to-contributor-role/.

Brodsky, David M., and Robert H. Swansbrough. "Tennessee: A House Divided." In *The 1988 Presidential Election in the South: Continuity Amidst Change in Southern Party Politics*, edited by Laurence W. Moreland, Robert P. Steed and Tod A. Baker, 201–20. New York: Praeger, 1991.

Brown, David L., and Stefan Rayer. "The Volume and Composition of Internal Migration to and from New York." In *New York State in the 21st Century*, edited by Thomas A. Hirschl and Tim B. Heaton, 228–40. Santa Barbara, California: Praeger, 1999.

Brown, Jen Corrine. *Trout Culture: How Fly Fishing Forever Changed the Rocky Mountain West*. Seattle, Washington: University of Washington Press, 2015.

Brown, Trevor. "Enzi and Cheney: How Do They Differ?" *Wyoming Tribune Eagle-WyomingNews.com*. December 15, 2013. http://www.wyomingnews.com/news/enzi-and-cheney-how-do-they-differ/article_8dd76b0f-ba67-5c28-b545-c940dda 85c4c.html#.VOuHanzF9Ao.

———. "Enzi leads in early poll." *Wyoming Tribune Eagle-WyomingNews.com*. July 20, 2013. http://www.wyomingnews.com/news/enzi-leads-in-early-poll/article_ f83e42ac-dde0-53ae-bf72-1ed349122733.html#.VOuHY3zF9Ao.

———. "Liz Cheney Promises Stiff Opposition to President Obama." *Wyoming Tribune Eagle-WyomingNews.com*. July 18, 2013. http://www.wyomingnews.com/news/liz-cheney-promises-stiff-opposition-to-president-obama/article_cc6e8ea1-df2a-583b-92be-17089b6ca7fa.html#.VOuHS3zF9Ao.

———. "Liz Cheney to Challenge Enzi for Senate Seat." *Wyoming Tribune Eagle-Wyoming News*. July 17, 2013. http://www.wyomingnews.com/news/liz-cheney-to-challenge-enzi-for-senate-seat/article_fafa7562-6620-57ff-94ed-616a8a4e1d76. html#.VOuHSXzF9Ao.

———. "Senate Race Money Is Pouring In." *Wyoming Tribune Eagle-WyomingNews. com.* October 16, 2013. http://www.wyomingnews.com/news/senate-race-money- is-pouring-in/article_fa52ea6f-d8af-5b50-b9e2-fa4d095ce75d.html#.VOuJBXz F9Ao.

Bruni, Frank. "Where Scott Brown Is Coming From." *New York Times Magazine,* Febru- ary 22, 2010: MM24. http://www.nytimes.com/2010/02/28/magazine/28Brown-t. html?mcubz=0.

Buckley, William F., Jr. "Sanctimonious Joe?" *NationalReview.com.* October 13, 2007. http:// www.nationalreview.com/article/222485/sanctimonious-joe-william-f-buckley-jr.

"Buckley to Attend Fund-Raiser." *The Hartford Courant.* September 6, 1979: 2.

Burden, Barry C., and Anthony Mughan. "Public Opinion and Hillary Rodham Clin- ton." *Public Opinion Quarterly* 63 (2) (2001): 237–50.

Burks, Edward C. "Weicker, Still an Unrepentant Maverick: Weicker Weathers 'Winds of Sentiment.'" *New York Times,* August 12, 1979: CN1.

Burris, Jeffrey William. "The Senatorial Election of 1970: Brock vs. Gore." *University of Tennessee Honors Thesis Projects,* 1994. http://trace.tennessee.edu/utk_chanhono proj/29.

Camia, Catalina. "Mitt Romney Building House in Utah." *USA Today,* May 15, 2013. https:// www.usatoday.com/story/onpolitics/2013/05/15/mitt-romney-house-utah/ 2162533/.

Carden, Dan. "Lugar Appeals Ruling that He Is Not Indiana Resident." *NWI.com,* March 21, 2012. http://www.nwitimes.com/news/local/govt-and-politics/elections/ lugar-appeals-ruling-that-he-is-not-indiana-resident/article_dcd1ede5-cf1c-596a- b4e1-691b76698d68.html.

Caro, Robert A. *The Years of Lyndon Johnson: The Passage of Power.* New York: Alfred A. Knopf, 2012.

"Carpetbagger." Box 25, folder "'Carpetbag' Issue," Robert F. Kennedy Senate Papers 1964–1968, John F. Kennedy Library, National Archives and Records Admin- istration, Boston, MA, n.d.

CBS Boston. "Scott Brown Not Running for Open Senate Seat." *CBS Boston,* February 1, 2013. http://boston.cbslocal.com/2013/02/01/ap-scott-brown-not-running- for-open-senate-seat/.

Celock, John. "Chris Sununu Says He Won't Run for New Hampshire Governor in 2014." *Huffington Post,* July 18, 2013. http://www.huffingtonpost.com/2013/07/18/ chris-sununu-governor_n_3617739.html.

Chabot, Hilary. "As N.H. Pols Buzz, Scott Brown Moves In." *Boston Herald,* Decem- ber 19, 2013. http://www.bostonherald.com/news_opinion/us_politics/2013/12/ as_nh_pols_buzz_scott_brown_moves_in.

Chan, Sewell. "Bloomberg Leaving Republican Party." *New York Times,* June 19, 2007. https:// cityroom.blogs.nytimes.com/2007/06/19/bloomberg-leaving-republican-party/.

Chase, John, and Liam Ford. "Senate Debate Turns Personal." *Chicago Tribune,* October 22, 2004: 1. http://articles.chicagotribune.com/2004-10-22/news/ 0410220071_1_mr-keyes-alan-keyes-debate.

Chicago Tribune. "Conservative New Hampshire Group Endorses Brown Rival for Senate." May 29, 2014. http://articles.chicagotribune.com/2014-05-29/news/sns-rt-us-usa-new-hampshire-senate-20140529_1_new-hampshire-republican-scott-brown-karen-testerman.

———. "Keyes Left off Illinois GOP Flier." *Chicago Tribune*, October 21, 2004: 33. http://articles.chicagotribune.com/2004-10-21/news/0410220013_1_primary-winner-jack-ryan-alan-keyes-illinois-republican-party.

Childs, Sarah, and Philip Cowley. "The Politics of Local Presence: Is There a Case for Descriptive Representation?" *Political Studies* 59, no. 1 (2011): 1–19.

Clark, Cal, and Janet Clark. "Wyoming Political Surprises in the Late 1980s: Deviating Elections in a Conservative Republican State." *Great Plains Quarterly* (1991): 181–97.

Cline, Drew. "Scott Brown Plans to Win over NH One Handshake at a Time." *New Hampshire Union Leader*, July 10, 2014: 7. http://www.unionleader.com/apps/pbcs.dll/article?AID=/20140710/LOCALVOICES03/140719950/-1/news&template=printart.

Clinton, Hillary. *What Happened*. New York: Simon and Schuster, 2017.

CNN.com Election Results: U.S. Senate Illinois Exit Polls. November 2004. http://www.cnn.com/ELECTION/2004/pages/results/states/IL/S/01/epolls.0.html.

Condon, William H. *Life of Major-General James Shields: Hero of Three Wars and Senator from Three States*. Chicago: Blakely, 1990. https://openlibrary.org/books/OL6775098M/Life_of_Major-General_James_Shields.

Confessore, Nicholas, and Danny Hakim. "Kennedy Drops Bid for Senate Seat, Citing Personal Reasons." *New York Times*, January 21, 2009. http://www.nytimes.com/2009/01/22/nyregion/22caroline.html.

Conley, Casey. "Scott Brown Goes from Senate to Cycle Assembly." *Fosters Daily Democrat*, June 14, 2015. http://www.seacoastonline.com/article/20150614/NEWS/150619571.

———. "Shaheen and Brown Agree: No West Africa Travel Ban." *Fosters.com*, October 11, 2014. http://www.fosters.com/article/20141011/gjnews_01/141019883.

Conway Daily Sun. "Massachusetts Governor Helps Rally Carroll County Democrats at Annual Grover Cleveland Dinner." September 15, 2014. https://www.conwaydailysun.com/news/massachusetts-governor-helps-rally-carroll-county-democrats-at-annual-grover/article_6e5ddfea-c427-5cdd-86e1-cf17c9b92c8e.html.

Cook, John. "Harold Ford Tries, Fails to Give a Straight Answer on Whether He's Paid New York Taxes." *Gawker*, February 15, 2010. http://gawker.com/5472029/harold-ford-tries-fails-to-give-a-straight-answer-on-whether-hes-paid-new-york-taxes.

———. "Harold Ford's Tennessee Tax Dodge." *Gawker*, February 12, 2010. http://gawker.com/5470445/harold-fords-tennessee-tax-dodge.

Cos, Grant C., and Brian J. Snee. "New York, New York: Being and Creating Identity in the 2000 New York State Senate Race." *American Behavioral Scientist* 44, no. 12 (2001): 2014–29.

Cowley, Philip. "Why Not Ask the Audience? Understanding the Public's Representational Priorities." *British Politics* 8 (2013): 138–63.

Crowley, Michael. "Ford Theater: The Crazy Logic of an Outsider/Insider Carpetbagger Candidacy." *New York*, March 5, 2010. http://nymag.com/news/intelligencer/64602/.

Cullen, Fergus. "Welcome to New Hampshire, Scott Brown." *New Hampshire Union Leader*, January 3, 2014: 18. http://www.unionleader.com/article/20140103/OPINION02/140109827.

Current, Richard N. *Those Terrible Carpetbaggers*. Oxford: Oxford University Press, 1988.

———. 1967. *Three Carpetbag Governors*. Baton Rouge: Louisiana State University Press.

Davey, Monica. "In a Star's Shadow, Republicans Strain to Find Opponent." *New York Times*, July 29, 2004: 6.

———. "The 2004 Campaign: The Illinois Primary; from Crowded Field, Democrats Choose State Legislator to Seek Senate Seat." *New York Times*, March 17, 2004. http://www.nytimes.com/2004/03/17/us/2004-campaign-illinois-primary-crowded-field-democrats-choose-state-legislator.html.

Dec, Mike. "Alan Keyes Announces for President!" *4president.org*. September 16, 2007. http://blog.4president.org/2008/2007/09/alan-keyes-anno.html.

DeCoster, Stan. "Buckley Was Gracious to the End." *The Day*, November 5, 1980: 5. https://news.google.com/newspapers?nid=1915&dat=19801105&id=DwAhAAAAIBAJ&sjid=DHUFAAAAIBAJ&pg=5587,618771&hl=en.

Democrats for Keating, Johnson, and Humphrey. "Kennedy: 'I Have the Negro Vote in My Bag!' " 1964.

Devenish, Colin. *Rage against the Machine*. Paperback. New York: St. Martin's Griffin, 2001.

Devine, Christopher J., and Kyle C. Kopko. *The VP Advantage: How Running Mates Influence Home State Voting in Presidential Elections*. Manchester: Manchester University Press, 2016.

Dewey, Thomas E. "Thomas E. Dewey Address for Senator Keating." October 7, 1964.

Diamond, Jeremy. "Apology, Geography Lesson Follow New Hampshire Debate." *CNN.com*, October 31, 2014. http://www.cnn.com/2014/10/31/politics/scott-brown-geography-fact-check/index.html.

DiStaso, John. "Former Sen. John E. Sununu Won't Run for Office in 2014." *New Hampshire Union Leader*, April 12, 2013.

———. "Is He In? Scott Brown Making Private Calls to Prominent NH Republicans." *New Hampshire Union Leader*, February 21, 2014. http://www.unionleader.com/article/20140221/NEWS0602/140219339.

Dooley, Erin. "New Hampshire Senate Debate Live Updates." *ABCNews.com*, October 30, 2014. http://liveblog.abcnews.go.com/Event/New_Hampshire_Senate_Debate_Live_Updates.

Dries, Bill. "Ford on Governor's Race: 'Not the Right Time.' " *The Daily News*, April 15, 2009. https://www.memphisdailynews.com/news/2009/apr/15/ford-on-governors-race-not-the-right-time.

Duquette, Jerold J. "The 'Scott Brown Era' in Massachusetts Politics." *New England Journal of Political Science* 7, no. 1 (2013): 120–41.

Easton, Lauren. "Updating AP style on Hillary Clinton." *Associated Press— Announcements.* November 30, 2015. https://blog.ap.org/announcements/ updating-ap-style-on-hillary-clinton.

Editorial. "Aron's Failed Lawsuit 1994 Senate Primary: Unsuccessful Candidate Sought Limits on What Opponents Can Say." *Baltimore Sun*, March 15, 1996. http:// articles.baltimoresun.com/1996-03-15/news/1996075083_1_aron-brock-ruthann.

———. "A Bear Market for Republicans." *The State Journal-Register*, July 14, 2004: 6.

———. "GOP: Grand Old Pot-shotters." *Baltimore Sun*, September 2, 1994. http://articles. baltimoresun.com/1994-09-02/news/1994245178_1_bill-brock-pierpont-franks.

———. "The GOP's Rent-a-Senator." *Chicago Tribune*, August 6, 2004. http:// articles.chicagotribune.com/2004-08-06/news/0408060313_1_mr-keyes-judy-baar-topinka-alan-keyes.

———. "Governor Bill Brock?" *Baltimore Sun*, February 1, 1993. http://articles. baltimoresun.com/1993-02-01/news/1993032037_1_republican-candidates-maryland-gop-bill-brock.

———. "Hey, Scott Brown Stop Flirting with NH." *New Hampshire Union Leader*, September 30, 2013. http://www.unionleader.com/article/20131001/OPINION01/ 131009992/-1/opinion01.

———. "The Kennedy Victory." *New York Times*, November 4, 1964: 38.

———. "N.H. Democrats Seek Dignity." *Nashua Telegraph*, April 13, 1986: A10.

———. "Nothing against Keyes, But How about an Illinoisan?" *Chicago Daily Herald*, August 5, 2004: 14.

———. "Plan B for Illinois." *New York Times*, August 10, 2004: 20.

———. "Sauerbrey Close Brock Not." *Baltimore Sun*, September 29, 1994. http://articles. baltimoresun.com/1994-09-29/news/1994272094_1_sauerbrey-glendening-brock.

Edsall, Thomas B. "The Obamacare Crisis." *New York Times*, November 19, 2013. http://www.nytimes.com/2013/11/20/opinion/edsall-the-obamacare-crisis.html.

Eilperin, Juliet. "Keyes to Face Obama in U.S. Senate Race; Ill. Election to Ensure Nation's 5th Black Senator." *Washington Post*, August 9, 2004: A08.

Elazar, Daniel J. *American Federalism: A View from the States.* 2nd. New York: Thomas Y. Crowell, 1972.

Elkins, Hilary. "Harold Ford Jr. Gets Stonewalled." *GQ*, February 25, 2010. http://www. gq.com/story/harold-ford-jr-gets-stonewalled.

"Endicott Peabody: Endicott "Chub" Peabody, a Quixote of Politics, Died on December 2nd, aged 77." *The Economist,* December 11, 1997.

Enten, Harry J. "If John Kerry Makes Secretary of State, Can Scott Brown Win His Senate Seat?" *The Guardian*, December 14, 2012. https://www.theguardian. com/commentisfree/2012/dec/14/john-kerry-secretary-state-scott-brown-senate.

Everett, Burgess. "GOP Senators to Cheney: We Like Mike." *Politico,* July 28, 2013. http://www.politico.com/story/2013/07/mike-enzi-liz-cheney-wyoming-senate-race-94846.html#ixzz2aRGFjP4Q.

"Excerpts: Shaheen to Address Supporters in Manchester on Primary Night." *JeanneShaheen.org*. September 9, 2014. http://jeanneshaheen.org/news/excerpts-shaheen-address-supporters-manchester-primary-night/.

Fairbanks, Eve. "150 Minutes with Carolyn McCarthy." *New York*, February 15, 2009. http://nymag.com/news/intelligencer/encounter/54343/.

Fenno, Richard F., Jr. *Home Style: House Members in Their Districts*. Boston: Little, Brown, 1978.

———. *Senators on the Campaign Trail*. Norman and London: University of Oklahoma Press, 1996.

———. *The United States Senate: A Bicameral Perspective*. Washington, DC: American Enterprise Institute Press, 1982.

Finucane, Martin. "Markey, Brown in Statistical Dead Heat, Poll Shows." *Boston Globe*, January 30, 2013. https://www.bostonglobe.com/metro/2013/01/30/new-poll-finds-markey-brown-statistical-dead-heat-hypothetical-senate-race/0jcrsghKfpTx5fbzVbaHXO/story.html.

Fiorina, Morris P., and David W. Rohde. "Richard Fenno's Research Agenda and the Study of Congress." In *Home Style and Washington Work: Studies of Congressional Politics*, edited by Morris P. Fiorina and David W. Rohde, 1–16. Ann Arbor: University of Michigan Press, 1989.

Fitzpatrick, Jody L., and Rodney E. Hero. "Political Culture and Political Characteristics of the American States: A Consideration of Some Old and New Questions." *Western Political Quarterly* 41, no. 1 (1988): 145–53.

Flanigan, Kaitlin, and Josh Brogadir. "Shaheen, Brown Clash in New Hampshire Senate Debate." *NECN.com*, October 21, 2014. http://www.necn.com/news/new-england/Jeanne-Shaheen-Scott-Brown-Set-To-Debate-in-New-Hampshire-Senate-Race-279946572.html.

Fleischer, Ari. "@AriFleischer." *Twitter*. July 16, 2013. https://twitter.com/AriFleischer/status/357249872174395393?ref_src=twsrc%5Etfw.

Ford, Gerald R. *A Time to Heal: The Autobiography of Gerald R. Ford*. New York: Harper & Row, 1979.

Ford, Harold, Jr. "Why I'm Not Running for the Senate." *New York Times*, March 2, 2010: A23. http://www.nytimes.com/2010/03/02/opinion/02ford2.html.

Ford, Liam, and David Mendell. "Keyes Sets Up House in Cal City." *Chicago Tribune*, August 13, 2014.

Ford, Liam, and Rudolf Bush. "Ryan Quits Race: State GOP Scrambles to Find Replacement to Face Obama; Republican Senate Nominee Cites Fixation on Divorce Files." *Chicago Tribune*, June 26, 2004.

Fortier, Marc. "Scott Brown to Host Donald Trump at N.H. Barbecue Event." *NECN.com*, January 12, 2016. http://www.necn.com/news/politics/Scott-Brown-to-Host-Donald-Trump-at-NH-Barbecue-Event-365010401.html.

Fowler, Linda L. "New Hampshire Senate: Down to the Wire in New Hampshire." In *Midterm Madness: The Elections of 2002*, 125–35. Lanham, Maryland: Rowman & Littlefield, 2003.

"Free-Agent Clinton Signs Five-Year, $37 Million Deal with Argentina." *The Onion*. March 17, 1998. http://www.theonion.com/articles/freeagent-clinton-signs-fiveyear-37-million-deal-w,604/.

Galdieri, Christopher J. "50 Takes on Trump: New Hampshire." *Utica College Center of Public Affairs and Election Research*. May 10, 2017. https://www.ucpublicaffairs.com/home/2017/5/10/50-takes-on-trump-new-hampshire-by-christopher-galdieri.

Gandy, Rob. "An Investigation of Politician Mobility in the United Kingdom." *British Politics* 9, no. 2 (2014): 182–209.

Gardner, Gerald. *Robert Kennedy in New York*. New York: Random House, 1965.

Gearan, Anne. "Mrs. Clinton May Find Tough Crowd in Upstate New York." *The Argus-Press*, July 8, 1999: 15. https://news.google.com/newspapers?nid=1988&dat=19990708&id=lGUiAAAAIBAJ&sjid=pawFAAAAIBAJ&pg=1987,625120&hl=en.

Gerstel, Steve. "Sleepers Could Pull Off Some Senate Surprises." *United Press International*, October 30, 1986.

Glass, Andrew. "Sen. Bob Smith Switches Back to GOP, Nov. 1, 1999." *Politico*, October 31, 2015. http://www.politico.com/story/2015/10/sen-bob-smith-switches-back-to-the-gop-nov-1-1999-215242.

Goslin, Joann. "Candidate Dupay Says Nuclear Issue Top Priority." *Nashua Telegraph*, July 20, 1986: 36. https://news.google.com/newspapers?nid=2209&dat=19860720&id=tZwrAAAAIBAJ&sjid=D_wFAAAAIBAJ&pg=5870,6226600&hl=en.

Graham, Kenneth L. *Fishing Wyoming: An Angler's Guide to More than 200 Sites*. Helena, Montana: Falcon, 1998.

Grier, Peter. "Liz Cheney Senate Bid off to a Rocky Start." *Christian Science Monitor*, September 5, 2013. http://www.csmonitor.com/USA/Politics/Decoder/2013/0905/Liz-Cheney-Senate-bid-off-to-a-rocky-start.

Grynbaum, Michael M. "Spitzer Resigns, Citing Personal Failings." *New York Times*, March 12, 2008. http://www.nytimes.com/2008/03/12/nyregion/12cnd-resign.html.

Gwirtzman, Milton. Memorandum to Robert F. Kennedy. Box 37, folder "Memoranda," Robert F. Kennedy Senate Papers 1964–1968, John F. Kennedy Library, National Archives and Records Administration, Boston, MA, n.d.

Haberman, Clyde, and Albin Krebs. "Notes on People: James Buckley Shifts Registration to Connecticut." *New York Times*, August 24, 1979: B5.

Haberman, Maggie. "Brown Gains on Shaheen in N.H." *Politico*, October 21, 2014. http://www.politico.com/story/2014/10/scott-brown-jeanne-shaheen-senate-new-hampshire-elections-112086.

Haddadin, Jim. "Shaheen Prods U.S. House on Transportation Funding Bill." *Fosters Daily Democrat*, March 28, 2012. http://www.fosters.com/article/20120328/GJNEWS_01/703289957.

Hakim, Danny. "For Nixon in-Law, G.O.P. Post and a Giuliani Clash." *New York Times*, September 29, 2009: A30. http://www.nytimes.com/2009/09/29/nyregion/29cox.html.

Hakim, Danny, and Nicholas Confessore. "Paterson Picks Gillibrand for Senate Seat." *New York Times*, January 24, 2009. http://www.nytimes.com/2009/01/24/nyregion/24senator.html.

Halberstam, David. "The Morning After in Keating's Suite: Dawn of Reflection." *New York Times*, November 5, 1964: 30.

Hamby, Peter. "Scott Brown in 2016: Why Not?" *CNN.com*, August 19, 2013. http://www.cnn.com/2013/08/19/politics/scott-brown-2016.

Hamilton, Alexander, James Madison, and John Jay. *The Federalist (with Letters of "Brutus")*. Edited by Terence Ball. Cambridge: Cambridge University Press, 2003.

Hancock, Laura. "Liz Cheney Wins Republican Primary for U.S. House." *Casper Star-Tribune*, August 16, 2016. http://trib.com/news/state-and-regional/govt-and-politics/liz-cheney-wins-republican-primary-for-u-s-house/article_e3b38943-8bba-5c87-8a02-7f87d9c53841.html.

Haq, Husna. "Senator Michelle Obama? Is the First Lady Eyeing a Senate Seat?" *Christian Science Monitor*, October 27, 2014. http://www.csmonitor.com/USA/Politics/Decoder/2014/1027/Senator-Michelle-Obama-Is-the-first-lady-eyeing-a-Senate-seat.

Henry, Diane. "Kissinger Holds Hartford Parley on Senate Race: Discusses Joining Contest for G.O.P. Nomination." *New York Times*, February 7, 1979: B2.

Hernandez, Raymond. "N.Y.'s Junior Senator Gains a Defender: The Senior Senator." *New York Times*, May 8, 2009: A1. http://www.nytimes.com/2009/05/08/nyregion/08gillibrand.html?_r=0.

Hibbing, John, and Sara L. Brandes. "State Population and the Electoral Success of U.S. Senators." *American Journal of Political Science* 27, no. 4 (1983): 808–19.

Hohmann, James. "How Shaheen Plans to Defeat Brown." *Politico*, March 30, 2014. http://www.politico.com/story/2014/03/new-hampshire-senate-race-2014-jeanne-shaheen-scott-brown-105149?o=1.

———. "Why Scott Brown Might Run for Governor, Not Senate." *Politico*, January 13, 2013. http://www.politico.com/story/2013/01/why-scott-brown-might-run-for-governor-not-senate-86102_Page3.html.

Hohmann, James, Tal Kopan, and Alexander Burns. "Cheney: 'I Have Decided to Discontinue My Campaign.'" *Politico*, January 6, 2014. http://www.politico.com/story/2014/01/liz-cheney-wyoming-senate-race-101767.

Huard, Jacqueline. "Weicker Reaffirms His Support of Bozzuto." *The Hour*, August 5, 1980: 3. https://news.google.com/newspapers?nid=1916&dat=19800805&id=8o4pAAAAIBAJ&sjid=Nm4FAAAAIBAJ&pg=1110,583268&hl=en.

Huetteman, Emmarie. "Liz Cheney to Run for Wyoming's Only House Seat." *New York Times*, January 30, 2016. https://www.nytimes.com/2016/01/31/us/politics/liz-cheney-to-run-for-wyomings-only-house-seat.html.

Humphrey, Tom. "Harold Ford Jr. to Lose TN Voter Registration." KnoxBlogs.com, August 31, 2010. http://knoxblogs.com/humphreyhill/2010/08/31/harold_ford_jr_to_lose_tn_vote/.

Isenstadt, Alex, and Tarini Parti. "Newsom Won't Run for Calif. Senate Seat; All Eyes On Harris." *Politico*, January 12, 2015. http://www.politico.com/story/2015/01/gavin-newsom-not-running-barabara-boxer-seat-114178.

Itkowitz, Colby. "Which Town Is Brown's Town?" *Washington Post*, June 11, 2014. https://www.washingtonpost.com/blogs/in-the-loop/wp/2014/06/11/which-town-is-browns-town/?utm_term=.ff3a9b25c598.

Jackson, John S. *The Making of a Senator: Barack Obama and the 2004 Illinois Senate Race*. Southern Illinois University Carbondale, Simon Review: Occasional Papers of the Paul Simon Public Policy Institute, 2016. http://opensiuc.lib.siu.edu/cgi/viewcontent.cgi?article=1004&context=ppi_papers.

Jacobson, Gary C. *The Politics of Congressional Elections*. 6th. New York: Pearson Longman, 2004.

Jaffe, Alexandra. "Scott Brown Forgets He's in New Hampshire." *The Hill*, December 6, 2013. http://thehill.com/blogs/ballot-box/senate-races/192295-scott-brown-forgets-what-state-hes-visiting.

Jensen, Tom. "Dems Favored for MA-Gov.—Unless Brown Runs." *Public Policy Polling*. May 7, 2013. http://www.publicpolicypolling.com/main/2013/05/dems-favored-for-ma-govunless-brown-runs.html.

———. "Uphill Battle for Cheney in Wyoming." *PublicPolicyPolling.com*. July 22, 2013. http://www.publicpolicypolling.com/pdf/2011/PPP_Release_WY_723.pdf.

Johnson, Benny. "Bartender Scott Brown." *National Review*, November 3, 2014. http://www.nationalreview.com/article/391703/bartender-scott-brown-benny-johnson.

Johnson, Rossiter, and John Howard Brown. *The Twentieth Century Biographical Dictionary of Notable Americans*. Vol. 9. 10 vols. Boston: Boston Biographical Society, 1904.

Kaiser, Robert G. "Sen. Ribicoff Announces Retirement." *Washington Post*, May 4, 1979: A3. https://www.washingtonpost.com/archive/politics/1979/05/04/sen-ribicoff-announces-retirement/ae6bd37a-bf5c-41d4-9672-9d0a2c6e5e42/?utm_term=.e3ca369b4e2f.

Kass, John. "Keyes' Antics Just What GOP Old Guard Wants." *Chicago Tribune*, September 5, 2004: A1–A2. http://articles.chicagotribune.com/2004-09-05/news/0409050366_1_selfish-hedonist-mr-keyes-illinois-republicans.

Kaufer, David, Shawn J. Parry-Giles, and Beata Beigman Klebanov. "The 'Image Bite,' Political Language, and the Public/Private Divide." *Journal of Language and Politics* 11, no. 3 (2012): 336–56.

"Kennedy and Reform." Box 30, folder "Keating, Kenneth," Robert F. Kennedy Senate Papers 1964–1968, John F. Kennedy Library, National Archives and Records Administration, Boston, MA, n.d.

Kennedy, Robert F. "Acceptance Speech for Democratic Nomination." Box 20, folder "9/1/64. Robert F. Kennedy Senate Papers 1964–1968, John F. Kennedy Library, National Archives and Records Administration, Boston, MA, September 1, 1964.

———. "Remarks Prepared for Delivery by Robert F. Kennedy." Box 21, folder "10/31/64, Democratic Rally Madison Square Garden," Robert F. Kennedy Senate Papers 1964–1968, John F. Kennedy Library, National Archives and Records Administration, Boston, MA, October 31, 1964.

———. "RFK TV Speech—Why I Am Running for Senate." Box 30, folder "Kennedy, Robert F.," Robert F. Kennedy Senate Papers 1964–1968, John F. Kennedy Library, National Archives and Records Administration, Boston, MA, 1964.

———. "Why I Would Like to Be Senator from New York." October 7, 1964.

"Kennedy-Johnson Accomplishments for New York." Box 20, folder "10/7/64, 'Why I Would Like to Be Senator From New York,'" *Journal-American*, Robert F. Kennedy Senate Papers 1964–1968, John F. Kennedy Library, National Archives and Records Administration, Boston, MA, October 7, 1964.

Kenny, Jack. "Alan Keyes Still Running for President." *New American*. October 1, 2008. https://www.thenewamerican.com/usnews/politics/item/2433-alan-keyes-still-running-for-president.

Keyes, Alan. "Alan Keyes Column." *Renew America*. Accessed August 18, 2017. http://www.renewamerica.com/columns/keyes.

Khoo, Michael. "White House Call Reshapes Senate Race." *Minnesota Public Radio*, April 18, 2001. http://news.minnesota.publicradio.org/features/200104/18_khoom_pawlenty/.

King, Dennis. *Lyndon LaRouche and the New American Fascism*. New York: Doubleday, 1989.

King, John, and Peter Hamby. "Liz Cheney Abandons Senate Bid." *CNN*. January 6, 2014. http://www.cnn.com/2014/01/05/politics/liz-cheney-senate-race/.

Kinzer, Stephen. 2004. "Candidate, under Pressure, Quits Senate Race in Illinois." *New York Times*, June 26, Late Edition ed.: A8.

———. "Ex-Coach Won't Run for Senate, and G.O.P. Woes Grow in Illinois." *New York Times*, July 15, 2004: A 14.

Kleefeld, Eric. "Gillibrand Inches Leftward, Now Supports Gay Marriage." *Talking Points Memo*, January 23, 2009. http://talkingpointsmemo.com/dc/gillibrand-inches-leftward-now-supports-gay-marriage.

Kludt, Tom. "Liz Cheney Says Opponent Mike Enzi Is 'Confused' (VIDEO)." *Talking Points Memo*. July 18, 2013. http://talkingpointsmemo.com/livewire/liz-cheney-says-opponent-mike-enzi-is-confused-video.

Koerner, Brendan. "Why Unseal Ryan's Divorce Papers?" *Slate*, June 23, 2004. http://www.slate.com/articles/news_and_politics/explainer/2004/06/why_unseal_ryans_divorce_papers.html.

Kornacki, Steve. "The Clintons Take New York." *Politico New York*, December 11, 2013. http://www.capitalnewyork.com/article/albany/2013/12/8537216/clintons-take-new-york?page=all.

Kraus, Jeffrey C. "Case: Showdown in the Empire State—Clinton versus Lazio." In *Campaigns and Elections: Issues, Concepts, Cases*, edited by Robert P. Watson and Colton C. Campbell, 229–38. Boulder, Colorado: Lynne Rienner, 2003.

Kraushaar, Josh. "Big Endorsement for Gillibrand." *Politico*, January 28, 2009. http://www.politico.com/blogs/scorecard/0109/Big_endorsement_for_Gillibrand.html?showall.

Kreiter, Marcy. "Who Is Harold Ford Jr.? Former Tennessee Rep. May Be Transportation Secretary in Trump Cabinet." *International Business Times*, November 22, 2016. http://www.ibtimes.com/who-harold-ford-jr-former-tennessee-rep-may-be-transportation-secretary-trump-cabinet-2450078.

Krol, Eric. "Facing 'Brutal' Campaign, Ryan Quits GOP Leaders Breathe Sigh of Relief, Begin Search for Replacement." *Chicago Daily Herald*, June 26, 2014: 1.

———. "Gidwitz Bows Out, but GOP May Have Another Senate Option." *Chicago Daily Herald*, July 2, 2014: 13.

———. "GOP List Down to a Surprising Pair: Former Bush Anti-Drug Official and Radio Talk Show Host From Maryland Up for Senate Candidacy." *Chicago Daily Herald*, August 4, 2014: 1.

———. "Keyes Makes GOP Wait; Maryland Conservative Gets the Offer, but He Delays Commitment." *Chicago Daily Herald*, August 5, 2014: 1.

———. "A Political Campaign Would Put a Halt to Mike Ditka's Lucrative Endorsements and ESPN Gig, Making a Run for the Senate . . . a Costly Venture." *Chicago Daily Herald*, July 14, 2014: 1.

———. "Ryan Denies Sex Club Claim Senate Hopeful Insists He Won't Quit over Ex-Wife's Allegations." *Chicago Daily Herald*, June 22, 2014: 1.

———. "Ryan Event Canceled When Hastert Bails Out; Spokesman Says Candidacy Not in Trouble." *Chicago Daily Herald*, June 24, 2014: 1.

———. "Salvi Says No to Senate Race Unless Bush Calls." *Chicago Daily Herald*, July 22, 2014: 1.

Krol, Eric, and John Patterson. "Political Glare Too Harsh for Ditka." *Chicago Daily Herald*, July 15, 2004: 1.

———. "Top Prospects Won't Take Ryan's Place." *Chicago Daily Herald*, June 26, 2004: 5.

Landrigan, Kevin. "Jim Rubens Becomes First GOPer to Officially Oppose NH's Shaheen." *Nashua Telegraph*, September 19, 2013.

Lane, Earl. "'Letter on STEM Education' Urges Parents to Demand Better Science Classes." *American Association for the Advancement of Science*. December 13, 2012. https://www.aaas.org/news/letter-stem-education-urges-parents-demand-better-science-classes.

Langfitt, Frank. "After Taking Many Blows, Brock Strikes Back at Aron." *Baltimore Sun*, September 9, 1994.

———. "Brock Leads Senate Race, Polls Show." *Baltimore Sun*, September 10, 1994. http://articles.baltimoresun.com/1994-09-10/news/1994253040_1_bill-brock-aron-unfavorable-rating.

———. "Brock Television Ads Call Sarbanes Soft on Crime." *Baltimore Sun*, October 13, 1994. http://articles.baltimoresun.com/1994-10-13/news/1994286043_1_senator-sarbanes-bill-brock-soft-on-crime.

———. "Brock Trails Sarbanes, Despite Heavy Spending." *Baltimore Sun*, November 5, 1994. http://articles.baltimoresun.com/1994-11-05/news/1994309044_1_bill-brock-sarbanes-brock-looked.

———. "GOP Candidates Narrow Sarbanes' Lead for Senate." *Baltimore Sun*, July 21, 1994. http://articles.baltimoresun.com/1994-07-21/news/1994202016_1_yesterday-poll-sarbanes-republican-candidates.

———. "Sarbanes Sweeps to 4th Term; Brock Says He Has No Regrets." *Baltimore Sun*, November 9, 1994. http://articles.baltimoresun.com/1994-11-09/news/19943 13162_1_sarbanes-maryland-republicans-brock.

Laskow, Sarah. "The Truck behind the Man." *Newsweek*, October 29, 2010. http://www.newsweek.com/truck-behind-man-74091.

Lavender, Paige. "Gov Brags that Scott Brown, Who Was Born in Maine, Was 'Born Virtually' in New Hampshire." *Huffington Post*, April 14, 2014. http://www.huffingtonpost.com/2014/04/14/scott-brown-new-hampshire_n_5145796.html.

Lee, Timothy B. "Larry Lessig Backs a Long-Shot Republican in His Campaign to Clean Up Money in Politics." *Vox*, July 29, 2014. https://www.vox.com/2014/7/29/5947835/larry-lessig-backs-a-long-shot-republican-in-his-campaign-to-clean-up.

Lerner, Max. "N.Y. Senate Race." *New York Post*, September 27, 1964: 41.

Leubsdorf, Ben. "Charlie Bass Passes on 2014 Senate Run against Incumbent Democrat Jeanne Shaheen." *Concord Monitor*, October 5, 2013.

———. "NH Republican Activist Karen Testerman to Run for US Senate." *Concord Monitor*, October 14, 2013.

———. "N.H. Senate Leader Jeb Bradley Won't Run for U.S. Senate in 2014." *Concord Monitor*, September 4, 2013.

"Lewis, James Hamilton (1863–1939)." *Biographical Directory of the United States Congress*, 2005. http://bioguide.congress.gov/scripts/biodisplay.pl?index=L000 284.

Lewis, Matt. "Alan Keyes Loses Constitution Party Bid." *TownHall.com*, April 28, 2008. https://townhall.com/tipsheet/mattlewis/2008/04/29/alan-keyes-loses-constitution-party-bid-n689396.

Lewis, Paul. "Scott Brown: Fallout from Hobby Lobby Decision Puts Senate Bid in Tight Spot." *The Guardian*, July 16, 2014. https://www.theguardian.com/world/2014/jul/16/scott-brown-republican-senate-campaign-hobby-lobby-women.

Lieberman, David. "Connecticut: Buckley Woos the Blues." *The New Republic*, October 10, 1980: 13.

Linskey, Annie. "Brown's Move to New Hampshire Fuels Talk of Senate Race." *Bloomberg.com*. December 16, 2013. http://www.bloomberg.com/news/2013-12-16/brown-s-move-to-new-hampshire-fuels-talk-of-senate-race.html.

Liu, Irene Jay. "Gillibrand Gets CSEA Endorsement." *Times Union*, July 31, 2009. http://www.timesunion.com/local/article/Gillibrand-gets-CSEA-endorsement-553224.php.

———. "Gillibrand Snags Endorsement over Sausage." *Times Union*, September 1, 2009. http://blog.timesunion.com/capitol/archives/17818/gillibrand-snags-endorsement-over-sausage/.

LoBianco, Tom. "Foes Allege Sen. Lugar Doesn't Really Live in Ind." *Associated Press*, February 15, 2012. http://archive.boston.com/news/politics/articles/2012/02/15/foes_allege_sen_lugar_doesnt_really_live_in_ind/.

Lueck, Thomas J. "Mrs. Clinton Explains Kiss in Middle East." *New York Times*, July 14, 2000: B4.

Lynch, Edward A. 2011. *Starting Over: A Political Biography of George Allen*. Lanham, Maryland: Hamilton Books, 2011.

Macalester, Gretyl. "Penguin Plunge Raises $600,000 over Weekend." *New Hampshire Union Leader*, February 2, 2014: 1. http://www.unionleader.com/article/20140203/NEWS/140209837.

Macneal, Caitlin. "Enzi Greeted with High Fives on Senate Floor following Cheney News (VIDEO)." *Talking Points Memo*. January 4, 2014. http://talkingpointsmemo.com/livewire/enzi-greeted-with-high-fives-on-senate-floor-following-cheney-news.

Madden, Mike. "Blanche Lincoln Stuns Bill Halter." *Salon*, June 9, 2010. http://www.salon.com/2010/06/09/bill_halter_blanche_lincoln_runoff/.

Madden, Richard. "POLITICS: A Hungry G.O.P. Eyes the Senate Race." *New York Times*, June 24, 1979: CN16.

Madden, Richard L. "Buckley and Dodd Sharpen Senate Campaign Barbs." *New York Times*, October 17, 1980: B2.

———. "Buckley and the '80 Senate Race." *New York Times*, September 2, 1979: CN20.

———. "Buckley Confronts 'Carpetbagger' Issue." *New York Times*, December 16, 1979: CN26.

———. "A Buckley-Dodd Debate Emphasizes Differences." *New York Times*, September 16, 1980: B1.

———. "Buckley Pleads for G.O.P. Unity in Contest against Dodd." *New York Times*, September 11, 1980: B4.

———. "Factors behind Buckley Victory: G.O.P. Convention: A Primary Warmup." *New York Times*, August 3, 1980: CN1.

———. "G.O.P. Senate Race Closer Than Expected: Both Contestants Have Delegates to Force Primary Bozzuto and Buckley in Tight G.O.P. Race." *New York Times*, June 15, 1980: CN1.

———. "James Buckley Says He Will Run for Ribicoff's Seat in U.S. Senate." *New York Times*, December 12, 1979: A1.

———. "McKinney Tells Why He Is Backing Buckley for Senate." *New York Times*, May 25, 1980: CN20.

———. "A Senator and His Party Boss at Loggerheads in Connecticut." *New York Times*, February 18, 1979: E6.

Madden, Richard L, and Matthew L. Wald. "Talking Politics: James L. Buckley." *New York Times*, June 22, 1980: CN1.

Mahoney, Joe. "Rick Takes Homegrown Approach to Lure Women." *New York Daily News*, October 21, 2000: 6.

Malcolm, Andrew. "Alan Keyes Stokes Obama Birth Certificate Controversy." *Top of the Ticket: Political Commentary from the* LA Times. February 21, 2009. http://latimesblogs.latimes.com/washington/2009/02/obama-birth-cer.html.

Mansbridge, Jane. "Should Blacks Represent Blacks and Women Represent Women? A Contingent 'Yes'" *Journal of Politics* 61, no. 3 (1999): 628–57.

Maraniss, David. "Before Race Began, Clinton Resolved Pledge Not to Run." *Washington Post*, July 15, 1992. https://www.washingtonpost.com/archive/politics/1992/07/15/before-race-began-clinton-resolved-pledge-not-to-run/696cb650-3dab-4fcc-97dd-8bdcbb4b50f5/?utm_term=.2efd204bcb69.

March, Richard. "Democrats Warn against LaRouche 'Nazi' Movement." *United Press International*, August 29, 1986.

Margolis, Dan. "N.Y. Progressives Begin to Line Up behind Gillibrand." *People's World*, February 18, 2010. http://www.peoplesworld.org/article/n-y-progressives-begin-to-line-up-behind-gillibrand/.

Markoe, Karen. "A Short History of New York's Two Major Parties." In *New York State Today: Politics, Government, Public Policy, Second Edition*, edited by Peter W. Colby and John Kenneth White, 62–70. Albany: State University of New York Press, 1989.

Marist Poll. "3/29: Gillibrand and Pataki in Virtual Dead Heat." *Marist Poll*. March 29, 2009. http://maristpoll.marist.edu/329-gillibrand-and-pataki-in-virtual-dead-heat/.

Marshall, Brenda DeVore, and Molly A. Mayhead. "The Changing Face of the Governorship." In *Navigating Boundaries: The Rhetoric of Women Governors*, edited by Brenda DeVore Marshall and Molly A. Mayhead. Westport, Connecticut: Praeger, 2000.

Martel, Frances. "Harold Ford, Jr. Goes on *Morning Joe* and Finally Sounds like a Senator." *Mediaite*, March 2, 2010. http://www.mediaite.com/print/harold-ford-jr-goes-on-morning-joe-and-finally-sounds-like-a-senator/.

Martin, Jonathan. "Dispute over Gay Marriage Erupts in Cheney Family." *New York Times*, November 17, 2013: A1. http://thecaucus.blogs.nytimes.com/2013/11/17/within-cheney-family-a-dispute-over-gay-marriage/?smid=fb-share&_r=1&.

———. "For Cheney, Realities of a Race Outweighed Family Edge." *New York Times*, January 7, 2014: A9.

———. "In Wyoming, a Cheney Run Worries G.O.P." *New York Times*, July 6, 2013: A1. http://www.nytimes.com/2013/07/07/us/politics/a-cheney-on-the-wyoming-ballot-if-so-a-problem-for-the-gop.html?hp&_r=2&.

———. "Lacking a House, a Senator Is Renewing His Ties in Kansas." *New York Times*, February 7, 2014. https://www.nytimes.com/2014/02/08/us/senator-races-to-show-ties-including-an-address-in-kansas.html.

Martinez, Dave. "Smith "Clear Winner" in Debate, Anti-Brown Candidate." *Girard at Large*. Manchester, NH, September 5, 2014. http://www.girardatlarge.com/2014/09/smith-clear-winner-in-debate-anti-brown-candidate/.

Marx, Claude R. "Gloves Come Off in State Campaigns: Gramm Visits Nashua with Rudman to Aid Campaign." *Nashua Telegraph*, October 16, 1986: 12.

"Massachusetts Vote: Scott Brown Profile." *The Telegraph*. January 19, 2010. http://www.telegraph.co.uk/news/worldnews/northamerica/usa/7023400/Massachusetts-vote-Scott-Brown-profile.html.

Matier, Philip, Andrew Ross, and Carolyn Lochhead. "Race for U.S. Senate: Gavin Newsom Out, Kamala Harris In." *SFGate.com*, January 13, 2015. http://www.sfgate.com/bayarea/article/Gavin-Newsom-won-t-run-for-Barbara-Boxer-s-6009753.php.

May, Clifford. "Buckleys Are Backing a Democrat?" *New York Times*, August 16, 1988: B1. http://www.nytimes.com/1988/08/16/nyregion/buckleys-are-backing-a-democrat.html.

McCormick, John. "Cheney Bid Divides Wyoming Republicans Puzzled by Timing." *Bloomberg*. July 17, 2013. http://www.bloomberg.com/news/articles/2013-07-18/cheney-bid-divides-wyoming-republicans-puzzled-by-timing.

McDaniel, Rodger. "Radical Liz Cheney No Good for Wyo. Politics." *Wyoming Tribune Eagle-Wyoming News*. July 13, 2013. http://www.wyomingnews.com/opinion/radical-liz-cheney-no-good-for-wyo-politics/article_9cc84bfa-37ae-59ce-81d4-cf34cbf8 8d2d.html#.VOuHR3zF9Ao.

McDermott, Kevin. "Illinois GOP Narrows Senate List to Two." *St. Louis Post-Dispatch*, August 4, 2004, Five Star Edition ed.: A 01.

———. "Illinois Republicans Pick Keyes as Senate candidate." *St. Louis Post-Dispatch*, August 5, 2004, Five Star Late Lift Edition ed.: B02.

———. "Keyes Enters Senate Contest." *St. Louis Post-Dispatch*, August 9, 2004, Five Star Lift Edition ed.: A01.

———. "Keyes May Expose GOP rift: 'If Jim Edgar or Jim Thompson Don't Like the Choice, They Should Have Stepped Forward and Given Us a (Expletive) Candidate!'" *St. Louis Post-Dispatch*, August 8, 2004, Sunday Five Star Late Lift Edition ed.: B06.

———. "Ryan Fiasco Adds to Burden of Struggling Illinois GOP." *St. Louis Post-Dispatch*, June 27, 2004, Sunday Three Star Edition ed.

McGhee, Geoff. "Rural Newspapers Doing Better Than Their City Counterparts." *Rural West Initiative*. July 14, 2011. http://web.stanford.edu/group/ruralwest/cgi-bin/drupal/content/rural-newspapers.

Merry, George B. "Classic Connecticut Battle: Buckley vs. Dodd." *Christian Science Monitor*, October 28, 1980. http://www.csmonitor.com/1980/1028/102837.html.

Millennium Council—Save America's Treasures, 2000. https://clintonwhitehouse4.archives.gov/WH/EOP/First_Lady/html/treasures/index2.html.

Mokrzycki, Michael. "Bruno Challenges Rudman to Limit Campaign Spending." *Nashua Telegraph*, April 12, 1986: 1.

Molotsky, Irvin. "Endicott Peabody, 77, Dies; Governor of Massachusetts in 60s." *New York Times*, December 4, 1997: B13. http://www.nytimes.com/1997/12/04/us/endicott-peabody-77-dies-governor-of-massachusetts-in-60-s.html.

Moody, Chris. "The Second Coming of Scott Brown." *Yahoo News*, April 14, 2014. https://www.yahoo.com/news/scott-brown-new-hampshire-2014-015538246.html.

Moore, Martha T. "N.H. GOP to Scott Brown: Are You In or Out?" *USA Today*, December 19, 2013.

Morning Insider. "A Proxy Battle, Senate-Style." *Crain's New York Business*, January 19, 2010. http://www.crainsnewyork.com/article/20100119/INS/100119881.

Morris, Allie. "Capital Beat: VP Chatter Includes Scott Brown." *Concord Monitor*, July 10, 2016. http://www.concordmonitor.com/Scott-Brown-Donald-Trump-Vice-President-Consideration-3286848.

"Mr. Kennedy's Childhood." Memorandum, "Mr. Kennedy's Childhood." Box 26, folder "Kennedy, Robert F.," Robert F. Kennedy Senate Papers 1964–1968, John F. Kennedy Library, National Archives and Records Administration, Boston, MA, n.d.

"Kennedy, Robert F." Robert F. Kennedy Senate Papers 1964–1968, John F. Kennedy Library, National Archives and Records Administration, Boston, MA.

Napolitano, Jo. "Illinois G.O.P. Finally Picks a Candidate." *New York Times*, August 5, 2004: A17.

National Governors Association. "New Hampshire: Past Governors Bios." *National Governors Association*, n.d. https://www.nga.org/cms/home/governors/past-governors-bios/page_new_hampshire.html.

Neal, Steven. *Happy Days Are Here Again: The 1932 Democratic Convention, the Emergence of FDR—and How America Was Changed Forever.* New York: William Morrow, 2004.

Neary, Ben, and Mead Gruver. "Liz Cheney: Time for 'New Generation' in US Senate." *Associated Press*, July 13, 2013. http://bigstory.ap.org/article/liz-cheney-challenge-us-sen-mike-enzi-wyo.

———. "Liz Cheney to Challenge GOP Sen. Mike Enzi In 2014." *Talking Points Memo.* July 16, 2013. http://talkingpointsmemo.com/news/liz-cheney-to-challenge-gop-sen-mike-enzi-in-2014.

New Hampshire Public Radio. "1972 Vice President Democratic Primary." *NHPR State of Democracy*, n.d. http://nh.electionstats.com/elections/view/63027/.

"New Hampshire Senate Debate." *C-SPAN.* October 30, 2014. https://www.c-span.org/video/?322395-1/new-hampshire-senate-debate#.

New Hampshire Union Leader. "Shaheen, Collins Call for Action to Avoid Potential Cuts to Portsmouth Naval Shipyard." February 4, 2013. http://www.unionleader.com/article/20130204/NEWS06/130209643/1013/NEWS11.

"New York." *2000 U.S. SENATE RESULTS*, n.d. https://transition.fec.gov/pubrec/fe2000/2000senate.htm#NY.

New York Graphic. "Senator Shields." *The Daily-Register Call*, January 22, 1879. http://0-find.galegroup.com.library.anselm.edu/ncnp/infomark.do?action=interpret&source=gale&prodId=NCNP&userGroupName=manc23575&tabID=T003&docPage=article&searchType=AdvancedSearchForm&docId=GT3014805463&type=multipage&contentSet=LTO&version=1.0&finalAut.

New York Post. "Does Hillary Agree with Suha?" November 23, 1999: 38.

New York Times. "Hillary Clinton Elected to Senate From New York." November 8, 2000. http://www.nytimes.com/2000/11/08/politics/hillary-clinton-elected-to-senate-from-new-york.html.

NHDP Video. "Brown Forgets Where He's Running." *YouTube.com*. July 15, 2014. https://www.youtube.com/watch?v=gPkVn6VduQE.

Nichols, John. "Even Republicans Fear Bush." *The Nation*, October 31, 2004. https://www.thenation.com/article/even-republicans-fear-bush/.

Nilsen, Ella. "Jim Rubens Tries to Win Over Votes as 'Reform' Candidate." *SentinelSource.com*, August 13, 2014. http://www.sentinelsource.com/news/local/jim-rubens-tries-to-win-over-votes-as-reform-candidate/article_ca0c1176-afc7-5886-a2ee-2089ff876d9a.html.

"1980 Senatorial General Election Results—Connecticut." *Dave Leip's Atlas of U.S. Presidential Elections*. n.d.

"1986 U.S. Senate Democratic Primary." *NHPR State of Democracy*, n.d. http://nh.electionstats.com/elections/view/60451/.

"1986 U.S. Senate General Election." *NHPR State of Democracy*, n.d. http://nh.electionstats.com/elections/view/60604/.

"1992 Vice President Democratic Primary." *NHPR State of Democracy*, n.d. http://nh.electionstats.com/elections/view/58606/.

"1992 Vice President Republican Primary." *NHPR State of Democracy*, n.d. http://nh.electionstats.com/elections/view/58605/.

"1964 Senatorial General Election Results—New York." *Dave Leip's Atlas of U.S. Presidential Elections*. May 4. http://uselectionatlas.org/RESULTS/state.php?year=1964&off=3&elect=0&fips=36&f=.

"Nomination of James L. Buckley to Be an Under Secretary of State." *Nominations, January 29, 1981*. January 29, 1981. https://www.reaganlibrary.archives.gov/archives/speeches/1981/12981a.htm.

Norris, Michelle. "Democratic Rep. McCarthy Blasts Gillibrand Pick." *All Things Considered*. National Public Radio. January 23, 2009. http://www.npr.org/templates/story/story.php?storyId=99816999.

N.Y. State Democratic Committee. "The Myth of Keating's Liberalism." 1964.

O'Brien, Michael. *John F. Kennedy: A Biography*. New York: Thomas Dunne Books, 2005.

Olesker, Michael. "Brock's Record Mostly a Secret to Marylanders." *Baltimore Sun*, October 2, 1994. http://articles.baltimoresun.com/1994-10-02/news/1994275068_1_make-brock-bill-brock-new-brock.

Oliphant, Thomas, and Curtis Wilkie. *The Road to Camelot: Inside JFK's Five-Year Campaign*. New York: Simon & Schuster, 2017.

O'Sullivan, Jim. "Scott Brown Nominated as Ambassador to New Zealand, Samoa." *Boston Globe*, April 25, 2017. https://www.bostonglobe.com/metro/2017/04/25/scott-brown-nominated-ambassador-new-zealand-samoa/tJeG43FRW4oevyqc-cYZXdP/story.html.

———. "Scott Brown Will Not Run for Governor in 2014." *Boston Globe*, August 21, 2013: A1. https://www.boston.com/uncategorized/noprimarytagmatch/2013/08/21/scott-brown-will-not-run-for-governor-in-2014.

O'Sullivan, Jim, and Travis Andersen. "Scott Brown Being Considered for Trump Cabinet Position." *Boston Globe*, November 18, 2016. https://www.bostonglobe.com/news/politics/2016/11/18/scott-brown-being-considered-for-trump-cabinet-position/1FQmz71id2nTVO80gqGsgN/story.html?s_campaign=bdc:article:stub.

Padilla, Bill. "Liz Cheney a Better Fit for Virginia Senate Election." *Wyoming Tribune Eagle-WyomingNews.com*. December 22, 2013. http://www.wyomingnews.com/opinion/liz-cheney-a-better-fit-for-virginia-senate-election/article_855a548d-d0a4-5d8f-b057-0005f48bece5.html#.VOuHUHzF9Ao.

Palermo, Joseph A. *In His Own Right: The Political Odyssey of Senator Robert F. Kennedy*. New York: Columbia University Press, 2002.

Patterson, Rachelle. "GOP: Senate Can Be Ours." *Boston Globe*, October 25, 1979: 6.

Paul, Rod. "Endicott Peabody 'Never Considered the Possibility of Being out of Politics.'" *Nashua Telegraph*, June 4, 1986: 34.

———. "Should Attorney General Be Elected?" *Nashua Telegraph*, May 22, 1984: 28. https://news.google.com/newspapers?nid=2209&dat=19840522&id=9ZsrAAAAIBAJ&sjid=evsFAAAAIBAJ&pg=5485,4664030&hl=en.

Pearson, Rick. "Keyes, State GOP Gearing Up Blame Campaign." *Chicago Tribune*, September 5, 2004: 6. http://articles.chicagotribune.com/2004-09-05/news/0409050304_1_selfish-hedonist-alan-keyes-illinois-republican-party.

Pearson, Rick, and John Chase. "How Illinois Gop Imploded." *Chicago Tribune*, January 16, 2005: 1. http://articles.chicagotribune.com/2005-01-16/news/0501160322_1_alan-keyes-illinois-republican-party-saviano.

Pew Research Center. *Religious Landscape Study*. Washington, DC: Pew Research Center, 2015. http://www.pewforum.org/religious-landscape-study/state/utah/.

Phillips, Macon. "President Obama on the Selection of Kirsten Gillibrand." *Obama White House*. January 23, 2009. https://obamawhitehouse.archives.gov/blog/2009/01/23/president-obama-selection-kirsten-gillibrand.

Pillifant, Reid. "The Last Gillibrand Fighter." *Observer*, November 9, 2009. http://observer.com/2009/11/the-last-gillibrand-fighter/.

Pindell, James. "Scott Brown Endorses Donald Trump." *Boston Globe*, February 2, 2016. https://www.bostonglobe.com/news/politics/2016/02/02/scott-brown-endorse-trump/Iz7bBu2IJoq4EDTFEIK3mM/story.html.

———. "Scott Brown to Formally Enter Senate Contest Thursday." *WMUR.com*, April 7, 2014. http://www.wmur.com/article/scott-brown-to-formally-enter-senate-contest-thursday/5189402.

———. "What's in a Twitter Name? Scott Brown drops 'MA' from His Handle." *WMUR.com*, November 27, 2013. http://www.wmur.com/article/what-s-in-a-twitter-name-scott-brown-drops-ma-from-his-handle/5186378.

Pitkin, Hanna Fenichel. *The Concept of Representation*. Berkeley and Los Angeles: University of California Press, 1967.

Plainview Old Bethpage Herald. "Congressman Israel Will Not Run for Senate." May 21, 2009. http://plainviewoldbethpageherald.com/2009/05/21/congressman-israel-will-not-run-for-senate/.

Polhamus, Michael. "Cheney Knocks Obama, Papers." *Jackson Hole News & Guide*, September 4, 2013. http://www.jhnewsandguide.com/news/top_stories/cheney-knocks-obama-papers/article_a4adf4d5-7977-546a-838b-6f66edc5f518.html.

Politico Staff. "Full Transcript: Mitt Romney's Remarks on Donald Trump and the 2016 Race." *Politico*, March 3, 2016. https://www.politico.com/story/2016/03/full-transcript-mitt-romneys-remarks-on-donald-trump-and-the-2016-race-220176.

Rahman, Rema. "Liz Cheney Wins Wyoming House Seat." *Roll Call*, November 8, 2016. http://www.rollcall.com/news/politics/liz-cheney-wins-wyoming-house-seat.

"Raw Video: Scott Brown Delivers Concession Speech." *WMUR.com*. November 5, 2014. http://www.wmur.com/politics/raw-video-scott-brown-delivers-concession-speech/29541380.

Rehfield, Andrew. *The Concept of Constituency: Political Representation, Democratic Legitimacy, and Institutional Design*. New York: Cambridge University Press, 2005.

"Residence in State (for H of R), Wed., Aug. 8, 1787." Box 25, folder "'Carpetbag' issue," Robert F. Kennedy Senate Papers 1964–1968, John F. Kennedy Library, National Archives and Records Administration, Boston, MA, 1964.

Richards, Clay F. "Negative Ads a Big Factor in '86 Campaigns." *United Press International*, October 31, 1986.

Richey, Warren. "Resolved: Where Maine Begins and N.H. Ends." *Christian Science Monitor*, May 31, 2001. https://www.csmonitor.com/2001/0531/p2s2.html.

Richman, Jesse. "Congress on the Line: The 2008 Congressional Election and the Obama Presidency." *White House Studies* 9, no. 1 (2009): 21–34.

Riede, Paul. "Ed Koch and 'Gingham Dresses': Upstate Never Forgets." *Syracuse Post-Standard*, February 1, 2013. http://www.syracuse.com/news/index.ssf/2013/02/ed_koch_and_gingham_dresses_up.html.

Rinker III, Earl A. "Earl Rinker Endorses Jim Rubens for US Senate." *NH Insider*, August 23, 2014. http://www.nhinsider.com/letters-to-the-editor/2014/8/23/earl-rinker-endorses-jim-rubens-for-us-senate.html.

Rizzuto, Richard. "Sen. Scott Brown Says He Now Supports a Federal Ban on Assault Weapons." *MassLive*, December 19, 2012. http://www.masslive.com/politics/index.ssf/2012/12/sen_scott_brown_says_he_now_su.html.

Rizzuto, Robert. "Despite Absence from Politics Poll Shows Republican Scott Brown Is Favorite for Governor Of Massachusetts in 2014 Race." *MassLive*, May 8, 2013. http://www.masslive.com/politics/index.ssf/2013/05/despite_absence_from_politics.html.

———. "Poll: Scott Brown Holding Slight Lead over Ed Markey in Massachusetts Senate race." *MassLive*, January 30, 2013. http://www.masslive.com/politics/index.ssf/2013/01/poll_scott_brown_holding_sligh.html.

———. "Scott Brown Carries Double Digit Lead over Ed Markey in Massachusetts Special Election." *MassLive*, January 25, 2013. http://www.masslive.com/politics/index.ssf/2013/01/scott_brown_carries_double_dig.html.

Roarty, Alex. "Republicans to Scott Brown: Oh, You're Serious?" *National Journal*, December 10, 2013.

"Robert L. Dupay." *NHPR State of Democracy*, n.d. http://nh.electionstats.com/candidates/view/Robert-L-Dupay.

Robillard, Kevin. "Harold Ford's Comments on Abortion Prompt Charges of Flip-Flopping." *Politifact*, January 19, 2010. http://www.politifact.com/truth-o-meter/statements/2010/jan/19/harold-ford-jr/harold-ford-flip-flopped-abortion/.

Roerink, Kyle. "Enzi Supporters Start Super PAC." *BillingsGazette.com*. September 10, 2013. https://billingsgazette.com/news/state-and-regional/wyoming/enzi-supporters-start-super-pac/article_66650f1e-74d1-5193-9576-75b89176a76d.html.

———. "Liz Cheney Features Daughters in Campaign Ad Touting Family's Wyoming History." *Casper Star-Tribune*, November 25, 2013. http://trib.com/news/state-and-regional/govt-and-politics/liz-cheney-features-daughters-in-campaign-ad-touting-family-s/article_81862c67-91ca-50cb-b65c-4ea861356105.html.

———. "Liz Cheney Listed as 10-Year Wyomingite, Gets Resident Fishing License Early." *Casper Star Tribune*, August 5, 2013. http://trib.com/news/state-and-regional/govt-and-politics/liz-cheney-listed-as--year-wyomingite-gets-resident-fishing/article_d764ebbc-7d00-5358-88f2-8029198beff7.html.

———. "Wyoming U.S. Senate Candidate Liz Cheney's Husband Caught in Voter Registration Snafu." *Casper Star-Tribune*, December 19, 2013. http://trib.com/news/state-and-regional/govt-and-politics/wyoming-u-s-senate-candidate-liz-cheney-s-husband-caught/article_f7fe8c69-4d5d-581f-920c-2326e9d66096.html.

Rogers, Alex. "Jeanne Shaheen Admits to Headwinds in New Hampshire Debate." *Time*, October 21, 2014. http://time.com/3530397/jeanne-shaheen-scott-brown-new-hampshire-debate/.

Rogers, Josh. "Shaheen, Brown Press Their Cases in Final Debate." *New Hampshire Public Radio*, October 31, 2014. http://nhpr.org/post/shaheen-brown-press-their-cases-final-debate#stream/0.

Ronayne, Kathleen. "Smith, Rubens go after Brown in GOP U.S. Senate debate." *Concord Monitor*, September 4, 2014. http://web.archive.org/web/20140908005802/http://www.concordmonitor.com/news/campaignmonitor/13424061-95/smith-rubens-go-after-brown-in-gop-us-senate-debate.

Rose, Derek. "Irish Eyes Will Be Smiling on . . ." *New York Daily News*, March 10, 2001: 10.

Rosenthal, Cindy Simon. *Women Transforming Congress*. Norman: University of Oklahoma Press, 2003.

Ross, Janell. "Hillary Clinton Will No Longer Be Called 'Rodham.' Here's Her Complicated History with Her Maiden Name." *Washington Post*, November 30, 2015. https://www.washingtonpost.com/news/the-fix/wp/2015/11/19/the-fascinating-history-of-when-hillary-clinton-has-chosen-to-use-her-maiden-name/.

Rucker, Philip. "A Detached Romney Tends Wounds in Seclusion after Failed White House Bid." *Washington Post*, December 1, 2012. https://www.washingtonpost. com/politics/a-detached-romney-tends-wounds-in-seclusion-after-failed-white-house-bid/2012/12/01/4305079a-38a9-11e2-8a97-363b0f9a0ab3_story.html?utm_ term=.805df2c4d864.

Rudman, Warren B. *Combat: Twelve Years in the U.S. Senate.* New York: Random House, 1996.

Russello, Gerald. "Mr. Buckley Goes to Washington." *The American Conservative.* April 14, 2011. http://www.theamericanconservative.com/articles/mr-buckley-goes-to-washington/.

Russo, Melissa. "NRA Shoots Down Gillibrand's 'Grade.'" *NBC New York.* September 29, 2010. http://www.nbcnewyork.com/news/local/NRA-Shoots-Down-Kirsten-Gillibrands-Rating--104050029.html.

Sakson, Steve. "Mayor Has 'No Intention' Of Running This Year." *Nashua Telegraph*, April 10, 1986: 64.

———. "Peabody Asked to Run against Sen. Rudman." *Nashua Telegraph*, April 4, 1986: 1, 12. https://news.google.com/newspapers?nid=2209&dat=19860404&id =wJ4rAAAAIBAJ&sjid=NfwFAAAAIBAJ&pg=4860,843604&hl=en.

———. "Rudman Campaign Chest 6 Times Opponents' Combined." *Nashua Telegraph*, August 28, 1986: 16. https://news.google.com/newspapers?nid=2209&dat=1986 0828&id=_p8rAAAAIBAJ&sjid=WPwFAAAAIBAJ&pg=6859,8742706&hl=en.

Sandler, Martin W. *The Letters of John F. Kennedy.* New York: Bloomsbury, 2013.

Sargent, Greg. "Scott Brown Lurches to The Right on Guns." *Washington Post*, May 27, 2014. https://www.washingtonpost.com/blogs/plum-line/wp/2014/05/27/ scott-brown-lurches-to-the-right-on-guns/?utm_term=.734605de3d4f.

Savransky, Rebecca. "Warren Congratulates Scott Brown on Ambassador Nomination." *The Hill*, April 20, 2017. http://thehill.com/homenews/senate/329732-warren-congratulates-scott-brown-on-ambassador-nomination.

Scala, Dante J. "New Hampshire: The Swing State Swings Right." In *Pendulum Swing*, 329–34. Hoboken: Pearson Longman, 2011.

———. "Politics in New Hampshire." *New England Journal of Political Science* 7, no. 1 (2013): 142–48.

———. *Stormy Weather: The New Hampshire Primary and Presidential Politics.* New York: Palgrave Macmillan, 2003.

Scharrer, Erica. "An "Improbable Leap": A Content Analysis of Newspaper Coverage of Hillary Clinton's Transition from First Lady to Senate Candidate." *Journalism Studies* 3, no. 3 (2002): 393–406.

Schinella, Tony. "Humphrey Backs Rubens in Race against Shaheen." *Patch.com*, January 10, 2014. https://patch.com/new-hampshire/concord-nh/humphey-backs-rubens-in-race-against-shaheen.

———. "Jeanne Shaheen to Support Scott Brown Ambassador Nomination." *Patch.com*, May 16, 2017. https://patch.com/new-hampshire/portsmouth-nh/jeanne-shaheen-support-scott-brown-ambassador-nomination.

Schlesinger, Arthur M., Jr. *Robert Kennedy and His Times*. Vol. 2. 2 vols. Boston: Houghton Mifflin, 1978.

Schlesinger, Joseph A. *Ambition and Politics: Political Careers in the United States*. Chicago: Rand McNally, 1966.

Schoenberg, Shira. "Jeanne Shaheen Uses Massachusetts Politicians to Attack Scott Brown in NH Senate Race." *MassLive*, October 21, 2014. http://www.masslive.com/politics/index.ssf/2014/10/jeanne_shaheen_uses_massachuse.html.

———. "Scott Brown 'Leaning Strongly' toward Another Massachusetts U.S. Senate Run, AP Reports." *MassLive*, January 30, 2013. http://www.masslive.com/politics/index.ssf/2013/01/scott_brown_leaning_strongly_t.html.

Schoenburg, Bernard. "Rauschenberger Won't Run; Drafting Ditka for Senate Race Excites Some in GOP." *The State Journal-Register*, July 9, 2004: 1.

———. "Ryan out of the Running; GOP Works on Recovering from Scandal." *The State Journal-Register*, June 24, 2004: 1.

Schullery, Paul. *Cowboy Trout: Western Fly Fishing as if It Matters*. Helena: Montana Historical Society Press, 1993.

Schumpeter, Joseph A. *Capitalism, Socialism and Democracy*. New York: Harper Perennial Modern Classics, 2008.

"Scott Brown: Proud to Serve." *YouTube.com*. May 12, 2014. https://www.youtube.com/watch?v=PEQ15NIE6_0&feature=youtu.be.

Seelye, Katharine Q. "Mrs. Clinton May Steal Mayor's Yankee Fan Base." *New York Times*, June 11: B5, 1999. http://www.nytimes.com/1999/06/11/nyregion/mrs-clinton-may-steal-mayor-s-yankee-fan-base.html.

———. "New Hampshire's Tight Senate Race Keeps Focus on Baggage." *New York Times*, October 26, 2014: A16. https://www.nytimes.com/2014/10/26/us/politics/new-hampshires-tight-senate-race-keeps-focus-on-baggage-.html.

"Senator for Three States." *United States Senate: Senate History*, n.d. https://www.senate.gov/artandhistory/history/minute/Senator_for_three_states.htm.

"Senators Born in Other States." Box 25, folder " 'Carpetbag' issue," Robert F. Kennedy Senate Papers 1964–1968, John F. Kennedy Library, National Archives and Records Administration, Boston, MA, 1964.

Shaheen, Jeanne. "Shaheen at Fundrasier." *C-SPAN*. November 16, 2013. https://www.c-span.org/video/?c4488581/shaheen-fundrasier.

Shaw, Dorsey. "Scott Brown's Campaign Ads Feature Green Screened Stock Footage." *Buzzfeed*, July 29, 2014. https://www.buzzfeed.com/dorsey/scott-browns-campaign-ads-feature-green-screened-stock-foota?utm_term=.jl3zP46wM#.hjleD09Rx.

Sheridan, Chris. "Michelle Obama for President?" *Al Jazeera—Reporter's Notebook*. October 28, 2016. http://www.aljazeera.com/blogs/americas/2016/10/michelle-obama-president-161028033947102.html.

Shesol, Jeff. 1997. *Mutual Contempt: Lyndon Johnson, Robert Kennedy, and the Feud that Defined a Decade*. New York: W. W. Norton, 1997.

"Shields, James (1806/1810–1879)." *Biographical Directory of the United States Congress*, 2005. http://bioguide.congress.gov/scripts/biodisplay.pl?index=S000362.

Silberfarb, Edward J. "Kennedy No Peril to Me—Wagner." *New York Herald Tribune*, August 29, 1964.

Simpson, Alan. "Simpsons Respond to 'Shut Up' Controversy." *Cody Enterprise*. September 27, 2013. http://www.codyenterprise.com/news/local/article_b840e2ea-279b-11e3-87fe-001a4bcf887a.html.

Sirkin, Gerald, and Natalie Sirkin. "The Unplanned Admirable Life of James Buckley." *Connecticut Commentary: Red Notes from a Blue State*. February 26, 2007. http://donpesci.blogspot.com/2007/02/.

Skalka, Jennifer, and Ofelia Casillas. "Keyes Takes Jabs at His Own Party." *Chicago Tribune*, September 1, 2004.

Skenazy, Lenore. "Hil Has Woman Troubles, Too." *New York Daily News*, April 5, 2000: 35.

Slosberg, Steven. "Buckley Assesses Chances in State." *The Day*, January 3, 1980: 1. https://news.google.com/newspapers?nid=1915&dat=19800103&id=IwohAAAA IBAJ&sjid=THUFAAAAIBAJ&pg=5740,414882&hl=en.

Smith, Ben. "Liz Cheney Takes On 'Radical' W.H." *Politico*, October 13, 2009. http://www.politico.com/story/2009/10/liz-cheney-takes-on-radical-wh-028212.

Smith, Ben, and Jonathan Martin. "Harold Ford's gilded New York." *Politico*, January 13, 2010. http://www.politico.com/story/2010/01/harold-fords-gilded-new-york-031455.

Smith, C. Fraser. "Maryland GOP May End Up Doing the Tennessee Waltz." *Baltimore Sun*, February 3, 1993. http://articles.baltimoresun.com/1993-02-03/news/1993034135_1_maryland-gop-maryland-republican-party-bill-brock.

Smith for U.S. Senate. "WMUR TV: BOB SMITH WINS US SENATE DEBATE." *NH Insider*, September 6, 2014. http://www.nhinsider.com/press-releases/2014/9/6/smith-for-us-senate-wmur-tv-bob-smith-wins-us-senate-debate.html.

Sollenberger, Mitch, Jack Rossotti, and Mark J. Rozell. "Reagan and the Courts." In *The Reagan Presidency: Assessing the Man and His Legacy*, edited by Paul Kengor and Peter Schweitzer, 93–114. Lanham, Maryland: Rowman & Littlefield, 2005.

Special to the *New York Times*. "Buckley Waging First Campaign in State Where He Was Raised." *New York Times*, September 10, 1980: B6.

St. Louis Globe-Democrat. "The Hero's Luck: Shields Nominated for the Short Term." January 16, 1879: 1.

States in the Senate: Minnesota. Nd. http://www.senate.gov/states/MN/timeline.htm.

Stein, Perry. "Erick Erickson Endorses Liz Cheney for Senate." *TPM*. July 13, 2013. http://talkingpointsmemo.com/livewire/erick-erickson-endorses-liz-cheney-for-senate.

———. "NRSC: 'Our Mission Is to Reelect Our Incumbents.'" *TPM*. July 16, 2013. http://talkingpointsmemo.com/livewire/nrsc-our-mission-is-to-reelect-our-incumbents.

———. "Rand Paul Voices Support for Sen. Enzi as Liz Cheney Considers WY Challenge." *TPM*. July 11, 2013. http://talkingpointsmemo.com/livewire/rand-paul-voices-support-for-sen-enzi-as-liz-cheney-considers-wy-challenge.

Steinhauser, Paul. "Brown Stokes More Speculation about Senate Run in NH." *CNN. com*, December 3, 2013. http://politicalticker.blogs.cnn.com/2013/12/03/ brown-stokes-more-speculation-about-senate-run-in-nh/.

———. "Incumbent Goes Up on Airways Again in Key Senate Race." *CNN.com*, May 12, 2014. http://politicalticker.blogs.cnn.com/2014/05/12/incumbent-goes-up-on-airways-again-in-key-senate-race/.

Stewart, Rebecca. "Lugar Beats Back Residency Challenge." *CNN Politics*, February 24, 2012. http://politicalticker.blogs.cnn.com/2012/02/24/lugar-beats-back-residency-challenge/.

Stolberg, Sheryl Gay. "Testing Presidential Waters as Race at Home Heats Up." *New York Times*, March 26, 2006: A26. http://www.nytimes.com/2006/03/26/politics/ testing-presidential-waters-as-race-at-home-heats-up.html.

Stonecash, Jeffrey M. "Political Parties and Partisan Conflict." In *Governing New York State*, edited by Jeffrey M. Stonecash, John Kenneth White, and Peter W. Colby, 83–101. Albany: State University of New York Press, 1994.

Strauss, Daniel. "Alan Simpson: Liz Cheney 'Destroying Family Relationships' Because of Senate Race." *TPM*. November 19, 2013. http://talkingpointsmemo.com/livewire/ alan-simpson-liz-cheney-destroying-family-relationships-because-of-senate-race.

———. "Liz Cheney's First Campaign Ad Touts Family's Ties to Wyoming." *TPM*. November 14, 2013. http://talkingpointsmemo.com/livewire/liz-cheney-releases-first-campaign-ad-focusing-on-family-s-ties-to-wyoming.

Strom, Ron. "MSNBC Pulling Plug on Keyes." *WorldNetDaily*. June 19, 2002. http:// www.wnd.com/2002/06/14279/.

Sullivan, Sean. "Scott Brown Won't Run for Governor of Massachusetts." *Washington Post*, August 21, 2013. https://www.washingtonpost.com/news/post-politics/wp/2013/ 08/21/scott-brown-wont-run-for-governor-of-massachusetts/?utm_term=.a5819 a69b67.

Sullivan, Sean, and Aaron Blake. "The Fix's Top 10 Senate Races of 2014." *Washington Post*, April 5, 2013. https://www.washingtonpost.com/news/the-fix/wp/2013/ 04/05/the-fixs-top-10-senate-races-of-2014-2/?utm_term=.6bf2a5f4b2e8.

Sullivan, Sean, and Ed O'Keefe. "Liz Cheney Will Challenge Sen. Mike Enzi." *Washington Post*, July 16, 2013. https://www.washingtonpost.com/news/post-politics/ wp/2013/07/16/liz-cheney-will-challenge-sen-mike-enzi/.

Sullivan, Timothy J. *New York State and the Rise of Modern Conservatism: Redrawing Party Lines*. Albany: State University of New York Press, 2009.

Taylor, Jane F. "Mrs. Endicott Peabody Explains Why Her Husband Seeks Vice Presidency." *Nashua Telegraph*, February 29, 1972: 20. https://news.google.com/new spapers?nid=2209&dat=19720229&id=4pgrAAAAIBAJ&sjid=sPUFAAAAIBAJ &pg=6804,3822085&hl=en.

Taylor, Jessica. "Ambition, Not Ideology Drives Liz Cheney's Senate Run." *MSNBC.com*. July 17, 2013. http://www.msnbc.com/the-daily-rundown/ambition-not-ideology-drives-liz-cheneys-se.

————. "Cheney Family Dispute Inflames Tensions in Wyoming Race." *MSNBC.com.*
      November 19, 2013. http://www.msnbc.com/the-daily-rundown/cheney-family-
      dispute-inflames-tensions.

Terris, Ben. "Kirsten Gillibrand's Improbable Path to Liberal Stardom." *The Atlan-
      tic,* October 26, 2013. http://www.theatlantic.com/politics/archive/2013/10/
      kirsten-gillibrands-improbable-path-to-liberal-stardom/280872/.

"The Typical Carpet-Bagger." *The New York Times.* December 12, 1880: 4.

Thomas, Evan. *Robert Kennedy: His Life.* New York: Simon and Schuster, 2013.

Thorson, Don. "The Battle of Mike Vs. Liz May Not End Well for Either." *Wyoming
      Tribune Eagle-WyomingNews.com.* August 12, 2013.

Thrush, Glenn. "King Iffy on NY Senate after Intel Appointment." *Politico,* June 29,
      2009. http://www.politico.com/blogs/on-congress/2009/06/king-iffy-on-ny-senate-
      after-intel-appointment-019473.

Thuermer, Angus M., Jr. "Breaking News: Cheney Pays $220 for Fishing License Ticket."
      Jackson Hole News & Guide. August 21, 2013.

Times Free Press. "Sen. Brock on Education." March 30, 2010. http://www.timesfreepress.
      com/news/opinion/freepress/story/2010/mar/30/fp2-sen-brock-on-education/
      11254/.

Tomasky, Michael. *Hillary's Turn: Inside Her Improbable, Victorious Senate Campaign.*
      New York: The Free Press, 2001.

Toner, Robin. "Ad Seen as Playing to Racial Fears." *New York Times,* October 26, 2006:
      A1. http://www.nytimes.com/2006/10/26/us/politics/26tennessee.html.

————. "Political Briefs." *New York Times,* May 2, 1996. http://www.nytimes.
      com/1996/05/02/us/political-briefs.html.

Tracy, Nancy M. "Senate Race Down to the Wire: Christopher Dodd." *Fairpress,*
      October 29, 1980: A1, A6.

————. "Senate Race Down to the Wire: James Buckley." *Fairpress,* October 29, 1980:
      A1, A6.

Trent, Judith S., and Cady Short-Thompson. "From First Lady to United States
      Senator: The Role and Power of Image in the Transmorgifying of Hillary
      Rodham Clinton." In *Images, Scandal, and Communication Strategies of
      the Clinton Presidency (Praeger Series in Presidential Studies),* edited by
      Robert E. Jr. Denton and Rachel L. Holloway, 113–41. Westport, CT: Praeger,
      2003.

Trotter, J. K. "Why Scott Brown Might Run for Governor Instead of John Kerry's Senate
      Seat." *The Atlantic,* January 14, 2013. https://www.theatlantic.com/politics/
      archive/2013/01/why-scott-brown-might-run-governor-insteadjohn-kerrys-
      senate-seat/319502/.

Trygstad, Kyle. "Gillibrand Racking Up Endorsements." *RealClearPolitics,* May 18,
      2009. http://www.realclearpolitics.com/politics_nation/2009/05/gillibrand_rack-
      ing_up_endorsem.html.

———. "New Hampshire: Local Republicans Skeptical on Scott Brown." *Roll Call*, April 5, 2013. http://www.rollcall.com/politics/new-hampshire-local-republicans-skeptical-on-scott-brown/.

Trygstad, Kyle, and Abby Livingston. "New Hampshire: Local Republicans Skeptical on Scott Brown." *Roll Call*. April 5, 2013. http://atr.rollcall.com/new-hampshire-local-republicans-skeptical-on-scott-brown/.

Tucker, Edith. "Congress Passes Funds to Open Berlin Prison." *Salmon Press*, November 22, 2011. http://www.newhampshirelakesandmountains.com/Articles-Berlin-Reporter-c-2011-11-21-155084.113119-Congress-passes-funds-to-open-Berlin-Prison.html.

Tumulty, Karen. "Scott Brown: Will He or Won't He Run for Senate from New Hampshire?" *Washington Post*, February 9, 2014. https://www.washingtonpost.com/politics/scott-brown-will-he-or-wont-he-run-for-senate-from-new-hampshire/2014/02/09/1b4fdce0-8ffe-11e3-84e1-27626c5ef5fb_story.html?utm_term=.05cf2ccdbfe6.

Tunnell, Ted. "Creating 'the Propaganda of History': Southern Editors and the Origins of Carpetbagger and Scalawag." *The Journal of Southern History* 72, no. 4 (2006): 789–822.

"2000 Presidential General Election Results—New York." *Dave Leip's Atlas of U.S. Presidential Elections*, n.d. http://uselectionatlas.org/RESULTS/state.php?fips=36&year=2000.

"2014 U.S. Senate Republican Primary." *NHPR State of Democracy*, n.d. http://nh.electionstats.com/elections/view/49560/.

"2006 Senatorial General Election Results—Tennessee." *Dave Leip's Atlas of U.S. Presidential Elections*, n.d. http://uselectionatlas.org/RESULTS/state.php?fips=47&year=2006&f=0&off=3&elect=0&class=1.

United Press International. "Keyes Vows More Provocative Campaigning." *United Press International*, September 14, 2004. http://www.upi.com/Top_News/2004/09/14/Keyes-vows-more-provocative-campaigning/77071095186946/.

———. "Tucker to Seek Re-Election." *United Press International*, June 4, 1986.

U.S. News & World Report. "Bobby Kennedy: Is He the 'Assistant President'?" February 19, 1962.

Van Meter, Jonathan. "In Hillary's Footsteps: Kirsten Gillibrand." *Vogue*, October 19, 2010. http://www.vogue.com/865477/in-hillarys-footsteps-kirsten-gillibrand/.

Viser, Matt. "Romney Was Recruited to Run for Senate in Utah by Hatch." *Boston Globe*, February 6, 2018. https://www.bostonglobe.com/news/politics/2018/02/05/the-seeds-mitt-romney-senate-bid-were-planted-marriott-meeting-with-orrin-hatch/YfY1zZxVK49WBrZiaz6LSK/story.html.

Wald, Matthew L. "Bozzuto vs. Buckley: Issues and Nonissues." *New York Times*, August 10, 1980: CN24.

———. "Buckley and Dodd Take Up Positions." *New York Times*, September 21, 1980: CN1.

———. "Dodd Makes Bid For Nomination to Ribicoff Post: Kennedy Backer Modifies Opposition to Carter." *New York Times*, January 10, 1980: B2.

———. "A Foe of Buckley Is Confident: Buckley's Foe in G.O.P. Says He Expects to Win." *New York Times*, July 22, 1980: B1.

———. "James Buckley Weighs Senate Bid." *New York Times*, November 2, 1979: B4.

———. "Talking Politics: Richard C. Bozzuto: The Candidates on the Issues." *New York Times*, June 15, 1980: CN1.

Waldron, Patrick. "Hastert Says He'll Back Keyes' Senate Campaign." *Chicago Daily Herald*, August 7, 2004: 3.

Wallace, Gregory. "Brown Stirs Speculation with Another New Hampshire Visit." *CNN. com*, April 13, 2013. http://politicalticker.blogs.cnn.com/2013/04/13/brown-stirs-speculation-with-another-new-hampshire-visit/.

Watson, W. Marvin, and Sherwin Markman. *Chief of Staff: Lyndon Johnson and His Presidency*. New York: Thomas Dunne Books-St. Martin's Press, 2004.

"WCBS-TV Interview with Senator Keating: Transcript." October 27, 1964.

Weatherford, Doris. *Women in American Politics: History and Milestones*. Thousand Oaks, California: CQ, 2012.

Weaver, Teri. "Syracuse, New York Leaders React to Death of NYC Mayor Ed Koch." *Syracuse Post-Standard*, February 1, 2013. http://www.syracuse.com/news/index. ssf/2013/02/syracuse_pols_react_to_death_o.html#incart_m-rpt-2.

Weaver, Warren, Jr. "Keating Assays Defeats in State: Says He Would Have Won if Goldwater Had Not Run." *New York Times*, November 25, 1964: 22.

Weiner, Rachel. "Scott Brown Not Ruling Out New Hampshire Bid." *Washington Post*, April 4, 2013. https://www.washingtonpost.com/news/post-politics/wp/2013/04/ 04/scott-brown-not-ruling-out-new-hampshire-bid/?utm_term=.ec7d22c77710.

Weisman, Jonathan. "In Fracas on Health Coverage, Some Democrats Feel Exposed." *New York Times*, November 16, 2013: A1. http://www.nytimes.com/2013/11/17/ us/politics/in-fracas-on-health-coverage-some-democrats-feel-exposed.html.

Whitworth, Damian. "Hillary Clinton Losing Support among Women: The Decline in the Polls Could Lead to Her Defeat in the N.Y. Senate Race." *Vancouver Sun*, February 24, 2000: A16.

"William Brock." *Bloomberg*. Accessed August 18, 2017. https://www.bloomberg.com/ profiles/people/1503150-william-e-brock.

"William E. Brock, CSIS Counselor and Trustee." *Center for Strategic and International Studies*. Accessed August 18, 2017. https://www.csis.org/people/william-e-brock.

Willis, John T., and Herbert C. Smith. *Maryland Politics and Government: Democratic Dominance*. Lincoln: University of Nebraska Press, 2012.

Wolvin, Andrew D. "Listening Leadership: Hillary Clinton's Listening Tour." *International Journal of Listening* 19, no. 1 (2005): 29–38.

Woodyard, Chris. "Scott Brown Drives His GMC Pickup To U.S. Senate Victory." *USA Today*, January 20, 2010. http://content.usatoday.com/communities/driveon/

post/2010/01/scott-brown-drives-his-gmc-pickup-truck-to-us-senate-victory/1#.
    WZrkqD6GPcc.

Wroblewski, Tom. "Gillibrand Boosts Stimulus, Obama Economic Team." *Staten Island
    Live*, April 15, 2009. http://blog.silive.com/politics/2009/04/gillibrand_boosts_
    stimulus_oba.html.

WSHM. "Scott Brown Will Not Run in the Special Election for U.S. Senator." *Western
    Mass News*, February 1, 2013. http://www.westernmassnews.com/story/20935790/
    scott-brown-will-not-run-in-the-special-election-for-us-senator.

Yokley, Eli. "Cynthia Lummis Will Not Seek Fifth Term in House." *The Hill*, November
    12, 2015. http://www.rollcall.com/news/home/cynthia-lummis-will-not-seek-
    fifth-term-house.

Zaller, John R. "Monica Lewinsky's Contribution to Political Science." *PS: Political
    Science and Politics* 31, no. 2 (1998): 182–89.

Index

Note: Figures and tables are indicated by *f* and *t* respectively.

CPSIA information can be obtained
at www.ICGtesting.com
Printed in the USA
LVHW111647150522
718815LV00007B/938